Telephone Interpreting:
A COMPREHENSIVE GUIDE TO THE PROFESSION

Nataly Kelly

Also by Nataly Kelly

From Our Lips to Your Ears: How Interpreters Are Changing the World
(in press)
www.fromourlips.com

Other Books of Interest

Business Without Borders
Donald A. DePalma
www.businesswithoutborders.info

For more details of these or any other publications written by Common Sense Advisory analysts, please contact:

Common Sense Advisory
100 Merrimack Street
Lowell, MA 01852-1708
USA
http://www.commonsenseadvisory.com
+1 978 275 0500

Cover design and interior layout by Grinning Moon Creative,
www.grinningmoon.com

Order this book online at www.trafford.com/08-1015
or email orders@trafford.com

Most Trafford titles are also available at major online book retailers.

Includes bibliographical references and index.
1. Translating services. 2. Telephone interpreting. I. Title.
P306.94.K45 2007
418'.02–dc22 2007000088
Note for Librarians: A cataloguing record for this book is available from Library and Archives Canada at www.collectionscanada.ca/amicus/index-e.html

ISBN: 978-1-4251-8501-5

We at Trafford believe that it is the responsibility of us all, as both individuals and corporations, to make choices that are environmentally and socially sound. You, in turn, are supporting this responsible conduct each time you purchase a Trafford book, or make use of our publishing services. To find out how you are helping, please visit www.trafford.com/responsiblepublishing.html

Our mission is to efficiently provide the world's finest, most comprehensive book publishing service, enabling every author to experience success. To find out how to publish your book, your way, and have it available worldwide, visit us online at www.trafford.com/10510

www.trafford.com

North America & international
toll-free: 1 888 232 4444 (USA & Canada)
phone: 250 383 6864 • fax: 250 383 6804
email: info@trafford.com

The United Kingdom & Europe
phone: +44 (0)1865 487 395 • local rate: 0845 230 9601
facsimile: +44 (0)1865 481 507 • email: info.uk@trafford.com

10 9 8 7 6 5 4 3 2

Contents

Acknowledgements

As with most research and writing projects of this magnitude, there are a great many individuals who lend support of diverse types, including practical, intellectual and moral. In the special case of this book, given its unique history and the process of its conception and creation over the span of many years, there are a great many individuals who had a share in making this publication a reality:

First and foremost, to the telephone interpreters who tirelessly interpret call after call each day – minute by minute, you save lives, you deliver babies into this world, you help individuals communicate who otherwise could not. You have been my friends, my colleagues, and my mentors throughout my career. I have learned tremendously from you, and I have always ventured to share these lessons so that others could benefit within our small community. Now, my goal is for the world to know you better and understand the value of your work. You are the inspiration, reason for being and backbone of this book.

Holly Mikkelson, Cynthia Roat and Izabel Arocha, for your careful commentary and supportive feedback of my work, your patience throughout the publishing process, and most importantly, your ability to truly understand and appreciate the unique and important role that telephone interpreting plays in the language access landscape.

Pamela Smith, Lauren Simon Irwin and Heather Burns, for expert navigation and sound advice that enabled me to keep this ship afloat in spite of not only choppy seas, but occasional gale force winds.

Renato Beninatto, Donald DePalma, Benjamin Sargent, Tahar Bouhafs, Gregory Mullen, Kelly Bradley, Karen McGahey, Mauricio Garza, Michael Powers, Simona Bertozzi, Melissa Gillespie, Tony Collett and the rest of the Common Sense Advisory team, for welcoming me so graciously into a dynamic, innovative and thought-leading group, of which I feel very lucky to be a part.

Louis Provenzano, Jeanette Anders and Winnie Heh from Language Line

Services, for believing in this book and the importance of its publication, for your generosity of spirit and for your devotion to further expanding our understanding of language services and their role in society. It is in great part thanks to you that the information in this book will reach readers and help advance the profession.

Rocío Txabarriaga, Mike Warner, Judith Walcott, Heather Rassi, Katrina Kosec, Alison Roycroft, Carla Lourenco Rodney, Laura Rittmuller, Mark Fynes, Darci Graves, Mary Phelan, Roseann Dueñas-Gonzalez, Marjory Bancroft, Katharine Allen, Robert Like, Elke Miot, Mirna Macias, Jorge Ungo, Annabelle Serrano, Guadalupe Flores, Rich Delperdang and Nancy Kellen, for your invaluable support as friends and colleagues.

Steven and Linda Fletcher, to whom I owe both my love of languages and my genetically predisposed willingness to fight for what I believe to be a noble cause; James Fletcher, Lynly and Isaac Triplett, Cindy and Corey Fletcher, Nathan and Hazel Fletcher, William and Luella Garner, Jennifer and Ken Morgan, Mary and Harry Kelly, for your unwavering encouragement throughout what has been an arduous but undoubtedly worthwhile journey.

Finally, but most importantly, I am forever indebted to my best friend and husband, Brian Kelly, for not only understanding my passion for this topic, but for feeding and fueling it. Your ever-available cure for writer's block – a cup of Irish tea and a few kind words – is what ultimately enabled this project to come to its fruition. Is tú clársach mo cheoil; is tú mionn mo mhuintire.

Definition of Terms Used

The list of terms below is by no means an all-inclusive list of terms related to the field of interpreting at large. This list defines some of the terms most frequently used in this book, especially terms that are common within the field of telephone interpreting.

Agent The call center representative at the telephone interpreting company call center who receives the inbound call from the end user and connects all parties.

Auditory acuity The ability to accurately decipher the words spoken by another party.

Auditory translation The transfer of a piece of written information in one language into the spoken language of another, whereby the information from a written document is read aloud in the source language to the interpreter and then rendered orally by the interpreter into the target language. Usually, the source of written information for auditory translation is limited to one or two short phrases or sentences.

Call center workforce The body of individuals working for a telephone interpreting company who work within a call center environment. The workforce usually includes a combination of telephone interpreters, agents, managers, and other key staff.

Call routing The process of sending the phone call to a telephone interpreter who speaks a given language and/or holds an industry-specific specialization (e.g. legal, health care).

Call volume The amount of calls requiring telephone interpreting services by a given client, industry, or for a given language, usually measured in minutes per month as opposed to number of calls.

Certification A process used by some telephone interpreting companies to guarantee the quality of its interpreters. May include a combination of requirements, including testing, training and monitoring.

Client The organization or individual consumer who contracts with the telephone interpretation service provider. May also refer to the end user.

Code of ethics A set of guiding ethical principles for members of a group, profession or organization.

Community interpreting Interpretation that is provided to enable individuals to obtain access to public or social services.

Conference interpreting Interpretation that is provided in order to enable members of an audience or attendees of an event to understand a speaker.

Consecutive interpreting Interpretation that is performed by the interpreter first listening to an utterance in one language and then rendering it into another language.

Consortium Refers to the states that are members of the Consortium for State Court Interpreter Certification in the United States.

Contingency plan A call routing plan that enables a telephone interpreting company to reach interpreters in the event of an emergency or disaster.

Customer Same as client.

End user The end user of interpreting services, normally either a private party or a representative of an organization that pays for the telephone interpretation service. May refer either to the individual end user or to the larger organization that contracts with a telephone interpreting provider.

Interactive voice response (IVR) An automated system that responds to voice commands, and commonly used to access telephone interpreting services.

Interpreting community The body of interpreters, interpreting educators and providers of interpreting services, across all industries and modes of delivery, including those who work specifically in telephone interpreting.

Language composition The percentage-based distribution of languages for which telephone interpreting services are required (e.g. 71% Spanish,10% Mandarin)

Language identification The process of determining the language for which telephone interpreting services are required. If the client is unable to identify the language, this process is usually completed by the agent.

Limited English proficiency (LEP) The preferred term within the United States to describe individuals who are not fully proficient in English.

Loudness The level of volume perceived by the listener, from among 280 levels that can be identifies by the human ear (Karpf, 2006).

Monitoring The process of observing telephone interpreters to evaluate performance, realized either through live (real-time) observation or through analysis of recorded calls.

Non-verbal cues The information that is available to the telephone interpreter through auditory perception, such as hesitations, changes in tone of voice and inflection. Certain non-verbal cues, such as facial expressions and gestures, could be perceived by the client and LEP individual when they are in the same location, but would not be available to the telephone interpreter.

Occupancy level See utilization rate.

Over-the-phone interpreting (OPI) See telephone interpreting.

Overflow Those interpreting services required by an organization that cannot be provided internally, and are therefore routed to a third-party telephone interpreting company.

Pitch The human perception of frequency (number of vocal vibrations). The human ear can perceive 1400 different pitches (Karpf, 2000).

Prosody Patterns of stress and intonation in speech, often characteristic of one's personal style or expression, or the 'personality' of one's voice.

Rate of speech The tempo at which an individual produces speech. The average rate of speech in British or American English ranges from 120 to 150 words per minute (Karpf, 2006).

Remote interpreter An interpreter who provides interpretation from a physical location that is different from the location of one or more of the other participants of the conversation.

Remote workforce The body of individuals working for a telephone interpreting company who do not work within a call center environment. This usually includes work-at-home interpreters, some managers and other key staff.

Side conversation Dialogue that occurs between the telephone interpreter and one other party without being interpreted to the third party. Also sometimes referred to as 'side talk'.

Sign language interpreter An interpreter who provides interpretation for a sign language, such as American Sign Language. Most of this book refers to telephone interpreting, and is therefore largely unrelated to sign language interpreting.

Simultaneous interpreting Interpretation that is performed by the interpreter listening to utterances in one language and rendering them into another language at the same time.

Spoken language interpreter An interpreter who provides interpretation for a spoken language, through any medium(e.g. telephone, on site, video)

Standards of practice Statements of enforceable guidelines for professional conduct, as stated in observable and measurable terms and as intended for minimum levels of practice.

Telephone interpreter An interpreter who provides interpretation via telephone.

Telephone interpreting Interpretation that is provided via telephone. Also sometimes called over-the-phone interpreting or telephonic interpreting.

Telephone interpreting company A for-profit or private organization that provides telephone interpreting services.

Telephone interpreting provider An organization that provides telephone interpreting services. May be for-profit or not-for-profit, and may also refer to a department within a larger organization, such as a telephone interpreting department within a hospital.

Telephonic interpreting See telephone interpreting.

Tone The quality of a speaker's voice, often associated with an emotional state. Depending on pitch and loudness, the human ear can perceive between 300,000 and 400,000 tones (Karpf, 2006).

Turn-taking The act of alternating utterances in a conversation that involves multiple speakers.

Utilization rate The ratio of minutes interpreted to minutes of an interpreter's availability.

Utterance The words, phrases and/or sentences spoken by a participant of a conversation.

Verbatim interpretation Interpretation that is rendered on a 'word-by-word' basis. This term is also sometimes used to refer to interpretation that is rendered with a high level of accuracy. There is debate in the field about the best way of defining and using this term.

Video remote interpreting Interpretation that is performed using videoconferencing technology. This term has historically been used in the sign language interpreting field.

Volume surge A sudden increase in the number of minutes of telephone interpreting services required.

Work-at-home interpreter An interpreter who provides interpreting services remotely from his or her residence.

Part 1

Introduction to Telephone Interpreting

Chapter 1
A Brief History of Telephone Interpreting

Society and the Changing Role of the Telephone

Every day around the world, millions of people use the telephone to conduct business and access services. Despite its current popularity, however, the telephone was not always used in this fashion. Many of us remember a time when, if our home phone rang in the evening, the person on the other line was most likely a friend or family member. Ever since businesses began using the telephone as a marketing tool in the 1980s and 1990s, that scenario has become increasingly less common, especially within the United States.

In years gone by, the use of the telephone was limited, due mostly to the high costs associated with using telephone services. Typically, it was more cost-effective for the average person to go in person to the business in question than to place a phone call. Even if one were to go to the trouble and expense of making a phone call, in those times, the amount and scope of services available over the phone were very limited.

With the advent of toll-free numbers, businesses began to make it easier for customers to access their services and purchase their goods via telephone. The prices of long-distance services began to drop dramatically, making it easier and more affordable for individuals to call even those numbers that were not toll-free. Owing to the lower costs of long distance calls, businesses began to recognize the cost-saving benefits of conducting business over the phone. As a result of this, the number of services available over the phone suddenly experienced tremendous growth.

A few decades ago, to pay automobile insurance premiums, consumers often went into a local agent's office with a checkbook in hand. With time, people began to send their checks to the insurance company via the postal service. These days, many insurance consumers prefer to call and make payments over the phone or pay via the Internet. Some insurance companies operate completely out of virtual offices, with no facilities whatsoever where a customer can walk in and speak to a live agent in person. This is a clear reflection of the increase in services that are provided remotely, as well as an indication that changes in technology influence consumer preferences for accessing those services.

Some individuals express concern regarding the increased number of services offered remotely via telephone and the Internet, arguing that this has resulted in certain impacts on social structure, including a decrease in one-to-one, personal services, the relationships that arise as a result of these, which can affect social dynamics and interaction among members of communities. However, recent changes in our relationship with the telephone have also brought a host of benefits.

To take a poignant example, if we go back in history to a time when emergency call centers did not exist, when an accident or emergency took place, people relied most heavily on family members and neighbors until – or if – police or emergency medical services could be notified. If an accident happened in a rural area with no telephone in the location, it was difficult, if not impossible to request police, fire or ambulance services in an emergency.

When call centers for emergency calls (e.g. 999 in the UK and 911 in the USA) began to appear, however, society's ability to access emergency services changed tremendously, and the lives, and no doubt the safety, of individual members of society, changed as a result of it.1 However, the increased ability to provide emergency response services is not the only social benefit of this new relationship between members of society and the telephone.

Only a few decades ago, if an individual with a chronic illness had a question regarding his or her care or a concern about a new or changing symptom, he or she would go in person to a provider's facility for an appointment. Depending on the level of information required, and the materials and services available at the facility, the patient might receive information on the disease, sometimes in writing, and sometimes in person from a health care educator. A few decades earlier, the individual would wait until the local family doctor came to visit the patient in the home.

Nowadays, with full-time disease management staff working in call centers, patients are able to address these needs in a different way. Much like the 'house calls' of long ago, when a doctor came to the door in person, today a dedicated nurse case manager places a telephone call to the patient in the home, sometimes several times a week, to remind the patient to take medications, to follow through on care plans, talk with health care professionals about changes in the patient's symptoms and receive education (El Boghdady, 2005).

Technological advances in communication have brought many social benefits. Members of society can reach services in new ways and, in many cases, those services can be extended to people who desperately require them, but would not have access to them without new technology.

In summary, the relationship between society and the telephone has evolved, and will continue to do so. As a result of this, many important factors that characterize our society and our economy have also changed – including the types of services and goods we consume, the individuals we interact with to obtain those services and goods and, most relevant for this book, the way we communicate with those individuals.

When discussing telephone interpreting, it is important to keep in mind all of these factors, because they provide the essential background with which to understand the relevance of telephone interpreting, both on its own, and in the discussions of these broader issues.

The Emergence of Telephone Interpreting

Telephone interpreting was first introduced in 1973 as a fee-free service in Australia. It was offered in response to the waves of immigrants arriving to the country and the resulting increased need for communicating in other languages. Originally, the service was offered in the cities of Melbourne and Sydney, and was used primarily for emergencies, but expanded to become a program with a more general scope and national availability (Department of Immigration and Multicultural and Indigenous Affairs, 2005).

In the United States, telephone interpreting was first offered in 1981, when a young police officer in San Jose, California, decided to team up with a colleague from the Defense Language Institute in Monterey, California, to form an organization that would help overcome barriers of language, such as those he had encountered in the course of his own work Language Line Services started off as a charity organization but quickly expanded beyond police clients into the health care market and incorporated as a for-profit organization headquartered in Monterey, California.

Over the course of the decade that followed, the size of the company's customer base grew exponentially. Before long, telephone interpreting services were being offered in many major industries, including financial services, telecommunications, health care, public safety, and more.

In the 1990s, a handful of other companies began to emerge on the U.S. telephone interpreting scene. Along with the decreased prices in long-distance calls and toll-free access, and the constant immigration trends, the demand for telephone interpreting in the United States began to experience enormous growth.

Just as the changing role of the telephone made services available to a wider group of people, telephone interpreting brought the services to an even larger group. People in many settings who had not been able to communicate with each other were suddenly able to do so. Through telephone interpreting, individuals could suddenly access emergency services and non-emergency services alike, even if they had limited proficiency in the dominant language of society.

Telephone interpreting exponentially increased the number of services available to people with limited English proficiency in the United States. While in-person interpreters were available for some settings, such as hospitals and courts, most people had no access whatsoever to an interpreter for their basic, everyday needs, such as calling their credit card company to request a payment extension or calling their doctor to schedule an appointment.

By the year 2000, a great many private companies, both small and large, were offering telephone interpreting services. By this time, long-time users of telephone interpreting services had begun to grow more sophisticated in their preferences, making additional demands of their service providers, including increased quality of interpretation, faster speeds of connection to the interpreters, and customer service.

As customers became more familiar with the services and the telephone interpreting market grew more competitive, individual providers began to seek out numerous ways to differentiate themselves from their competitors. Some of these strategies included focusing on a specific market segment, such as health care or government, and establishing certification programs in order to provide a minimum quality commitment to customers.

In addition, telephone interpreting began to gain popularity outside of private companies. For example, large hospitals systems began to use telephone interpreting as a way to pool resources. Many large organizations began to follow suit and open up their own call centers with in-house telephone interpreters. Similarly, non-profit language banks used volunteer interpreters over the phone as a way to cut costs and expand their reach, as well as the number of languages offered.

Today, telephone interpreting in the United States is still provided mainly through for-profit companies. In 2005, the US telephone interpreting market was estimated at approximately US$200 million, without including those telephone interpreting services provided internally, such as the services being used at hospital systems and other large organizations, as mentioned above.

Also, while many segments of the market are veteran consumers of telephone interpreting services, other segments are only just beginning to learn about the services' existence. Therefore, the size of the market for telephone interpreting (or some other form of remote interpreting) stands only to increase as time goes on.

Certain countries, such as the United States, Australia and the United Kingdom have been using telephone interpreting services for many years. However, in many parts of the world telephone interpreting is still new. Where individuals and organizations fall on the curve of implementation for telephone interpreting really depends on geography, market sector, and other factors.

The Evolution of Quality

When telephone interpreting first began to emerge in the United States, there were still many lessons to be learned. Since this type of service had not previously been offered by private, for-profit companies, numerous facets of telephone interpreting that are common today, such as quality guarantees and minimum acceptable levels of service, evolved over time. Due in part to the rapid growth of the market demand for the service and the arrival of competitors on the scene, telephone interpreting providers began to invest in quality control.

Few people outside the field may realize it, but ongoing quality control is an essential and standard part of the daily operations of most large-scale telephone interpreting providers. This topic will be covered in more detail in later chapters, but it is important to recognize that some of the quality control processes that exist within telephone interpreting companies have been in place for decades.

A few of the leading telephone interpreting providers in the United States have gone so far as to validate their quality-control programs through leading industry experts, including notable professors of major universities with programs in interpretation and translation. Some of them have published articles and presented at professional conferences on the subject of quality control for telephone interpreting.

In addition, a handful of providers in the United States have gone a step further to create actual certification processes for their interpreters, both for general purposes and for specific industries. Given that there is currently no government-administered or non-profit association certification test or program in place for telephone interpreters, it is understandable that private companies would address this demand, in order give practicing telephone interpreters tangible proof of their qualifications and skills.

This is not to say, however, that all providers can be considered equal. While some telephone interpreting companies adhere to rigorous processes to ensure the highest quality to their customers, others are reluctant to identify what process they use, if any, to train, test and monitor their interpreters.

It is, in part, this lack of transparency among some providers, coupled with the lack of any non-profit or government qualification process for telephone interpreters, that has contributed to the opinion among some members of the interpreting community that the quality of telephone interpreting cannot be trusted. This opinion is reflected often in comments made in the field that telephone interpreting is inferior to in-person interpreting – usually only with only anecdotal evidence to support these opinions. A later chapter of this book attempts to shed some light on that discussion by taking a closer look at potential advantages and disadvantages of telephone interpreting for various settings.

Perhaps one of the most problematic aspects of the field is the general lack of models for a code of ethics and standards of practice for telephone interpreting. Some private companies have developed their own internal codes of ethics for their telephone interpreters. However, until now, there have been no publicly available standards of practice for telephone interpreters. It is understandable that some members of the interpreting community, and even the public, would express unease with regard to the quality of telephone interpreting. How can telephone interpreters be expected to uphold standards of quality, when no standards have ever been published?

For this reason, this book includes both a model code of ethics (Chapter 9) and model standards of practice (Chapter 10). The model code of ethics consists of several principles that telephone interpreters can constantly refer back to while carrying out their job to ensure ethical conduct. The model standards of practice build on the model code of ethics by stating specific standards of practice that telephone interpreters should uphold in relation to each principle.

In addition to serving as useful reference materials for telephone interpreters and service providers, the models also serve to educate anyone who might need to use a telephone interpreting service. By becoming familiar with the models, even those who are completely unfamiliar with telephone interpreting can gain a clear understanding of the criteria that ultimately determine the quality of a telephone interpreting service.

The definition of the term, 'profession' varies depending on the context and source. For the purposes of this publication, and out of respect for all practicing telephone interpreters who strive to uphold high levels of quality, the field of telephone interpreting will be regarded as a profession of its own, albeit, a relatively new and evolving one. In addition, this publication, which marks the first major book publication to contribute to the body of knowledge available on the subject, serves as a testament to the levels of accuracy, completeness, and overall quality that can and should be attained through telephone interpreting when a defined set of standards are in place.

NOTE

1. THE FIRST EMERGENCY TELEPHONE SYSTEM SERVING POLICE FIRE AND EMERGENCY MEDICAL SERVICES (999) WAS INTRODUCED IN BRITAIN IN 1937. THE FIRST 911 CALL IN THE UNITED STATES WAS PLACED IN 1968 IN HALEYVILLE, ALABAMA (DISPATCH MONTHLY, 1995).

Chapter 2
How It Works

In a traditional telephone interpreting transaction, there are usually four parties involved: the client, the LEP (limited English proficient) party, the agent, and the telephone interpreter.

From the client's perspective, accessing telephone interpreting services is rather simple. The client, normally an employee at a company that provides products or services to individuals who speak a different language, accesses the telephone interpreting services in four simple steps:

1. *Dialing the service:* The client contacts the telephone interpreting service provider.

2. *Data collection:* The telephone interpreting service provider's agent receives the call and requests the client's billing information, as well as the language being requested.

3. *Interpreter connection:* The agent connects a telephone interpreter for the appropriate language to the line.

4. *Session initiation:* The telephone interpreting session begins.

Let's break down each step a bit further:

Step 1: Dialing the Service

The client contacts the telephone interpreting service provider. Normally, the client will have the number for the telephone interpreting service posted in a visible location for easy access. In other cases, the client organization will have a speed-dial button pre-programmed with the number for the telephone interpreting service . In most cases, the company has signed up for a subscription to telephone interpreting services at an agreed rate and has been provided with the telephone number to access the service.

Step 2: Data Collection

The telephone interpreting service provider's agent receives the call and requests the client's billing information, as well as the language being requested.

Types of answering systems

- *Live agent* – A representative, usually a call center worker, answers the call and takes the information manually, entering it into a billing system.
- *Interactive voice response (IVR)* – The call is answered by an automated system that responds to the company employee's voice commands.

Billing information

Services are usually accessed through a unique client account number or client number. Some telephone interpreting companies allow these numbers to be client-defined; other companies assign them to the client. Some phone systems enable the telephone interpreting company representative to see which company is calling by synchronizing user identification information with the telephone interpreting provider's caller identification technology.

This allows a live agent or IVR to greet the individual with the client's name: 'Hello [*client company name*]! Thank you for calling [*telephone interpreting company name*]'.

As well as tracking the account number and client name, telephone interpreting companies are often able to track the identifying information for the individual placing the call, by means of a personal identification number or user name. This enables the client company to track its call statistics in order to analyze the information and determine the differences and similarities between the various locations that access the service. For example, a client company may have one personal identification number, and might assign unique user names to each department that uses the services. This way, the client company can track the types of telephone interpreting sessions, as well as how the duration and language requested might vary from one department to the next.

The analysis of call data also enables the client company to identify trends in usage over a given period of time. This, in turn, allows the client company to make well-informed business decisions related to the provision of language services to its customers, which may help them improve language access and general levels of customer service. Also, the analysis of these statistics may support the client company in making additional business decisions to enhance operations, revise processes, and improve overall effectiveness.

Real-world example

Springfield General Hospital handles its language barriers with patients by employing bilingual staff in several of its more commonly requested languages and uses a telephone interpreting company for four different areas of the hospital: emergency room (ER), patient rooms, reception and billing. Upon analysis of the call data provided by the telephone interpreting provider, the hospital sees that the average monthly usage over the previous year breaks down as follows:

Hospital area	*Usage in minutes per month*
ER	3000
Patient Rooms	9000
Reception	5000
Billing	4000
Total	*23000*

However, in the past month, call volumes have increased across all four departments, as follows:

Hospital area	*Usage in minutes per month*
ER	4000
Patient Rooms	14000
Reception	6500
Billing	4000
Total	*29500*

From this, the hospital learns that, in most departments, the call volume has increased by around 20–25%. However, in the patient rooms, the call volume has grown at a greater rate. This indicates that something different may be happening with patient rooms.

By cross-referencing data from the human resources department, the hospital can identify that the reason for the increase is that the hospital has faced recent difficulties in locating bilingual nursing staff to support the needs of its patient population. Since the hospital nursing staff is the primary user of the telephone interpreting services in patient rooms, the hospital can easily correlate the reason for the larger call volume increase in that area.

The hospital can also review and organize the call data by language. Over the past year, the hospital has had the following call volumes by language:

Language Usage in minutes per month	
Spanish	17000
Vietnamese	3000
Mandarin	2000
Tagalog	1000
Total	*23000*

However, in the past month, the hospital has noticed a puzzling deviation to the normal usage patterns. The calls for Spanish stayed exactly the same, while the calls for other languages increased substantially.

Language Usage in minutes per month	
Spanish	17000
Vietnamese	4750
Mandarin	4425
Tagalog	3325
Total	*29500*

Upon further analysis, the hospital was able to identify the reason for the deviation. The hospital's finance department had migrated to a new billing system in the previous month. Letters were sent out in Spanish to inform the patients of the differences between the new and the old system along with a sample copy of a bill for services under the new system.

However, for the other languages, no information was sent out to explain the change in the system. This resulted in mass confusion for the patients who speak other languages, because they did not understand their bills, and many thought they had been billed twice by mistake when they saw that two bills had been sent, because they did not understand that one was a sample. Therefore, the call volumes increased dramatically for those languages, as did the need for interpreting services.

What can the hospital learn from this experience? Providing translated letters to the patients in the other major languages served would have prevented some of the confusion and reduced call volumes. The hospital did not have internal staff available to translate the letter for the other three languages, but it might have saved money in the long run by paying for a professional translation company to provide translation services. This would have decreased the amount of minutes for which interpreting services were used.

In other words, through the data tracking that is provided as part of the standard service offered by most telephone interpreting companies the hospital in this example could enhance its overall effectiveness as a business and assess its areas of deficiencies in communicating with its patients in other languages. This real-world example provides a clear picture of the usefulness of gathering the client and user identification for each interpreted interaction, as well as tracking the usage information by language. Only a handful of interpreter firms offer real-time information on their web portals to better assist with the management and control of telephone interpreting usage.

Language request

In addition to the data collection process (step 2), the telephone interpreting company agent will ask the client company representative to state the language for which they require interpretation services. The telephone interpreting company will often provide a helpful sheet to the client company to assist them in identifying other languages. Some telephone interpreting companies also provide basic training to enable them to phonetically identify the names of the top languages requested by the client company in that language, e.g. 'español' for Spanish, 'nihongo' for Japanese.

Language identification

In some cases, it may be difficult or impossible for the client company representative to identify the customer's language. When this occurs, the client company representative will inform the telephone interpreting company agent of the problem and ask for additional assistance. Often, the telephone interpreting company agents have extensive experience and training on identifying languages based on their phonetics and can recognize the language within a matter of seconds. If the client company representative has used an IVR and does not know the language needed, he or she would need to choose the option to be connected to a live agent to receive assistance in identifying the language needed.

Step 3: Interpreter Connection

The agent connects a telephone interpreter for the appropriate language to the line. The effectiveness and speed of this step of the process depends on a tremendous amount of preparation and planning on the part of the telephone interpreting service provider. Most telephone interpreting companies provide access to services for 100 or more languages on a 24/7 basis. In addition, many telephone interpreting companies commit (in writing) to providing their customers a minimum speed of answer and connection time, which is usually a matter of mere seconds. Many parts of the telephone interpreting company must work together collaboratively to ensure that this commitment can be upheld.

Human resources

In order to provide an on-demand service, one of the most important issues to resolve is ensuring that there are enough interpreters available to handle any unpredictable changes in call volumes. As news reports remind us on a near-daily basis, there is a shortage of qualified interpreters in many areas of interpreting, such as court interpreting and healthcare interpreting.

For telephone interpreting, this shortage is compounded by the fact that there are even fewer academic and training programs. It is for this reason that telephone interpreting companies must provide a full spectrum of testing and training services to ensure that enough qualified interpreters are available.

Scheduling

Once qualified interpreters have been identified, screened, and tested, there is the additional consideration of ensuring access to those interpreters. Moreover, the company needs to ensure various levels of access to a given number of interpreters at specific times of day, as well as specific days of the week. This is where the telephone interpreting company's scheduling department plays a primary role. Rather than simply scheduling interpreting services for a given day and time, the telephone interpreting company's schedulers face the additional challenges of using trends to forecast growth in the volume of calls requiring telephone interpreting services. The company must also ensure that the lines are fully staffed, based on informed estimates of call volumes as broken down by time of day, day of week, and language.

Most telephone interpreting providers of 100 or more languages on demand work with a mixture of full-time employees, part-time employees, and freelancers. Depending on the call volumes, the company may be scheduling thousands of interpreters at any given time, across many different time zones, and throughout numerous countries. This further complicates the task of providing an on-demand service such as telephone interpreting, making it important for most large-scale providers to have a large percentage of interpreters who work pre-assigned schedules.

When providers rely exclusively or primarily on freelancers instead of scheduled workers, this can sometimes result in a lower level of ability to provide interpreters quickly in the languages needed, putting the customer at increased risk, especially where emergency settings may be concerned.

Governmental employment regulatory bodies in some countries take a strong stance on the issue of using contractors versus employees. There are often strict limitations in place regarding the scheduling, training, supervision and monitoring of contractors. Employees that work for an organization directly can be managed in a way that allows for scalability and potential spikes and surges in telephone interpretation usage.

In addition, to accommodate occasional unforeseen surges in volume, schedulers must take into account the average rate of interpreter utilization. Calls can then be sent to interpreters who are not occupied on other calls when the call volume increases. Most companies employ a model that involves both full-time interpreters and contractors, for this purpose.

The telephone interpreting industry, like many other service industries, can be greatly affected by outside events: policy decisions at local, state, and federal government levels, immigration trends, consumer spending patterns, and especially by extreme or inclement weather.

For example, when hurricanes struck the Gulf Coast of the United States in 2005, all residents of the affected areas, including many who spoke very limited English, suddenly needed to access emergency services. Calls began to stream into emergency call centers in record volumes. In addition, many people from outside of those areas began to call homes, businesses and non-profit agencies in an attempt to communicate with and/or locate their loved ones. These unforeseen circumstances will sometimes occur, and for this reason, many telephone interpreting companies rely on emergency disaster back-up or contingency plans, which enable them to quickly tap into additional staffing resources.

Many of the situations that require interpretation via telephone are emergency in nature and therefore service must be available at all times. Complete business continuity and extensive redundant systems are required by the interpreting firm and critical to meet any technological failure either by the client within their operation or by the interpreting firm.

In addition to the individuals affected by such events, the interpreters themselves could be affected. If a telephone interpreting company were to have a fully operational call center in one of the areas damaged by the hurricane, that call center may have lost electricity, and the interpreters might not have been accessible. For this reason, many telephone interpreting providers are supported by back-up generators and systems for such emergency situations.

Some companies rely on a remote workforce of interpreters that operate from a home office environment. If large concentrations of these interpreters are in a given area, they too might be affected by a natural disaster. Often, remote workers do not have a back-up system available, so this is another potential area for which telephone interpreting companies must establish a back-up staffing plan.

It is also possible for physical phone lines to be damaged by a natural disaster. For this reason, telephone interpreting providers must have access to additional back-up equipment and technologies that will enable them to continue providing service in the event of physical damage to actual equipment. All of these things can have dramatic impacts on the telephone interpreting company's ability to access its pool of interpreters. Therefore, the scheduling department of a telephone interpreting company will often pay close attention to these and other events, in order to ensure that enough interpreters are available.

Technical support

In addition to identifying qualified telephone interpreters and ensuring that enough are available to meet the customer demand, the means of accessing the interpreters must be fully protected. Also, to guard against technical problems that may result from factors that are beyond the telephone interpreting its control, the company must ensure that it has a contingency plan in case these problems inhibit the its ability to access the interpreters when needed.

The technical support department often uses specialized call routing software to immediately notify the appropriate parties when lines are compromised in anyway. If there is physical damage to the phone lines that connect customers with interpreters working in a call center in New York, for example, the telephone interpreting company's technical team can use the call routing software to route the calls to call centers in Chicago, Dallas, and Portland, to ensure that the calls are distributed evenly across various centers. This way, the calls can be routed to other interpreters, and an individual call center will not be burdened with the entire volume of calls normally destined for another center, on top of existing call volumes. This process temporarily increases utilization rates for interpreters working in areas where lines are not affected; however, it enables the company to account for the temporary overflow and continue to accept all interpretation requests while the problem is being resolved.

Real-world example

A telephone interpreting company that provides on-demand services in 120 languages has a pool of 2000 interpreters, broken down as follows:

Full-time employees	1000
Part-time employees	600
Freelancers	400

The 1000 full-time employees are employed in call centers as follows:

Dallas	200
Chicago	200
Mexico City	200
Buenos Aires	200
Miami	200

The company knows that its Miami call center is shut down for an average of 3 days each year during the hurricane season. The scheduling department ensures that the line coverage is supported fully at this time of year. However, a string of tropical storms in succession causes the Miami call center to close down for seven consecutive days. The scheduling department has staffed the interpreter workforce in the remaining centers with a projected occupancy of 70%. But the unforeseen days in which the Miami center is inoperable, mean that the overall occupancy across all centers increases to 80%. Occupancy across freelancers increases to 85%. These occupancy levels stay in place for an additional day while the IT department ensures that damaged telephone lines are restored. Thus, all departments work together collaboratively to continue to provide services to clients per the speed of answer and connection times to which the company has committed.

Step 4: Session Initiation

The telephone interpreting session begins. Once the interpreter has been connected to the line, the interpreted session can begin. The telephone interpreting company agent will then dial the interpreter, usually aided by a dialing software system. The interpreter will answer in accordance with the procedures outlined by the telephone interpreting company, and the telephone interpreting company agent will then conference all parties together. Once everyone is on the line, the agent will introduce the interpreter. The way the agent introduces the interpreter varies, depending on the individual telephone interpreting company.

However, the customer usually is provided with the interpreter's language, first name, and identification number. This information is stated either by the agent, the interpreter, or a combination of the two. For example, the agent might state only the language, and the interpreter might state the identification number and name. Or, the agent might simply say, 'I have your interpreter on the line', and the interpreter might provide the rest of the information. Once the interpreter has been introduced, the interpreted session can begin.

Real-world example

Now that we've explained the details of the process, let us look at a sample of how the scenario would play out in an actual call.

A client company representative receives a call from a customer that does not speak the same language.

CLIENT: Thank you for calling [*company name*]. How may I help you?
LEP CALLER: Vietnamese?
CLIENT: One moment, please.

The client representative then dials the interpreting service.

AGENT: Thank you for calling. May I have your account number, please?
CLIENT: Yes, it's 713978928.
AGENT: Thank you. And your user ID?
CLIENT: 7777.
AGENT: What language please?
CLIENT: Vietnamese.

The agent connects the interpreter.

AGENT: [*company name*]? I have your interpreter for Vietnamese on the line. Please proceed with the call, interpreter.

Once the agent has provided this cue, the interpreter knows to provide an introduction and offer to assist.

INTERPRETER: This is Tony, your interpreter for Vietnamese. How may I help you?

CLIENT: My name is George with [*company name*]. What is the reason for your call today?

INTERPRETER: [*in Vietnamese*] My name is George with [*company name*]. What is the reason for your call today?

The interpreted session continues from this point forward.

Chapter 3
Industry Trends

Telephone interpreting may have a relatively short history, but it is a field that is constantly evolving, and many interesting developments are currently underway. In this chapter, we will take a look at three major areas of trends in the industry: (1) human resources; (2) quality improvement; (3) service offerings.

In many settings, there are several driving forces that trigger change in the way services are delivered. Certain trends relate to supply and demand, as both the services themselves and the providers of the services are changing the way the services are delivered. Some trends come about as a result of the ever-changing market composition and changes in the types of services needed. Also, many trends are driven by advances in technology. Combined, these three elements help to explain most of the current trends in the telephone interpreting realm.

Trends in Human Resources

Call centers

While call centers have long been a part of the daily operations of many telephone interpreting companies, the way they are used is constantly evolving. In the past, many companies used call centers to house call center agents, who simply answered calls from incoming clients and forwarded them to interpreters who would, in turn, interpret the calls.

Call centers have also been used for decades by providers of telephone interpreting services in order to house telephone interpreters in a central location. Historically, this has been extremely important in emergency call settings in which connection time between the client and the interpreter is crucial. However, in more recent times, large telephone interpreting companies have set up call centers full of interpreters that handle calls for a variety of settings, not limited to emergency calls.

Home offices

As the popularity of telecommuting has increased over the years, many telephone interpreting companies have turned to work-at-home interpreters as a way of meeting a constantly-growing market demand for on-demand interpreting services in a large number of languages. While home-based interpreters have long been a staple in the telephone interpreting industry, changes in technology have improved the ability to manage such resources.

Some telephone interpreting companies began to equip their fulltime telephone interpreters with computers, specialized telephone headsets, and other equipment. Because the remote workforce was such a common feature of the industry, many companies began to specialize in providing over-the-phone training and testing for interpreters, combined with a plethora of written materials delivered in hard copy to the interpreters' home offices. In addition, some companies continue to hold regional interpreter conferences and events that allow interpreters to interact in person and take training programs in a group setting.

In recent years, some telephone interpreting companies have taken things a step further. Taking advantage of the latest technology, employers now provide web-based training and testing to telephone interpreters in remote locations, maximizing resources and creating consistency independent of location. Some companies also provide access to special websites for their interpreters, with web access to glossaries, training materials, message boards, and more.

International growth

When many large companies began to move call center resources to offshore centers, the largest telephone interpreting companies began to mirror that trend. Initially, this served as a strategy for certain companies to decrease cost while maximizing profit, but the practice soon became more commonplace. Before long, some telephone interpreting companies were faced with a choice of either moving business off shore or being driven out of business entirely because of increasingly lower prices.

As a result, most major players in the telephone interpreting world operate at least one offshore call center. For companies based in the United States, these centers are located primarily in Latin American countries, because of the high demand for Spanish interpreting services in the US market.

However, costs and competition are not the only reasons for offshore interpreting resources. Given the shortage of interpreters throughout the United States and the ever-growing demand for services, many companies have found that recruiting in other countries helps to supplement in-country resources and provide the on-demand access that customers require.

Trends in Quality Improvement

Consumer education

By the late 1990s, consumers had become more sophisticated and better educated about interpreting services. Many organizations employed many types of language service providers, including on-site interpreters, and began to understand more about standards and method for providing high-quality interpreting services. As a result, consumers began to apply the same standards of quality to telephone interpreting services, and started to ask questions of their providers, such as 'How do you train your interpreters?', 'How do you test them for interpreting skills?' and 'What are your quality control processes?' Some providers already had extensive quality control mechanisms in place, complete with codes of ethics, standards, and more.

Given the highly competitive nature of the industry, providers were initially reluctant to share this information externally. However, as customers began to ask questions, providers knew that this would need to change. The need for secrecy began to decrease as the need for transparency to customers became a priority. As a result, some companies began to share information about their programs with customers and members of the interpreting community. Thankfully, most of the trends in quality improvement that the industry has witnessed over the past decade seem as if they are here to stay.

Training and testing

In part due to these changes in the market, and in part due to a genuine recognition of the need to improve quality on the part of certain telephone interpreting companies, some providers began to invest significant amounts of time and money in training and testing interpreters. Most large telephone interpreting companies had already been providing at least some form of training to their interpreters – they knew it was an essential part of their business. However, the type and amount of training began to shift.

Instead of developing all resources in-house, telephone interpreting companies began to look outside of their sphere at recognized programs in other areas. Many companies began to develop relationships with reputable individuals from other areas of interpreting (often in specialty areas, such as health care, conference, and court interpreting) that could contribute to their internal programs.

As well as changing the way they viewed training, telephone interpreting companies began to change the way they viewed assessment. As with training, they had been providing assessment, in many cases, from the onset, primarily as a recruiting mechanism. However, as customers grew more sophisticated, providers saw a need to create assessment tools that would uphold the scrutiny of experts in the interpreting field.

In fact, just as they had done for training, some of the larger companies created testing programs in conjunction with well-known consultants from other fields of interpreting, in order to ensure quality to their customers. Tests became common both for general interpreting skills and for industry-specific terminology knowledge in various fields, such as health care, insurance, finance, and court interpreting.

Monitoring

Monitoring of interpreter performance, conducted either via live observation or through call recording and post-call monitoring, was also a common industry practice for some of the larger telephone interpreting companies. Using monitoring specialists and a complex set of performance criteria, some telephone interpreting companies emulated standards for monitoring call center employees to ensure quality, while others created their own guidelines that were in some ways related to guidelines for interpreting in other fields.

Implementing a monitoring service was important, both for purposes of proving to large customers with call centers that their telephone interpreting provider was giving monitoring a similar priority, and for purposes of measuring and improving quality of performance.

Certification programs

As training, testing and monitoring programs grew more complex, companies began to introduce certification programs, as a new way of providing customers with peace of mind regarding quality, while packaging the diverse component types that comprised their quality programs. Some companies went so far as to develop long-term, continued relationships with panels of expert advisors in this area. Others began to offer their programs externally, primarily in response to the market demand for interpreter training and testing services.

Quality in telephone interpreting: Fact or fiction?

The short answer to the above question is: both. It is important to note that, while some telephone interpreting companies have gone to great lengths to develop training, testing, and monitoring programs in order to improve the quality of the services they provide, other telephone interpreting companies may still offer little, if any such programs to their interpreters.

In the field of community interpreting at large, it is not uncommon for interpreters to be hired for on-site positions without any training, testing or prior experience whatsoever. There is a common misconception that anyone who can speak two languages can work as an interpreter. In practice, even individuals who are fully fluent in two languages may not always be effective interpreters, even with training. Concerned individuals in all areas of interpreting struggle to correct the misconception that any bilingual person can interpret, and to educate individuals and organizations on the importance of quality. However, just as uninformed and/or unscrupulous organizations hire unqualified interpreters to interpret in hospitals and courts across the nation, some telephone interpreting providers do not place a value on the quality of their interpreters, and will simply hire anyone who claims to have interpreting experience.

With good reason, some members of the interpreting community have expressed concern over the quality of telephone interpreting. A concern for quality is always a positive sign for the professionalization of the field. Low-quality bargain-basement providers who do not put an emphasis on quality exist in every industry. However, to judge the entire industry on those companies would be neither fair nor accurate, taking into consideration that some providers have gone to great lengths to ensure quality. Sharing information with consumers on the importance of quality is one strategy for addressing this problem, and various sections of this book may help to accomplish this.

Some telephone interpreting providers have no concern for quality or simply lack the knowledge, experience, and resources to ensure it, but this is not unique to telephone interpreting and is commonplace in many areas of interpreting in the United States. For example, in the legal field, where testing and training programs have existed for decades, there are still reports of interpreters for state courts who were hired to interpret without any prior experience or training. In the health care field, bilingual staff members are often asked to interpret without any training, simply because they are already present and seem to fit the job description. In the field of educational interpreting, even fewer training and testing programs exist for spoken language interpreters.

In general, the same basic rule applies to telephone interpreting that applies to all areas of interpreting. Interpreters must first be provided with a code of ethics and professional standards of practice. Once this material is in place, interpreters can be trained on it, and they can then be evaluated (both through testing and monitoring) on how well they adhere to those guiding ethical principles and standards.

Until the publication of this book, there were no publicly available models for these purposes. Some telephone interpreting providers have shared their codes of ethics with customers and via websites and brochures for marketing and sales purposes, but neither a published non-company-specific code of ethics nor a standards document for telephone interpreting was previously available that would serve as a foundation for the field at large.

It is imperative, for all stakeholders – professional companies concerned with quality, consumers of telephone interpreting services, and the interpreters themselves – to request that such ethical principles and standards be implemented and followed across the entire industry. If this does not take place, all stakeholders continue to remain at risk.

For example, even though most professional interpreting associations require the use of first person interpretation and many educators and associations actually advise strongly against using reported (third person) speech (see NAJIT, 2004), some telephone interpreting companies continue to train interpreters to use this as an interpreting method. This is presumably because it increases the length of billable minutes, and because some consumers are so accustomed to this method that they actually request it. This practice on the part of any provider goes against the professional standards of the field at large. Until telephone interpreting companies can be held to a common set of ethical principles and standards, it may be difficult to ascertain quality.

As a rough estimate, approximately 80% of telephone interpreting services provided within the United States are handled by only a handful of large-scale providers who have long-standing quality programs in place for testing, training, monitoring, and certifying their interpreters. Therefore, the answer to any query about the quality of telephone interpreting services is that it varies, depending on the provider. For this reason, it is important for consumers to become more informed and not only request copies of their providers' standards and codes of ethics, but to hold the providers accountable for following them.

Trends in Service Offerings

On-site interpreting

One service offered by some telephone interpreting companies is on-site interpreting. Some critics believe that telephone-interpreting providers seek to one day completely replace on-site interpreters with telephone interpreters, which they perceive as inferior. At least in the case of providers who offer on-site services, this could not be further from the truth. Companies that provide both types of interpreting have a good understanding of the differences between them and, because they offer both types, can be very forthcoming about the pros and cons of each.

On-site interpreting is preferable to telephone interpreting in certain situations, for example, when training or visual learning is taking place – such as when a nurse is demonstrating the use of medical equipment to a patient. In certain settings, telephone interpreting cannot replace on-site interpreting, at least, not with current technologies. On the other hand, there are also many cases in which on-site interpreters cannot replace telephone interpreters.

When two people are communicating via telephone, a telephone interpreter is the only logical option, and this is one of the reasons that telephone interpreting was born in the first place. For example, in an emergency 911 call, it would be impossible to use an on-site interpreter, since both parties are communicating over the telephone.

Translation and localization services

Another set of services offered by some telephone interpreting companies includes translation of written materials and localization of websites and other electronic media. Some companies provide this as simply a byproduct of the multiple requests from customers, and outsource the work to a professional translation agency.

Other companies actually operate a full-service, professional translation department internally, and take great pride in creating consistency for their customers across their entire portfolio of services. These companies can ensure, for example, that the terminology used in the company's written materials in other languages is also used by its telephone interpreters (and on-site interpreters, if that service is also available). As with any service, when comparing the translation services offered by telephone interpreting companies, it is best to become educated about the quality of services by asking as many questions as possible. With all language services, the informed consumer will receive the best quality of service.

Terminology management

When a telephone interpreting company also operates a professional translation service, there is an opportunity for consistent branding and a corporate image across multiple languages. For this reason, some companies have begun to offer terminology management services.

By creating databases of commonly used terms and translations, the telephone interpreting company's translation department can ensure consistency in branding for its customers, not only throughout the organization's written materials, but on their website, in their voice prompts, in their television advertisements, and lastly, in the calls that are interpreted by the company's telephone interpreters.

Companies that offer this service often provide the interpreters with client-specific glossaries to ensure consistency in terminology. This service is of tremendous value to any company attempting to create brand loyalty and build a strong presence for their company in markets where other languages are required. By creating a link between the written and spoken marketing communications, a company can ensure consistency of messaging, regardless of language.

Testing and training services

As mentioned earlier, some telephone interpreting companies have started to offer their internal testing and training programs externally, in order to provide customers with the ability to test and train their in-house bilingual employees and interpreters. The types of programs available depend on the company, and some companies have set up entire divisions within their organizations to focus specifically on such services. Some companies provide both written and oral language proficiency testing, and some also provide interpretation testing.

Bilingual agents

Another current trend in the telephone interpreting world is for companies to provide certain call-handling services in other languages. Sometimes, customers request of their telephone interpreting provider that the interpreter answer the call and greet the caller in his or her native language, and then transfer the caller to a company representative. From that point onward, the 'agent' acts as an interpreter for the caller.

This can be somewhat confusing to the caller, especially in a telephonic environment, in which voices can be easily confused. With several speakers on the line, if the roles are not clear, the caller could become frustrated about having a direct in-language service and then switching to an interpreting service, which takes considerably longer. For this reason, training is imperative to make sure that these issues are taken into account.

A troubling trend in this category of service is that some call center outsourcing companies are beginning to try their hand at providing telephone interpreting services. With little or no experience in the interpreting community, let alone in the area of telephone interpreting, it is hard to know how they will incorporate industry best practices of testing, training and monitoring into their services. Many companies that are new to telephone interpreting underestimate the level of skill required for this type of work, let alone the sheer quantity of resources required to provide customers with a high-quality level of service.

This is not to say that bilingual agent services should be entirely avoided by telephone interpreting companies. In fact, given the changing market demands, it is likely that they will be an important area of growth. However, when customers require both bilingual agents, and telephone interpreting services, they must be fully aware of the provider's qualifications, and standards of quality for providing both of these apparently similar but quite different services.

Dual receiver phones

Some telephone interpreting companies also offer telephones with two receivers, one for each speaker. This prevents the parties from having to pass the phone back, and forth to each other or having to use a speaker phone when both people are on the phone with an interpreter. This can be extremely helpful in many situations, and across a wide variety of industry settings. Some end users mount their phones to carts, and wheel them from one area to another, as needed, while others transport theirs in a carrying case or store them away. The way these phones are used varies greatly from one setting to the next.

In general, each phone has a speed dial button that is programmable to enable the quickest possible call to the telephone interpreting services. Some phones also allow the end user to dial different departments to request other services. These phones are typically available in both corded and cordless models. They are sometimes affixed to a mobile cart, and sometimes are stored in a central location within a facility for ease of access. More commonly, however, multiple phones are installed at various points of contact where interpreting services might be required, such as bank teller stations, counters at stores, the reception area, etc.

Video remote interpreting

Commonly used in the sign language interpreting world, video remote interpreting (VRI) services are now being offered by some telephone interpreting providers. Often, telephone interpreting customers also require sign language interpreters, and VRI service allows the provider to offer them. Traditionally, the interpreters providing VRI service are based in call centers. Some providers offer the service on-demand, while others require advance scheduling.

So far, telephone interpreting companies have offered VRI service only in some of the most commonly requested spoken languages. As technology improves, it is likely that more languages will be offered, and the popularity of the service may increase. Currently, however, it is far more expensive than telephone interpreting.

There are also certain other advantages of telephone interpreting that are currently not offered by video interpreting. For example, a patient may feel uncomfortable having certain exams and procedures performed while a camera is pointed in his or her direction. With video interpreting, it can also be more difficult for the interpreter to position him or herself in a way that is unobtrusive. Individuals tend to stare at the screen instead of looking at each other, thereby reducing non-verbal communication between these parties. For the near future, it is likely that video and telephone interpreting will compliment each other and provide different advantages, rather than replace each other.

Part 2

Working as a Telephone Interpreter

Chapter 4
Profile of the Ideal Candidate

Certain basic characteristics are required of all interpreters, no matter what mode or environment they happen to work in. The two most essential requirements of all interpreters are native or near-native fluency in both working languages and the ability to transfer meaning from one spoken language to another in an accurate and complete manner. These two core characteristics are the primary foundation for all interpreters, including telephone interpreters.

Still, there are numerous differences between telephone interpreting and its sister professions of conference interpreting and community interpreting. Because of these differences, the best interpreter for each of these three professions may not necessarily be the same person. Indeed, while there may be some overlap, the individuals best suited to each profession do not always possess the same set of skills and characteristics.

As discussed in earlier chapters, the trend for industry specialization for individual telephone interpreters may one day be predominant in the world of telephone interpreting. However, for the purposes of this chapter, the profile of an ideal telephone interpreter will be based heavily on the scenario most common at present, in which telephone interpreters jump within a matter of seconds from one form of interpreting in a given setting to a completely contrasting situation.

One of the biggest differences between telephone interpreting and other types of interpreting is the vast array of situations that the telephone interpreter encounters within a day's work. Conference interpreters, court interpreters and medical interpreters all encounter unique and diverse situations on a daily basis, of course, and many of these are completely unpredictable. In any setting, an interpreter can never be sure of what he or she will encounter throughout the course of work. However, in the world of telephone interpreting, the interpreter must not 'expect the unexpected' only once in awhile, but on an ongoing basis.

If we were to compare the general work of an interpreter to that of driving an automobile, we might say that a conference interpreter is akin to a limousine driver, in that his or her client usually has a higher profile in society and access to greater economic resources. We might also say that community interpreters are like drivers of public transport, because they are most likely to encounter many levels of society, including those individuals with limited resources. The telephone interpreter, by contrast, is found behind the wheel of an ambulance, a tour bus, a tractor, a delivery van and a sixteen-wheeler – all in one day.

For this reason more than any other, in order to be successful at their, job telephone interpreters should possess a distinct set of qualities. It is important to recognize that many of the key ingredients for success in telephone interpreting are skills that can be learned, practiced and perfected by most individuals with the two core competencies identified earlier (fluency in both languages and ability to transfer spoken language accurately and completely).

However, in addition to mastery of skills and adherence to standards for telephone interpreting, there are certain factors that are good indicators of a candidate's ability to succeed as a telephone interpreter that cannot always be easily taught or trained. These factors can be placed into two categories: professional experience and personal qualities.

Professional Experience

Consecutive interpreting experience

One of the most basic factors for success in telephone interpreting is that the candidate should have as much consecutive interpreting experience as possible. Because telephone interpreting is provided, with rare exceptions, exclusively in consecutive mode, the interpreter must be highly proficient at consecutive interpreting. In particular, telephone interpreters need to have excellent memory and note-taking skills, since they are often subjected to lengthy segments of information.

Telephone interpreters rely more heavily on vocal cues to request a pause in order to interpret, but with multiple speakers on the line, the interpreter's request may not always be heard. In on-site settings, an interpreter can use vocal cues as well as physical gestures and/or eye contact to request a pause. By contrast, this decreased ability to manage the length of the speakers' utterances means that the telephone interpreter is normally required to employ enhanced memory and note-taking skills.

While the skills for mastery of consecutive interpreting can definitely be taught, the majority of telephone interpreting companies expect candidates to have met this basic requirement prior to applying for a job. Experience in this mode of interpreting can be gained via various educational programs at universities and colleges throughout the world, and some interpreting associations offer ongoing workshops and training sessions to help prospective interpreters in their development.

Aside from completing a formal educational or training program, the best way to gain experience is to practice. The practice scenarios in later chapters serve to help interpreters gain additional experience in consecutive interpreting.

For individuals who have worked in other fields of interpreting prior to entering the field of telephone interpreting, it is often surprising at first to see that many excellent interpreters from other fields are not necessarily excellent telephone interpreters at the onset. There are many reasons for this, but one of them is undoubtedly unfamiliarity with the setting. This includes the telephone interpreter's decreased ability to request a pause from the speaker, which leads to an increased reliance on the consecutive interpreting skills of long-term memory and note-taking. This is not to say that a skilled interpreter from another field cannot become a skilled consecutive interpreter; in fact, interpreters with previous professional background are often able to learn telephone interpreting skills quickly. However, it does take time and experience to attain a mastery of any type of new delivery, and mastery of another type of interpreting does not necessarily equate to an immediate mastery of telephone interpreting.

Work experience in a telephonic environment

Another good indicator for success in telephone interpreting is actual experience working over the phone, even if that experience is unrelated to interpreting. Using the telephone to communicate with family and friends is something nearly everyone has done. However, spending longer in a telephonic environment, especially in a business setting, enables an individual to gain a better understanding of the unique aspects of communicating over the phone.

Specifically, by working over the phone, an individual often gains a better knowledge of how to best utilize inflection, tone of voice, loudness, pronunciation, breath control and various other techniques in order to communicate clearly and effectively. In addition, the individual may have improved his or her listening skills and overall auditory acuity.

Most importantly, an individual who has experience working in a telephonic environment has often developed skills that enable him or her to counteract the lack of visual cues by relying more heavily on auditory cues for both receiving and transmitting information. In other words, an individual with experience working over the phone is often better able to transmit an idea orally in the absence of visual cues by better utilizing pitch, tone of voice, etc.

When monitoring telephone interpreters, one can easily pick out those with less experience in an over-the-phone setting. Interpreters with less telephone experience tend to sound 'flat', especially if they have worked previously in an on-site environment where they relied more heavily on visual cues and were not trained in the importance of transferring auditory information. This type of interpreter usually concentrates fully on rendering the speech accurately and completely, but tends to ignore inflection and tone of voice and adopts a tone that is more 'neutral' or monotone.

Experienced telephone interpreters, as well as individuals with substantial experience in telephone environments, are often able to convey the source meaning in a way that is more authentic by effectively using the proper techniques to ensure that the source meaning is rendered in a way that increases the likelihood of it being understood with its original character and intent.

Community interpreting experience

An ideal candidate for a telephone interpreting position should also have experience in community interpreting. Community interpreting is normally provided to members of the public, and a great number of telephonic interpreting encounters can be listed under that umbrella, but there are also many situations that fall outside the scope of community interpreting.

For example, if a telephone interpreter receives a call between a consumer and the representative of a catalog, this is not really a scenario that belongs in the community interpreting realm. However, many of the calls that are interpreted telephonically, particularly in areas of health care, social services, public safety, and government, definitely fall into this area.

Customer service experience

One thing that uniquely distinguishes telephone interpreting from many other types of interpreting is the focus on customer service. Because telephone interpreting is, at the end of the day, provided by companies that are all competing for business, customer service skills are required for employment with most telephone interpreting companies. Although opportunities to actually provide customer service are limited, the interpreter must have proper training in this area.

In the freelance world, a complaint or comment about the interpreter's service might be made directly to the interpreter. On the other hand, the individual or department contracting with the interpreter might simply choose not to work with that interpreter in the future. However, with telephone interpreting, the end user of the service is, in many cases, connected directly to the interpreter from the beginning of the call and may not interact with any other representative from the telephone interpreting company. In this case, the interpreter takes on the role of receiving valuable information from customers regarding their levels of satisfaction with the service.

In the course of a day's work, the telephone interpreter might hear the following comments:

- 'Interpreter, when I called earlier I was left on hold and disconnected.'
- 'I've noticed that our average connection time for Hmong interpreters has decreased over the last month.'
- 'We've hired three bilingual representatives, so we won't be using your services as often in the future.'
- 'I'd like to get these instructions translated into Vietnamese for the patient. Is that a service your company offers?'
- 'How do you say, 'Please hold' in Japanese? Sometimes my customer hangs up before I can connect the interpreter.'
- 'I'll be calling the patient back in three hours. Can I request the same interpreter?'

For all of these examples, and more, the interpreter must be prepared not only to provide a response that will be acceptable to the client, and in accordance with the telephone interpreting company's internal policies and guidelines, but to do so while using exceptional customer service skills, including a friendly tone of voice and polite forms of expression. Also, in many cases, the interpreter must document and pass on the customer feedback so that the telephone interpreting company can follow up accordingly.

It is common for telephone interpreting companies to request that interpreters document customer feedback, either through an on-line information submission via an interpreter portal on the company website, or by faxing, e-mailing or mailing a form that serves this purpose. This enables the company's client relations department to follow up and get back to the individual representative from the company with an appropriate response.

Ultimately, the same level of customer service is expected for the limited English proficient (LEP) individual as well. However, opportunities to interact with this individual, who is normally not the person who pays for the services, are usually more limited. The LEP person is also not normally aware of the issues of common concern to the individuals who access telephone interpreting services, such as connection speed, for example. If the LEP individual has a complaint or commendation about the interpretation service being provided, the telephone interpreter must simply interpret these comments to the client. Obviously, if any specific feedback would be useful for the telephone interpreting company, the interpreter would share this feedback with the company as well.

Personal Qualities

While professional experience is extremely important and may give the recruiter a fair idea of an individual's aptitude for learning the necessary skills of telephone interpreting, there are other qualities that will ultimately determine the individual's ability to achieve success in the long term. Many of the qualities that follow may seem to be inherent to an individual's personality. While that is true to a certain extent, many interpreters are able to use specific techniques to overcome deficiencies in these qualities.

Versatility

As described in the driving analogy earlier, a telephone interpreter wears many different hats, all within the course of one day's work. Here are a few common types of calls that a telephone interpreter may encounter in an average work day:

- An organ donation bank is places a call to the LEP parents of a child recently killed in an automobile accident. The decision regarding donation must be made within the next 24 hours. The client asks the interpreter to use a very caring, concerned and comforting tone, and to use as many polite forms of expression as possible when addressing the mourning family members.
- An automobile insurance company calls an attorney's office to take a recorded statement from the LEP driver who was involved in an accident with the insured party. The attorney intervenes and argues with the insurance adjuster during the recording.
- A state-administered food stamp program calls a LEP recipient to ensure that his or her proper address is on file.
- An LEP person calls the gas company to request instructions on how to read the gas meter and be enrolled in a budget billing program.
- A technical support representative returns a call to an LEP customer

to help resolve a problem with an Internet connection.

- A police officer calls to take a report from an LEP witness to a crime of shoplifting in a local grocery store.
- An LEP individual calls a state agency to file for unemployment benefits.
- An American bachelor calls his LEP girlfriend in another country to have a personal conversation, share his feelings for her and make arrangements for his next visit to her country.
- An airline gate attendant calls to explain to an LEP passenger that a flight has been rescheduled.
- Along distance phone company calls to tell an LEP customer about a new promotional rate plan for international calls.
- A delivery room nurse calls to give instructions to an LEP woman in the final stages of labor.

As these examples make clear, a telephone interpreter's daily work can cover a broad gamut of experiences. A telephone interpreter may also be used in many different interactions that result from a single event. For example, when an accident occurs with an LEP individual, a telephone interpreter might be used in each of the following interactions resulting from that event:

- The LEP driver calls 911 and reports the accident through a telephone interpreter.
- The police officers who arrive on the scene call the telephone interpreting service to take a report from the LEP driver.
- The ambulance personnel calls the telephone interpreting service to ask the LEP person questions about how she is feeling.
- The doctor at the hospital asks the LEP additional questions through the telephone interpreter to ascertain a correct diagnosis.
- The LEP person calls her insurance company to give them a statement; the adjuster calls the telephone interpreting service to interpret the interview.
- The adjuster then calls the LEP passengers to take statements through the interpreter.
- The LEP driver calls her insurance agent through the telephone interpreter to verify coverage and deductible amounts.
- The physiotherapist calls the telephone interpreting service to explain the rehabilitation exercises to the LEP person.
- The pharmacist calls the telephone interpreting service to answer

the LEP speaker's questions about the medication.
- The billing department of the hospital calls the LEP patient through a telephone interpreter to request payment.

This scenario provides just an overview of the many steps in which a telephone interpreter might be involved as a result of one incident. There are many other examples of this, but it serves to provide an understanding of the immense scope of activities and scenarios that occur in a telephone interpreter's course of work.

For this reason, high-performing telephone interpreters must be versatile and flexible. They must be able to adjust to the ever-changing circumstances of the various call types that they encounter. Individuals who prefer a more stable and predictable environment may not be best suited to telephone interpreting. Also, individuals who are not adaptable may find telephone interpreting very difficult.

With practice and proper training, most skilled interpreters with the professional experience described above can learn to be versatile and flexible.

However, as is the case with any job, unless this is something desirable for the individual, it may result in lower levels of job satisfaction, which could result in decreased performance. For this reason, it is important to take into consideration an interpreter's versatility as a possible indicator of success in the telephone interpreting profession.

Many interpreters find that they enjoy the variety of situations, for many reasons. In terms of increasing one's vocabulary, this is a constant endeavor for all interpreters, no matter what type of interpreting is performed. However, with telephone interpreting, the scope of terminology is so large and diverse that it encompasses many terms that may not normally come up in other types of interpreting.

Also, interpreters who work over the phone often find that they are exposed to a greater number of regional varieties of their working languages.

For example, an interpreter who speaks primarily Mexican Spanish and works in the Southern part of the United States would normally expect that the majority of his or her clients will speak a Southern variety of American English, and the non-English speakers will, for the most part, speak a variety of Mexican Spanish.

However, if this same interpreter begins to work over the phone, suddenly this is no longer the case. The interpreter may be interpreting for a speaker of British English and Ecuadorian Spanish one minute, and for a speaker with a New York variety of American English and a Puerto Rican

Spanish speaker the next. This may drastically increase the interpreter's exposure to new terminology, particularly with regard to regional variations in either language. While some interpreters may find this to be extremely challenging, other interpreters thrive on the constant opportunity to learn and be exposed to new regional variations of terms.

Willingness to learn

There may be a direct correlation between an interpreter's willingness to learn and his or her versatility. Part of the job of a telephone interpreter is to never be complacent. A telephone interpreter is constantly learning, and that learning is not limited to new terminology, although this is often one of the most important areas of ongoing study for any interpreter.

For a telephone interpreter, nearly every bill, advertisement, promotion, service, catalog and conversation that takes place outside of the interpreter's work is also a potential source of terminology that may come up in the course of a call. Each time a new product is launched or a new social program is created, the names of those products and programs are likely to come up in the interpreter's work. When a government department or procedure is renamed, this will also affect the telephone interpreter's work.

When a new billing program is announced or a class action lawsuit is filed, the related terminology will often appear in telephone interpreting calls. Also, because of the regional variations mentioned in the discussion of versatility, the interpreter never stops learning regional variations. Of great importance to the telephone interpreter are Anglicisms and loan words from one language to another. Whenever there is human migration, languages and cultures collide. A natural part of this interaction is that the speakers of one language will often take words from another language, sometimes preserving their original meaning, and sometimes helping the meaning evolve into something only slightly related, or in some cases, completely different.

While all interpreters experience this to a certain degree, one might argue that telephone interpreters experience it to a greater extent because of the variety of scenarios in which they interpret. Many of the fields for which telephone interpreting is commonly utilized have concepts that may not even exist in some languages and cultures.

For example, for languages that are spoken primarily in places with tropical climates, the word 'heater' may be unfamiliar to most speakers, or the actual term in that language may be used to refer only to an industrial heater. Therefore, when those speakers move to an area with sub-zero temperatures, they may learn the word 'heater' in English and continue to use it, even when speaking in their own language.

There are numerous other examples of terms like this from other fields (such as 'liability insurance', 'full coverage' and 'deductible' from insurance) that may often be used by speakers of other languages in some form when they move to a country that requires insurance coverage in order to drive an automobile. Also, terms such as 'welfare' and 'food stamps' may not exist in a speaker's country of origin, and therefore it is often more natural for these terms to be left in English for the speaker, even when using the speaker's native language.

The reason that this issue is an important one in the field of telephone interpreting is that, owing to the scope of industries and scenarios that are encountered in the interpreter's normal work, Anglicisms and regional varieties are often quite common. Many interpreters come from a strong educational background with a focus on grammatical and structural aspects of a given language. Therefore, it is tempting for many interpreters to judge a person's language usage as 'right' or 'wrong'.

However, if the goal of an interpreter is to facilitate communication by rendering an accurate and complete interpretation, then the interpreter must be open to viewing all regional varieties of a language as valid ways of communicating, whether or not they are defined as 'correct' or 'incorrect' by a dictionary. For this reason, a telephone interpreter should view each speaker as a potential resource for better understanding a regional variety of a language. In order for this to happen, the interpreter must have a willingness to learn.

A willingness to learn is an important part of the job of a telephone interpreter not only for the purpose of becoming ever more efficient and versatile, but for maintaining impartiality. If an interpreter automatically assumes upon listening to a speaker that, because of a regional variation, he or she is speaking incorrectly, the interpreter is, however unconsciously, making judgments about that individual. This can have a negative effect on the interpreter's ability to remain unbiased throughout the interpreted interaction.

Therefore, an interpreter's willingness to learn, and even more importantly, a willingness to acknowledge that the communication takes priority over the textbook definition of what is 'right' and 'wrong' for a given language, may be considered one of the most important factors for success as a telephone interpreter.

Patience

Telephone interpreting differs from other types of interpreting in another unique way. In many types of interpreting, there is a clear sense of who is in control of the interpreted session. For example, in conference interpreting, there is normally an individual in charge and a sense of order to the turn-taking of the speakers. Also, in a court setting, the judge is ultimately the person in charge, and an attorney will have some control over the questioning of witnesses. It is clear that the witness has less control over the proceedings and is present to answer questions when directed to do so. In a medical setting, the health care practitioner is in control of the situation and usually is responsible for guiding the questions and getting responses from the patient in order to make a diagnosis or to formulate a plan of treatment.

However, in telephone interpreting, this is often not the case. In many calls, it is unclear who, if anyone, is in control of the call. In many cases, the person initiating the call is the one with the most control, because this individual is usually calling for a specific purpose. The caller, therefore, usually guides the call toward a specific outcome.

Interpreters with experience in other fields may have a hard time adjusting to this dynamic. To better explain this point, let us look at the example below. For purposes of clarity and simplicity, as well as to illustrate why an interpreter's patience may be tested, the example is given entirely in English.

CLIENT: Thank you for calling A1 Services. May I have your account number?

INTERPRETER: Thank you for calling A1 Services. May I have your account number?

CALLER: Yes, the reason I am calling is that I got a bill for a past due amount, but I already sent my payment in last week.

INTERPRETER: Yes, the reason I am calling is that I got a bill for a past due amount, but I already sent my payment in last week.

CLIENT: OK. In order to help you, I'll need your account number.

INTERPRETER: OK. In order to help you, I'll need your account number.

CALLER: That's the problem, no one ever listens when I call. This is the third time this has happened to me. I want to know why my payments are not being credited to my account!

INTERPRETER: That's the problem, no one ever listens when I call. This is the third time this has happened to me. I want to know why my payments are not being credited to my account!

CLIENT: If you won't give me your account number, can I have your billing address please?

INTERPRETER: If you won't give me your account number, can I have your billing address please?

CALLER: It doesn't matter, because even when I lived at my previous address, the same thing happened. My payments were never credited on time and there were always late charges.

INTERPRETER: It doesn't matter, because even when I lived at my previous address, the same thing happened. My payments were never credited on time and there were always late charges.

CLIENT: Interpreter, why isn't she understanding? Can't she just give me her account number so I can help her?

At this point, the interpreter's company guidelines will often dictate how the interpreter should proceed. In some cases, the interpreter might just interpret what was said. In others, the interpreter might say, 'This is the interpreter speaking. Would you like the interpreter to ask for the account number again?' In either case, the interpreter will normally try to put the responsibility for attaining the account number back in the hands of the client, since the interpreter is there to facilitate the exchange, but not to retrieve specific information. In other words, if the client needs the account number, all the interpreter can do is interpret the questions. The interpreter cannot, in any case, simply rephrase or repeat the question.

However, this is precisely one of the difficulties for many telephone interpreters. In many cases, an exchange like the one above might go on for what seems like an endless period of time, especially when the client is apparently turning to the interpreter for help and sympathy. Therefore, it would be easy to lose patience, especially when the client is also losing patience and the information being requested seems to be so simple.

Nevertheless, it is important to remember that the non-English speaker in the above example has the right to vent her frustrations with the company, and the interpreter should never try to prevent that from happening. Perhaps this exchange would end in the representative simply giving up on the caller and transferring her to speak with a manager, allowing a better solution in the end.

Because of the telephone interpreter's obligation to provide good customer service to the client, the telephone interpreter often feels 'stuck in the middle' when the client is audibly frustrated and not able to obtain the desired outcome to the call. Therefore, the interpreter must, above all, exercise a great level of patience and interpret the exchanges faithfully, even if the same question is interpreted numerous times to no avail, without getting caught up in the meaning or attempting to influence the outcome of the call in any way.

While patience is not necessarily a quality that can be taught to an interpreter, most telephone interpreting companies provide training to interpreters that enables them to role-play situations like the above scenario, which commonly occur in the telephone interpreter's daily work. By practicing these types of scenarios and learning techniques that enable an interpreter to remain detached and neutral while still providing good customer service to both parties, an interpreter may not become a more patient person, but may learn how to better perform under such circumstances.

Still, an individual with a great amount of patience may not be as easily frustrated by these situations, and is therefore more likely to perform well as a telephone interpreter with only a minimal amount of mentoring and coaching in this particular area.

In summary, the ideal candidate for a telephone interpreting position will have experience in consecutive interpreting, community interpreting, customer service and work in a telephonic environment. In addition, the ideal candidate is a person who is patient, versatile and eager to learn. In practice, it is not always easy to recruit individuals that meet all of these criteria. Often, as is the case with any employment position, a novice telephone interpreter may have strengths in a particular area and need improvement in others. However, if a candidate comes close to attaining these qualities or strives toward them, it will undoubtedly increase his or her chances for success in telephone interpreting.

Chapter 5
Finding Employment as a Telephone Interpreter

The first step toward finding employment in the telephone interpretation world is to learn more about the types of entities that are currently providing telephone interpreting services. In this chapter, we discuss the various types of organizations in which a telephone interpreter might find employment. To simplify the classification, we address each type of employer in terms of volume of service provision.

Large-scale Providers

This category refers specifically to companies whose revenue comes primarily from providing telephone interpreting services, also commonly referred to as over-the-phone interpretation (OPI). These companies are the largest providers of such services and are normally worldwide in scope. In addition, these companies normally provide telephone interpreting services on demand, 24 hours per day, 7 days per week, in 100 or more languages.

Major telephone interpreting companies often have numerous call centers throughout the world, although they may also employ interpreters who work from remote home offices. These companies may be based anywhere in the world, although the largest companies are currently headquartered in the United States and Europe.

Because these telephone interpreting companies are normally quite large and employ thousands of individuals, they tend to be the provider of choice for large-scale interpretation contracts, some of which may equate to millions of minutes of telephone interpretation services annually. These companies also normally handle calls from a wide variety of industries, and may therefore offer various types of interpreters or specializations (certified court interpreters, emergency services interpreters, health care interpreters, etc.).

In addition, these providers normally have full-time staff interpreters for all shifts in the languages most commonly requested working in a call center environment and rely on freelance or remote workers primarily to accommodate surges in call volume and less commonly requested languages.

Mid-scale Providers

These companies normally also count telephone interpreting as their primary source of revenue, but they are not necessarily be worldwide in scope. They also provide telephone interpreting services on demand on a round-the-clock basis, but may not always staff as many full-time telephone interpreters as large-scale providers do. Their interpreters may work out of a limited number of call centers, but providers of this size normally rely heavily on work-at-home interpreters to service their calls.

These companies are headquartered in various countries throughout the world, and may also be awarded large interpretation contracts, although they may not always have the scale and infrastructure in place to handle the largest contracts for service of more than a million minutes per year. While these companies may also handle calls from a wide variety of industries, some mid-scale telephone interpretation providers have focused more heavily on a specific segment of the market, such as health care, legal or government interpreting.

Small-scale Providers

The providers of telephone interpretation services in relatively small volumes are diverse and numerous. The small-scale provider normally does not count telephone interpreting as its primary source of revenue, if in fact it is a for-profit organization. Quite the opposite of organizations that are worldwide in scope, the small-scale provider normally provides services to a relatively small geographic area – although this is not always the case. In addition, it is rare for a small-scale provider to provide services on a round-the-clock basis.

These providers may work exclusively with a small number of in-house staff interpreters, although their primary jobs may be other than that of telephone interpreter. Alternately, these providers may work with a small number of ex-house freelance interpreters. Small-scale providers of telephone interpreting services are normally limited to a specific industry or application. To better understand these organizations, we will divide them into subcategories.

Agencies

It is increasingly common for even very small translation agencies and interpreting agencies to provide telephone interpreting services to their clients. Using existing relationships with freelancers, agencies may call upon these interpreters to provide services over the phone. When this occurs, interpreters are not normally provided with training on the specifics of telephone interpretation, and they do not usually go through a structured program in order to become a telephone interpreter. When an agency provides telephone interpreting services, the party requesting the services also pays for the services.

Government entities

In several countries around the world, particularly in countries where a very high proportion of public resources is devoted to social services, government bodies have made excellent headway in structuring their own centers to enable the provision of telephone interpreting services to the public. These government entities are often dedicated to providing interpreters for services that are requested through an office of the government, such as health care, legal services, social services, and education. Since the services are provided by the taxpayer, neither the LEP person nor the English speaker pays for the interpretation services.

In most cases, interpreters for government-run services are provided with ample training in telephone interpreting, and are tested as part of the recruiting process. These entities often offer full-time employment, although that may consist of a mixture of on-site and telephone interpreting assignments. Some entities are devoted exclusively to telephone interpreting.

Non-profit organizations

In many communities, non-profit organizations have stepped in when private and public organizations have failed to provide interpretation services. While non-profit organizations traditionally provide on-site interpreters, many have instituted formal programs for contacting interpreters over the phone, as a means of increasing access to interpreter services.

Normally, the 'client' or requester of services from these organizations is the minority-language speaker. In most cases, interpreters are required to have some level of training in interpreting, although not necessarily in telephone interpreting, as this may be a minor part of their work. In most non-profit organizations, the interpreters work on a voluntary basis and are unpaid. Likewise, the member of the community does not pay a fee for the interpreting services.

Call centers

At the opposite end of the spectrum from non-profit organizations, we find call centers for private companies. More often than not, the telephone interpreter at a call center is actually employed as a bilingual call-taker who may interpret for employees in another division or area of the company when those employees receive calls from an individual who does not speak their language. As these calls are highly specialized and relevant to the company in question, the interpreters are normally very familiar with the subject matter.

However, most call center employees do not receive training as telephone interpreters. They may, however, be screened for language proficiency, though this does not necessarily guarantee that they are qualified to interpret. Because these employees may not always be available to take a call, most companies with call centers use a large-scale telephone interpreting provider as a back-up for the overflow calls that their internal interpreters cannot service.

Hospitals

Interpreters who work at hospitals may also be asked to provide interpretation over the phone. This is more common in large hospitals with multiple facilities, as a means of decreasing travel time for the interpreter and providing greater access. Also, some hospitals have networks of shared interpreters who may provide interpreting services over the phone.

The level of training for interpreters in hospitals varies greatly with each hospital. Some hospitals, especially larger ones in urban settings, have in-depth training programs for interpreters, while others, often those with either lower demand for interpreting services or fewer financial resources, provide limited training. Most of the hospitals that use interpreters over the phone are large enough to be so familiar with providing interpreting services that they need a need training program for all their staff interpreters. However, very few hospitals train interpreters in the specifics of telephone interpreting, probably because this is something they ask their interpreters to do only on an occasional basis.

To find employment as a telephone interpreter, it is best to first determine if you would like to make this your sole profession, or if you would simply like to add it as an additional skill to your portfolio. Depending on how interested you are in telephone interpreting, you may want to work as a freelancer or as a part-time or full-time employee.

In order to work as a professional telephone interpreter on a full-time basis, you would most likely need to seek employment with either a large or mid-scale provider, although some small-scale government entities in certain countries might also offer full-time employment. The largest employers of telephone interpreters throughout the world are also, obviously, the large-scale providers. It is for this reason that, unless otherwise specified, this book mainly focuses on this type of employment when referring to telephone interpreting.

Chapter 6
Home Office vs. Call Center

Now that you are familiar with the various types of organizations that employ telephone interpreters, it is helpful to learn about the two categories of work environments most common to the profession. While many individuals associate working from their own residence with all the pleasures invoked by the concept of returning home after a long day of work outside their house, the reality of working from home is often a far cry from the image of domestic bliss that most people conjure.

Most humans are social creatures by nature and crave interaction with others, so the turnover rate for home-based telephone interpreters is often higher than for interpreters who work in call centers. This may be due, in part, to the level of job satisfaction experienced by individuals who work at home (in isolation) versus those who work in call centers (among other interpreters). There are numerous other factors to consider with regard to working from home, due to the differences between this type of setting and the traditional office setting to which most workers are accustomed.

In order to provide an analysis of the pros and cons of each environment, it may prove beneficial to answer a few questions, which will allow you to determine which environment might be best suited to your individual situation. There are no 'right' or 'wrong' answers. These questions serve, not to provide you with a final score, but rather, as a guide for self-assessment of your ability to work in either a home or call center environment as a telephone interpreter.

Answering each question honestly and then reviewing the response analysis that follows will support you in determining which work environment is best for you. It is also recommended that you read the response analysis for both answers to gain the greatest possible insight into the specifics of each setting as addressed in the question.

Self-Assessment

1. When I talk to a friend on the phone, I am more likely to be found:
   (a) Listening intently and focusing all my attention on the person on the other line, normally sitting down.
   (b) Carrying out other activities, such as driving, cooking or other mindless tasks.

2. When I receive feedback from a teacher or boss, I prefer:
   (a) To receive feedback in person.
   (b) To get the feedback in writing or over the phone.

3. I would describe my preferred learning style as:
   (a) Interactive – I learn best when I am able to observe examples in action and can interact with others.
   (b) Reflective – I learn best when I can inwardly process what I have learned and implement it on my own with minimal feedback.

4. My home environment is:
   (a) Normally full of activity and people, with televisions and/or music playing most of the time.
   (b) Fairly quiet, with very little activity and noise.

5. In the neighborhood where I live:
   (a) I often hear traffic noise from inside my house during the day, such as cars honking, and an occasional ambulance or police siren.
   (b) There is rarely, if ever, any noise from traffic or sirens, or my house provides a good barrier to outside noise, so that I cannot hear it from within.

6. The electrical situation in my home can best be described as:
   (a) Power outages occur whenever there is an electrical storm, and they tend to occur several times a year.
   (b) We rarely, if ever, have an electrical storm, and if so, our power is usually restored immediately.

7. In my home, I have the following pet(s):
   (a) Animals that are capable of making loud noises, such as dogs and/or birds.
   (b) Cats, fish, and/or other animals that are not capable of making loud noises, or no animals whatsoever.

8. To heat and cool my house, I use:
   (a) Radiator heat and/or window air conditioning units.
   (b) Central heat and/or air conditioning, OR I live in an area that does not require heat or air conditioning.

9. Noise from my neighbors can be described as:
   (a) I sometimes hear noise from lawn mowers, sirens, music, television, etc. through my walls, ceiling and/or windows.
   (b) I hear very little, if any, noise from my neighbors.

10. In my former employment, I socialized with co-workers (in person):
   (a) Quite frequently.
   (b) Not very frequently.

11. My home phone line is:
   (a) Sometimes prone to interference from other phone lines, radio signals, static, etc.
   (b) Usually clear as a bell; I rarely, if ever, have any interference.

12. My neighbors, family and friends:
   (a) Sometimes stop by unannounced.
   (b) Rarely, if ever, stop by unannounced.

13. In my home, I have:
   (a) A workspace that is located in another room, such as a living room or other high-traffic area.
   (b) A dedicated office space, completely separate from other rooms.

14. I become sick with a cold or flu:
   (a) Occasionally.
   (b) Rarely, if ever.

15. I enjoy my free time by:
   (a) Getting out of the house.
   (b) Spending time at home alone or with family.

16. I would describe my social network as:
   (a) Extensive – I belong to one or more groups (churches, clubs, etc.) in my community and interact with a wide range of individuals.
   (b) Close-knit – I prefer to spend time with a few close friends and family members.

17. Which statement most closely describes your ultimate goal as an interpreter?
    (a) My ultimate goal is to be the best possible interpreter I can be and focus on my own development as a skilled professional.
    (b) My ultimate goal is to contribute to the field of telephone interpreting and share my learning/knowledge with others.

18. In my professional career thus far, I have:
    (a) Experience working from home.
    (b) No experience working from home.

19. I see working from home as:
    (a) A dream job for someone who wants to stay at home with their children during the day.
    (b) A challenging job that would present difficulties in balancing home and work life.

20. In my home, I have the following equipment:
    (a) A computer, printer, fax, telephone headset, and shredder.
    (b) Few, if any, of the above.

Response Analysis

Please locate your responses beneath each question in order to determine which type of telephone interpreting would be the best match for you.

Question 1

If you answered (a):

You may be a good candidate for working from home since you are accustomed to making a conscious effort to limit your activity while taking a phone call, thereby focusing intently on the speaker. Conversely, you may find that working in a call center may be more difficult, because the surrounding activity may distract you and cause you to lose your focus.

If you answered (b):

You may find it difficult to work from home. Many individuals who are accustomed to 'multi-tasking' while on the phone carry this behavior over to their work as a telephone interpreter. While this behavior is acceptable for personal phone calls, it can be hazardous to a telephone interpreter. Therefore, you would be more likely to succeed as a telephone interpreter in a call center environment, where the increased activity in the surrounding area will probably not be distracting to you.

Question 2.

If you answered (a):

You may thrive in a call-center environment, where you are likely to interact with monitors and supervisors in an in-person setting. A remote work situation, where the supervisor would more likely communicate with you over the phone or in writing, would probably not be the best setting for you.

If you answered (b):

You may thrive in a work-at-home situation, in which the majority of your interactions with your supervisor will probably take place in writing or via telephone.

Question 3.

If you answered (a):

You are in the majority. Numerous studies indicate that most people learn best by example. Because you are in this group, you would probably benefit from working in a call-center environment, where you can observe other individuals 'live' and in action.

If you answered (b):

You may work well in a remote, home-based environment. However, you may still benefit from learning from examples. If the telephone interpreting company you wish to work with does not currently do so, you may suggest that their training materials should incorporate real-world scenarios of actual call experiences. Many telephone interpreters find that it is much easier to understand the processes and skills used for telephone interpreting when listening to sample scenarios. Even if you are only hearing the examples as opposed to seeing them in action, this will probably be beneficial.

Question 4.

If you answered (a):

You may want to avoid working in a home office setting. The more activity, noise, and traffic in your household, the more difficult it will prove to change these patterns. If you do choose to work at home, you will need to identify all potential areas of interruptions and noise in order to find a realistic way of eliminating them. For many people in this situation, it may be easier to work in a call-center environment than to drastically alter the normal way of life of the other members of your household.

If you answered (b):

Your home environment would be ideal for a work-from-home position. However, you must take into account your answers to all other questions as well, in order to ensure that a home office setting would be right for you.

Question 5.

If you answered (a):

Your home environment would not be suitable for remote working. The outside noises that are beyond your control could greatly impair your ability to interpret effectively over the phone. For example, a poorly-timed car horn could prevent you from hearing a crucial number for the address in an emergency call where police are to be dispatched. This could affect not only the interpretation, but also life or death an individual's. Therefore, it would not be recommended for you to work from home as a telephone interpreter; however, you may be suited to work in a call center.

If you answered (b):

Your environment would support you in working at home as a telephone interpreter. However, bear in mind that a quiet home environment is not the only factor to consider when deciding between working at home or in a call center.

Question 6.

If you answered (a):

It would not be advisable for you to work from home. In a call center, electrical supply is usually backed up with generator power and alternative sources. In addition, most telephone interpreting companies have fully redundant systems in place for their call centers. The same is not true when the interpreter works from home, since the power sources are not in the telephone interpreting company's control.

If you answered (b):

Power outages would probably be of less concern, and you would probably not have any problems that would affect your ability to provide telephone interpretation from your home.

Question 7.

If you answered (a):

It would be very difficult for you to work from home. You probably would not be able to control the noises of dogs, birds, and other animals capable of making noise, unless you can work on a different floor or in a location that is fully sound-proofed and protected from any such noises. Many work-at-home interpreters have been dismissed from telephone interpreting employment because of exactly these types of interference. You would be better advised to seek a position in a call center.

If you answered (b):

The pets in your home do not provide any potential interference, so you would be able to work in a home office, should you desire to do so. As always, however, it is important to weigh the other factors when making your decision.

Question 8.

If you answered (a):

A work-at-home position may prove to be very difficult for you, for a few reasons. First, the noise from window units and radiator heat can often be very loud. While perhaps this noise would not normally be too noticeable for normal activities in the home, telephone interpreting demands complete background silence in order to ensure the best possible auditory acuity. A call-center environment, where noise elements are controlled by the company, may be more advisable.

If you answered (b):

You have the ideal home environment for a telephone interpreter's home office.

Question 9.

If you answered (a):

Again, you may be better suited for a call-center position when looking for telephone interpreting work. Noise from neighbors is another element that falls outside your control and, unfortunately, external sources of noise are an important consideration for determining a work-from-home interpreter's ability to provide a service of the highest quality.

If you answered (b):

Your environment would be very conducive to telephone interpreting work from your home office.

Question 10.

If you answered (a):

A call center environment may be more agreeable to you, since you will have the opportunity to socialize with other individuals in a face-to-face setting on an ongoing basis.

If you answered (b):

You would probably thrive in a home-based work environment. You may very well still socialize with colleagues via phone, e-mail or other means. If you are not accustomed to socializing in person with co-workers, the isolation aspect of working from home as a telephone interpreter should not be as challenging for you.

Question 11.

If you answered (a):

Your phone line may pose a risk to your ability to work from home as a telephone interpreter. Any interference on your phone line could create a problem for the customer. Also, if interference from other lines is an issue, customer confidentiality could be of concern. If this is your situation, you should by no means accept employment as a telephone interpreter.

If you answered (b):

Working from home may be possible, but be sure to ask others in your household if they have ever experienced any problems with the line. Or, ask the previous owner, neighbors, and/or landlord. Spending 8 consecutive hours a day on the phone is quite different from spending 30–60 minutes per day, and will often provide a much clearer idea of any issues related to the phone line quality. Therefore, the more information you can gather, the better informed you will be to make your decision.

Question 12.

If you answered (a):

You may want to think twice before working from home. Can you realistically request that neighbors, family, and friends refrain from stopping by during your work hours? Many interpreters respond by saying, 'That's no problem; I'll just tell them all not to stop by during my workday'. In practice, this is often very difficult to coordinate. Let's say that you instruct all potential visitors that you will be working during the day, and they adhere to this. However, many telephone interpreters have work schedules that may vary from one day to the next. For example, one week an interpreter may work from 8–5 on Monday, Wednesday, and Friday, and from 12–8 on Tuesday, and Thursday. The following week, perhaps the interpreter will be asked to work on a Sunday, with a day off during the week. Unless you have a way of notifying individuals of your daily work schedule and keeping them apprised of all variations, the best solution is to ensure that no one can interrupt your work schedule. One strategy may be to advise visitors that you will no longer be able to attend to unannounced visits. However, many people do not understand that telephone interpreting requires absolute silence. Therefore, they may think, 'It won't hurt if I stop by and ring the doorbell, just to see if anyone is home.' The only problem is that, the ring of the doorbell, depending on its proximity to your office environment, may cause you to miss a crucial piece of information. This can create a very stressful work environment for the work-at-home telephone interpreter.

If you answered (b):

You are likely to be able to handle telephone interpreting from a home office with relative ease. You may not have to deal with unexpected visits as often as others, but you may still want to keep potential visitors apprised of your new position so that they will make an effort not to disturb you while you are working. Also, you may want to leave a note on your door for your FedEx or UPS delivery person to indicate that you are unavailable.

Question 13.

If you answered (a):

It may not be possible for you to work from a home office, unless you are somehow able to turn your situation into (b). Without a dedicated office space, it may be difficult to create an environment that will be conducive to a telephone interpreting role. A call-center environment may prove to be more beneficial.

If you answered (b):

You are in the ideal situation to work from home as a telephone interpreter. However, in addition to having a dedicated workspace, you may want to take other factors into account. Is the space located near a street? If so, would you have a quieter environment in a different room? Is the room sound proofed? Will you be able to hear noise from adjoining rooms, such as television sounds from the living room or sounds of running water from the bathroom or kitchen? If so, you may want to reconsider your selection and/or the location of your workspace.

Question 14.

If you answered (a):

You may benefit from knowing that some studies, such as the study published in Health Psychology (Pressman et al., 2005), have indicated that there may be a correlation between an adult's frequency of social interaction and the ability of the immune system to fight off illnesses. Moreover, if you become sick easily, this might be exacerbated by working at home. Working in a call-center environment is not in any way a shield against illness, but it may provide more opportunities for forming relationships with work colleagues and expanding your level of social interaction, which, in turn, could potentially help boost your immune system.

If you answered (b):

You may be a better candidate for working from home. However, you may wish to take additional health precautions in order to boost your immune system to compensate for possible loneliness and a lack of social interaction. Most importantly, telephone interpreters working exclusively from a home office should be sure to schedule plenty of opportunities for social interaction into their non-working hours.

Question 15.

If you answered (a):

Working in an at-home capacity may be appealing to you. In order to physically leave their workspace, many work-from-home interpreters find that it is highly necessary to spend free time outside the home. Therefore, individuals who already spend a good amount of their free time outside of the home may find this to be an easy transition.

If you answered (b):

You probably view your home as a place of solace and rest, to return to after a day of work in an external environment. If you work in a call-center environment, you will be able to continue to view your home in this manner. However, if you begin to work from home, your view of 'home life' may very well change. For this reason, if you do decide to work from home and you enjoy spending free time at home, it would be advisable to situate your workspace in a completely separate location, so that you can have a clear division between 'work' and 'play'.

Question 16.

If you answered (a):

You would probably be less affected by a work-at-home situation, since you have an extensive network of social activities outside of work that will allow you to have plenty of interaction with other individuals. However, you may feel more drawn to a call-center environment because of the additional social opportunities afforded by that type of environment. Therefore, it is important to consider these issues when deciding between the two.

If you answered (b):

Working from home might prove challenging because of the lack of social interaction. If you have very few opportunities for make contact with other individuals, a work-at-home environment might limit these interactions even further, which could be detrimental. If you do decide to work from home, you may want to make a concentrated effort to expand your social network outside of your work life to prevent feelings of isolation and loneliness.

Question 17.

If you answered (a):

You will probably be able to adapt to a home office environment, since your goal does not require much interaction and involvement with other individuals. You will more than likely be able to achieve your goal while working at home, closely analyzing and tracking your own professional development. However, this does not prevent you from being a successful call center interpreter. You could probably thrive in either environment, but the circumstances surrounding each type of work would affect the likelihood of achieving your goal in a different way.

If you answered (b):

You would probably be more suited to a call center-environment, in which you would have more opportunities to work with others. However, some telephone interpreting companies also provide many opportunities for interacting with others and sharing knowledge with peers in an over-the-phone environment. If this is one of your professional goals, you should talk to the telephone interpreting employer to learn more about the potential for career development within that company.

Question 18.

If you answered (a):

You have some exposure to a home office environment. Obviously, as you are seeking employment as a telephone interpreter, you will be able to apply your experience in your former home office employment to your current job search. Therefore, it would be important to evaluate your experience and ask yourself if a home-based or a call-center position would be best suited to your professional work preferences.

If you answered (b):

You may want to gather information about working from a home office to help you in your decision. It may be advisable to speak to interpreters and other workers with experience in a home office setting to inquire about the pros and cons, as well as the practical considerations of that type of environment versus a call-center environment. Being fully aware of all considerations and having a fuller picture will allow you to make the most informed decision.

Question 19.

If you answered (a):

You may be surprised by the reality of telephone interpreting work. A telephone interpreter must have a background of complete and total silence. Any noise whatsoever could interfere with the interpreter's ability to hear and transfer the information correctly. For this reason, a telephone interpreter working from home with children would need to have appropriate child care arrangements during his or her working hours. Likewise, a telephone interpreter would not be able to complete domestic tasks while providing the necessary level of focus and concentration for the work at hand. In other words, if you answered (a), it will be necessary for you to have a full and realistic picture of the scope and seriousness of a telephone interpreter's work.

If you answered (b):

You have a more realistic picture of the complexity of balancing home and work life. With this knowledge, you may find it more practical to work in a call-center environment, or you may choose to accept the challenge and work in a home-based environment as a telephone interpreter, depending on how you answered the other questions. In either case, you are more prepared to work from a home office than an individual who answered with (a).

Question 20.

If you answered (a):

You are probably prepared to work from home as a telephone interpreter. These items are the basic and essential equipment required by almost any telephone interpreting company for your employment as a work-at-home interpreter. In addition, if you currently have this equipment in your home, you probably already have a dedicated space that can be used for your telephone-interpreting work. Therefore, you are moreprepared to begin work in a home-office environment and to start work as soon as you gain employment with a telephone-interpreting company.

If you answered (b):

It may be preferable for you to work in a call-center environment. If you do not already have this basic equipment in your home, it would require investment on your part, and you may have difficulty obtaining the equipment and ensuring proper set-up when you gain work-at-home employment. Many telephone interpreting companies will pre-screen applicants to ascertain their readiness in terms of having the necessary equipment for home-based employment. Therefore, you may not be able to obtain such employment until you have acquired the necessary equipment.

Conclusion

By honestly answering the 20 questions presented in this section, and by reading the response analysis that followed, you have already made substantial progress both in learning more about the differences between a home-office and a call-center telephone-interpreter position, and in identifying which setting might make most sense for you. Also, you have gained a better understanding of additional factors for consideration to allow you to carry out additional research and consider your options more fully.

Chapter 7
Working From a Home Office

For most people, working at home often implies a certain level of autonomy and control that is not found within a traditional work environment. Many individuals associate working from home with the freedom to work as they choose, dress as they prefer, and set up their office as they see fit. However, working from home as an interpreter does not imply total freedom and autonomy. Many conditions of the interpreter's work are actually dictated by the employer, and fall completely or mostly outside of the interpreter's realm of control.

In addition, society sometimes confuses home-based workers, especially women, with part- or full-time homemakers. Often, people assume that people in work-at-home employment have more time free to concentrate on domestic tasks. While it is true that the lack of commuting does free up additional time in the day that could be devoted to other, non-work-related efforts, there are several aspects of working from home that require a greater investment of time than an office environment does.

For example, a worker in an office or call center does not have to worry about purchasing, installing, and maintaining any equipment. The office's local IT department handles every aspect of the equipment. However, home-based interpreter will need to devote time to purchasing, installing, and maintaining their own equipment. When technical issues occur, in addition to working a full day's schedule, the home-based interpreter may need to spend hours working to resolve the problem.

Normally, a cleaning crew comes in to an office environment to ensure proper sterilization and cleaning of all equipment and workspaces. The work-at-home interpreter, however, does not have access to commercial-grade equipment and cleaning products, let alone a staff that comes in to carry out the actual tasks associated with this requirement. Therefore, this aspect of maintaining a proper work environment will also take up some extra time, and the interpreter will need to accomplish this outside of the normal work schedule.

Also, office workers have increased opportunities to interact with others during periodic breaks and mealtimes. When working from home, the interpreter will most likely not have any opportunities to socialize with other peers and co-workers during breaks. Therefore, if the interpreter wishes to socialize or even make small talk with other interpreters, this normally occurs outside of the interpreter's normal work hours, whereas in an office environment, this type of interaction would be considered part of the average workday.

This is not to say that the lack of travel time to the office is not a huge benefit of working from home; it most certainly is. However, it is important to recognize that that benefit brings additional considerations that might counteract or offset the very characteristics that made the benefit so attractive in the first place.

This is just one example of many that will follow throughout this chapter, but it serves to put the job of the telephone interpreter into a clearer context, so that the interpreter can actually envision what the daily work life will be like. And, in order to present a fair and realistic vision of the actual work, we will be looking at multiple practical considerations that ultimately serve to prepare you to work as a home-based telephone interpreter, and to ensure the quality of telephone interpreting services that you are able to provide.

In order to help guide you through the process of analyzing these considerations, the remainder of this section is divided up into a series of Real-World Considerations that enable you to take a closer look at the requirements of working as a professional telephone interpreter in a home office environment. After reading each consideration and the paragraphs that provide more detail, you will find Real-World Tasks that you will need to accomplish in order to make your home-based work environment a reality.

Real-World Consideration 1: Home Office

Before you can begin to work from home as a telephone interpreter, you must set up your home office. The first step is to determine which room of your house will be used exclusively for your work. Ideally, this room should be positioned in a place within the home that is as far away as possible from areas of high traffic and typical sources of noise.

If you do not have a room that can function exclusively as an office, you may want to reconsider your decision to work from home. Any room that would be accessed by others, such as a living room, family room or bedroom, would not lend itself well to telephone interpreting. Professional telephone interpreters wishing to work from home need to have a dedicated room for their work in order to prevent distractions and interruptions from others and to provide a high level of quality.

A telephone interpreter's home office must be equipped with a minimum of the following: a phone line used exclusively for work purposes, a telephone with a headset, a desk, a chair, and ample lighting. In addition, the telephone interpreter must have on hand all necessary supplies for carrying out the interpreting work, such as paper, pens or pencils, and any training materials provided by the employer.

One of the most important tasks in setting up the office environment is to have a separate work line installed in the home office. The phone line should run directly into the home office, and a telephone connection (jack, socket) should be installed near the planned or existing location of the desk. It is not advisable to install jacks for the work line in other rooms of the house, because this exposes the work line to the possibility of others in your household connecting equipment to the line – either on purpose or by accident.

Another essential part of setting up your home office will be selecting a telephone with a headset. This will be the device that enables you to hear clearly and provide an accurate interpretation. Some providers may supply you with a list of acceptable models of headsets. Others may require that you purchase your own. Your headset/phone must have a minimum of the following: a mute button, volume control, a microphone/mouthpiece, and earphones that will cover one or both ears.

It is extremely important to avoid using a cordless phone or cordless headset. In addition to an increased chance of possible line interception, cordless phones, and headsets run on battery power and run the risk of losing charge during a phone call. Also, cordless phones are more likely to experience interference with other pieces of equipment. In urban areas, some cordless phones have been known to pick up conversations from other homes, as well as signals from other sources. For all these reasons, it is advisable to use only corded phones and headsets.

The desk you select should be large enough to accommodate whatever equipment you will have on hand for your work, as well as a free space at least 8 inches wide and 12 inches long, to hold a standard-size notebook for use while interpreting. The desk should be an actual desk, designed for work purposes, and not a kitchen table, night stand or other piece of furniture. When choosing a chair, it is important to select one that is comfortable and allows you to maintain a healthy, upright, and natural sitting position.

You will be spending most of your work hours (roughly 8 hours per day if you are doing full-time work) sitting in this chair. An ergonomically-designed office chair is best suited to telephone interpreting work. When trying out different models, be sure to sit in a way that would allow you to take notes at your desk (as opposed to leaning back in the chair). This will give you the most realistic impression of how the chair will feel when you are actually using it for your work.

The choice of lighting depends on the size of the room, the number of windows, the type of window dressing (if any), and objects that might create reflections and glare. In addition, an individual's preference will dictate to some extent the amount and type of lighting desired for the home office. It is of special importance to ensure that the desk area itself is properly lighted. It is helpful for interpreters to review and observe basic ergonomic guidelines for illumination of office environments, in order to prevent visual strain and maintain eye safety (Canadian Centre for Occupational Health Safety, 2003).

Real-world tasks

- Designate a room of your house as your home office. Make sure it is located in the quietest possible area of the home.
- Install a dedicated work telephone line in your home, with a connection in your new home office.
- Obtain a corded telephone and/or headset with a mute button, volume control, a microphone/mouthpiece, and monaural or binaural earphones.
- Set up a desk that provides enough space for all equipment and ample room for paper to take notes.
- Get a comfortable chair with an ergonomic design.
- Ensure proper lighting of the workspace, especially near the desk area.

Real-World Consideration 2: Additional Equipment

In addition to the aforementioned minimum items needed to work from home as a telephone interpreter, you may want to consider obtaining some additional pieces of equipment that can serve to enhance your job performance and help you work more efficiently.

One piece of equipment that many interpreters find helpful is a telephone amplifier that connects to the telephone and/or headset and increases the volume levels of the speakers' voices. Sometimes, especially when calls are placed using defective or antiquated telephone lines or equipment, the voice of either party may seem faint and difficult to hear. For this reason, many telephone interpreters use an amplifier to boost the volume and decrease the likelihood of needing to ask for a repetition, or the possibility of misunderstanding a word or phrase due to insufficient volume.

Another piece of equipment that is often recommended, if not required, by the employer, is a paper shredder. Because of the confidential nature of the information that interpreters are exposed to in the course of each workday, most telephone interpreting companies require interpreters to destroy all records of their calls at the end of each business day. This helps the employer to protect the security of the information provided during the interpreted calls.

Also, while not technically required for providing telephone interpreting services, some interpreters find that it is very useful to have a computer on hand. However, computers cannot be used to take notes, owing to the noise generated by using the keyboard, which can be very distracting for the other parties. In spite of this limitation, many interpreters find it helpful to use the computer to search electronic glossaries and to research related information in between calls.

Additionally, if an interpreter does have a computer in the home office, it can be useful in to have an Internet connection, which enables the interpreter to e-mail electronic reports to managers, if necessary. Some telephone interpreting companies have web portals for interpreters so that they can access work-related discussion boards, chat rooms, and training materials on line. However, it is important to remember that the Internet can also be a source of distractions, so Internet activity should be limited to times when the interpreter is not actively interpreting.

Finally, a printer may also be helpful for an interpreter's home office, so that any electronic documents provided by the employer can be printed out and available in an accessible location. However, as with other sources of noise, the printer should not be used while the interpreter is taking calls.

Real-world tasks

- Consider obtaining a telephone amplifier.
- Obtain a shredder for destroying all call notes and confidential information.
- Consider having a personal computer available in the home office.
- Install an Internet connection, if desired.
- If necessary, purchase, and install a printer.

Real-World Consideration 3: Work Schedule

Working a schedule that fits with one's lifestyle is one of the most important considerations for any home office worker. However, telephone interpreters may sometimes have to operate under even stricter requirements than other home-based workers. For example, sales people who work from home can, to some degree, set their own schedule and prioritize their work according to their home environment. For example, if a sales person needs to pick up her daughter every day from school at 3:30pm, she can schedule her calls and meetings with prospective clients according to that priority.

However, in many cases, this could prove to be difficult, if not impossible, for a telephone interpreter. The telephone interpreter normally receives a schedule from the scheduling department. Since the schedules are generated according to business needs, the interpreter might not always receive his/her desired schedule. Some telephone interpreting companies allow more flexibility with scheduling, but many large companies recruit according to very specific scheduling needs. It might be possible to obtain a schedule that would allow the interpreter to be free by 3:30pm each day, but this could not always be guaranteed.

If working as a contractor on a freelance basis, the interpreter might have more flexibility with scheduling his or her work time around personal priorities. With some telephone interpreting companies, contractors can log in whenever they choose. However, since contractors are normally compensated on a per-minute basis, there is no guarantee of how much income they will be able to generate.

Also, even if the contractor plans to log out by 3:00pm in order to pick up a child at 3:30pm, there are potential scenarios that would prohibit the interpreter from leaving according to plan. For example, if the contractor receives a call at 2:59pm, and this call lasts for 45 minutes, the interpreter will not be able to simply refuse the call, let alone disconnect from it once the call begins.

For these reasons, it is important for a prospective work-at-home telephone interpreter to think about his or her ideal schedule prior to approaching an employer. If seeking full-time or part-time employment, the interpreter should do everything possible to make sure that the schedule offered by the employer is one that suits his or her lifestyle. Otherwise, the schedule could end up affecting not only the interpreter's stress level, but also the overall quality of interpretation delivered to the client.

If the interpreter's schedule ends at 3:00pm each day, and the interpreter must pick up a child by 3:30pm, the interpreter will no doubt be stressed each time a call comes in toward the end of the shift. In fact, an interpreter could be tempted to 'speed up' the call process by omitting information in an effort to make the call end sooner. This would violate the interpreter's code of ethics and standards. Also, even if the interpreter does not intentionally do anything to alter the call flow, he or she might provide inferior service because of the stress associated with having a non-work obligation that is not being met because of the interpreter's work situation.

Of course this situation is not limited to work-at-home interpreters. It is common for individuals in a variety of workplaces to be required to work late occasionally. The problem is that, when an individual works from home, the line between work and home life can be blurred more easily. Also, even if the line is clearly drawn for the interpreter him or herself, it may not be so clear for society.

If an interpreter is consistently late to pick up her child from school, the teacher may ask, 'Why are you late again? Don't you work from home?' This question might imply, 'If you work from home, you have ultimate control over your schedule, unlike me. I have to stay here until each child is picked up. What's your excuse for being late?' What the teacher might not realize is that the work-at-home interpreter is in a similar situation. The interpreter cannot get off the phone and leave the home office until the call is fully ended.

If the parent were coming from a non-home-based office environment, however, the teacher (and society) would probably have less trouble comprehending the reason for the parent's tardiness, because this is a setting that they are accustomed to and can identify with.

To prevent such misconceptions and misunderstandings, it is important for the interpreter to speak with others involved in his or her daily life and educate them on the scheduling requirements. If the interpreter has a predetermined schedule, the schedule should be posted in a visible location for all family members to see. Also, copies of the schedule should be provided to others to enable them to understand exactly what times of day will be off-limits for visits to the home and phone calls.

Because the interpreters' ability to work according to their schedules up to the very minute is so important, it is recommended that, before beginning actual interpreting work, interpreters synchronize all their clocks to ensure that these reflect the same time as the employer's clock. This will ensure that all the interpreters can take the maximum time allotted by their breaks without fear of missing calls.

Real-world tasks

- Write down your family's typical weekly and daily schedule, identifying all times and dates for which you would not be available to work due to other obligations.
- Draft a few ideal work schedules that fit with your family schedule, with specific start and end times, as well as break and meal times.
- If you are offered a telephone interpreting position that does not coincide with your ideal schedule, but you still wish to accept the offer, work with your family to see where you can be flexible in modifying the family schedule.
- Once you have accepted a position, share your detailed schedule with your family, friends, and others, so that they are aware of what times they can and cannot reach you.
- Synchronize clocks with the employer's clock in order to ensure accurate shift end and start times, as well as break times.
- Plan a specific area for breaks that will allow you to be near your phone, just in case you make a mistake and accidentally take your break at the wrong time.

Real-World Consideration 4: Children

One of the most obvious signs of an unprofessional telephone interpreting service is the sound of a child talking or crying in the background. Just as it would be inappropriate for an on-site employee to have children sitting on his lap inside his cubicle, or running freely around the halls of an office building, it is completely unacceptable for telephone interpreters to have a child in the room while they are interpreting. Children should not be present in the interpreter's home office during work hours. In fact, no children should be in the interpreter's home, unless someone else is there to supervise their activities, so that no noise can be heard from within the interpreter's home office.

Some interpreters take a work-at-home position because they want to spend more time with their children. However, to even attempt to work as a telephone interpreter while watching children means making a compromise. Either the interpreter sacrifices the ability to fully pay attention to the work at hand, potentially making critical errors that could endanger people's lives and well-being, or the interpreter sacrifices the ability to focus on watching the child, which puts the child's well-being at risk.

Therefore, the only solution for mothers and fathers who wish to work at home as professional telephone interpreters is to arrange for someone else to watch the children during the interpreter's work hours. It is simply not professional for the interpreter to attempt to hold down a telephone interpreting position while watching children. Working as a telephone interpreter commands the utmost in focus and concentration, and the level of quality required by a professional organization is simply not within reach if the interpreter tries to do the job of two people simultaneously.

Another common misconception about work-at-home telephone interpreting positions is that there will be plenty of free time between calls. Perhaps for this reason, some individuals who seek work-at-home telephone interpreting employment overestimate the amount of time that they would have available to spend with their children.

In reality, telephone interpreters are often kept so busy that they may only have a matter of a few seconds between calls, providing barely enough time to take a sip of water and rest one's voice briefly. There is definitely not enough time between calls to have a meaningful interaction with another person.

The only time the work-at-home interpreter would have free to spend with children would be during breaks and at meal times, but these times are dictated, not by the interpreter, but by the employer. For example, if an interpreter has a scheduled break from10:30–10:45am, the interpreter must be back in the office and ready to receive a call at 10:45am exactly. If the phone rings, and the interpreter does not answer promptly, the interpreter's failure to answer is recorded in the system.

If the interpreter continues failing to answer calls that come in subsequently, the interpreter may be completely removed from the line and, depending on the employer's policy, may not be compensated for the time lost due to poor attendance. The requirements of each employer may vary, but no telephone interpreting company can afford to employ interpreters who do not answer the phone promptly during their scheduled work hours.

Real-world tasks

- Find another adult to be responsible for childcare during your scheduled work hours.
- If the adult will be in the home with the child during your scheduled work hours, develop a plan with the adult to determine which rooms the child will be spending time in, to ensure that no noise enters the workspace.
- If the child has any toys that make noise, indicate to the childcare provider which rooms can be used for play with these toys.

Real-World Consideration 5: Other Family Members

Children are not the only family members that could be of concern when creating a boundary between home and work life. If an adult requires fulltime care, as in the case of a person with special needs or an elderly family member, the same precautions should be taken as with children, to ensure that the person's well-being is given the priority it deserves, without jeopardizing the quality of the interpretation.

Even adults that do not require supervision are potential causes of distractions and interference with the home-based interpreter's work life. For example, an adult might turn on a television or stereo in another room assuming that in the sound will not carry into your home office, when in fact, it could create a major distraction, both to the interpreter and to the other parties on the line.

Or, a well-meaning family member might hear through your office door that you are not currently speaking, and open the door and say something to you, assuming that you are not on a call. However, if you were listening and taking notes, this interruption could completely divert your attention and, worse still, could cause you to miss part of what the speaker was saying.

Many noises that most people do not think could create distractions (such as the noise of water running in a nearby kitchen or bathroom, the beep of a washing machine, or the noise of someone coughing or sneezing in the next room) can actually be audible to the other person on the line. While these noises may seem like unoffending "background noise" to the interpreter, and in fact could go unnoticed by the interpreter, any such noises could create a perception on the part of the client that the interpreter is not in a professional work environment. For this reason, it is extremely important for the interpreter to address all these issues when preparing to work from home.

Real-world tasks:

- Find another adult to be responsible for the care of any adults, such as elderly or special needs family members, during your scheduled work hours.
- For every television and stereo in your home, determine an acceptable level of volume for work hours. To do this, enter your workspace and have another person begin to raise the volume until it is audible from your desk. Then, reduce it until it is no longer audible from your workstation.
- Make a note indicating the acceptable level of volume for each television and stereo, such as, 'Do not raise above [level] during

work hours.' Post the note in a visible location. This way, even if a visitor comes to your home who is not familiar with this rule, a reminder will be in place to prevent any unwanted distractions from occurring.

- Test other noise-making appliances in your home, such as your washing machine, dryer, and dishwasher. If they can be heard from your workstation, post a note that indicates that they should not be used during work hours.
- While you are in your home office, get someone to speak in a normal tone of voice in each room in your house. If you can hear the voice from certain rooms, request each member of the family to avoid speaking, either on the telephone or to others, in those rooms during your work hours.

Real-world Consideration #6: Pets

Members of the household that many prospective telephone interpreters fail to consider are any animals live inside the house. Of particular importance are dogs, cats, birds, and other pets that might make noise of any kind. The sounds of a dog barking or a bird squawking in the interpreter's background environment are as unprofessional as the sounds of children, and are not tolerated by any professional employer of telephone interpreters.

If a pet will be inside the house during an interpreter's work hours, the interpreter must ensure that the noise created by the pet will not be audible, either to the interpreter, or the other parties on the telephone. For this reason, the interpreter should confine a pet to areas of the house where its noise will not have an impact on his or her ability to concentrate. Aside from the obvious noises made by pets, such as barking and meowing, it is helpful to consider other sounds as well, such as the noise of the pet moving throughout the house, eating its food, playing with toys, and any other noises it commonly makes throughout a typical day.

Finally, in addition to the noises that pets may make, it is important to consider their care during your work hours. If a dog needs to go outside, a telephone interpreter cannot abandon a call to go and open the door. Also, pets have other needs, such as feeding and grooming, that an interpreter cannot take care of while interpreting.

Real-world tasks

- Determine which areas of your house, in addition to your workspace, are off-limits for pets during your work hours.

- If the pet has any toys that make noise, advise all other adults in the household that these toys should not be given to the pet during work hours.
- If there is a need to feed or spend time with the pet during your work hours, determine who will be in charge of doing this.

Real-World Consideration 7: Friends, Neighbors, and Extended Family

Other individuals that may be a normal part of your home life include your neighbors, friends, and members of your extended family. If these people are aware that you are at home, they might not think twice about stopping by to visit with you. However, as a work-at-home telephone interpreter, you will not be able to stop to chat with them as freely as they might assume.

For this reason, it is recommended that you share your work schedule with all people who might be tempted to visit you in your home, and that you make it clear to them that your house will be off-limits during those hours. It is not even recommended that you make plans to have them stop by during a break, because there will be many instances when your break does not occur at the planned time, due to a call going on longer than normal.

Some friends and neighbors may actually see you through your office window and think it is acceptable to stop by. Also, even if you do share your schedule with them, many people still do not understand that you cannot put your work on hold, even for a few seconds, to stop and speak with them. For this reason, be sure to emphasize that the calls you interpret include emergency calls, and that by stepping away from the call, you could put someone's life in danger. Perhaps this will drive the point home to others that you have no real opportunity to see them during your scheduled work hours.

If this does not solve the problem, you may want to consider hanging a sign on your door during your shift indicating that you are not available to answer the door. Also, if your doorbell is loud enough to be heard from within your office, you may need to consider disconnecting it in order to eliminate the potential distraction.

Another particular problem with neighbors can be the noise generated from their homes. For example, if a neighbor starts mowing the lawn during your shift, this could create a distraction. Or, perhaps one of your neighbors is having some construction work done at home. Whenever possible, notify your neighbors of the nature of your job and the importance of maintaining a quiet work environment, and share your schedule with them so that they can assist you in keeping the noise to a minimum during your work hours.

Real-world tasks

- Talk with friends, neighbors, your extended family and others about your job. Ask them to avoid coming to your home during your work hours.
- Consider hanging a sign on your door or disconnecting your doorbell to further prevent unwanted distractions.
- Ask your neighbors to be especially mindful of noise that could impact your work during scheduled hours.

Real-World Consideration 8: Other Noise Sources

When striving to ensure a quiet work environment, it is important to plan for the uncommon and occasional sources of noise that could affect your work. For example, within the household, other appliances that could generate noise might include air-conditioning units, space heaters, humidifiers, fans, exercise machines, microwaves, hair dryers, and musical equipment. If you live with others, it is important to establish a set of rules regarding any potential noise, in order to eliminate distractions whenever possible.

A common yet often overlooked source of noise is the post man or delivery person. If you place an order, you may want to ask the sender to ship the package without requiring your signature, so that you will not be interrupted with the ringing of the doorbell, and you will not miss the delivery. If you are expecting a package but are not sure if a signature will be required, you might be able to leave a note that requests that the package be left at the door. Alternatively, if you are concerned for the safety of the package, you might put a note on the door asking the delivery person not to ring the bell, and indicate that you will go to the local office to collect the package.

In addition, there are sometimes external sources of noise that are beyond your control. These might include heavy rain, thunder, high winds, and hail, or perhaps the sirens of police, ambulance, and fire trucks in your neighborhood. Hopefully, these occasions will be limited in frequency, but it is best to have an emergency plan in place for these instances when, or if, they do occur. Your plan might include temporarily disconnecting your headset and moving to a room with a connection for your work telephone line that is less exposed to the noise. If that is not possible, you could consider asking your employer to temporarily route your calls to your home line, if you have a room available with a jack for your home line that would provide a quieter environment.

Real-world tasks

- Make a list of all appliances in your home that create noise. If the noise can be heard from within your office, establish a set of ground rules for your family to observe during your work hours.
- For mail carriers and delivery persons, place a note on your door indicating what to do with the package.
- Have an emergency back-up plan for times when disrupting external noises occur.

Chapter 8
Quality in Telephone Interpreting

In the interpreting community at large, the topic of telephone interpreting quality has been hotly debated. Mainly citing personal experiences or single incidents, many critics have stated that the quality of telephone interpreting is below par or, at best, that it is inferior to the quality of interpreting that can be provided by an in-person interpreter.

To the author's knowledge, none of these statements regarding the quality (or lack thereof) of telephone interpreting has been backed up by any empirical evidence or in-depth research studies. Despite the lack of hard data regarding quality, telephone interpreting continues to be plagued by the popular view that it is an inferior but necessary alternative to on-site interpreting. In this chapter, we will review some of the most common myths about telephone interpreting and quality.

Myth 1: Lack of Non-Verbal Information

'Telephone interpreting provides a lower quality of interpreting, due to the total lack of non-verbal information.'

One of the most popular comments made by critics is that telephone interpreting is inferior to other types of interpreting because telephone interpreters are unable to process visual cues provided by body language. However, no research has been conducted that shows that a lack of vision directly impairs an interpreter's ability to interpret precisely and accurately. It is true that a lot of communication in general is non-verbal.

It is important to remember that 'non-verbal' does not necessarily mean 'visual'. Telephone interpreters are able to process a great many non-verbal cues, such as hesitations, inflection, tone of voice, and vocal volume. Only the visual element is missing in telephone interpreting. And just how vital is that?

Many interpreters who are visually impaired or legally blind have become outstanding interpreters with superior abilities. To date, no evidence has been provided to support the idea that a blind interpreter's lack of ability to process visual cues affects his or her ability to render a high quality interpretation. As with so many other jobs, blind people often rely more heavily on other senses to obtain information that allows them to perform at the same level as sighted people.

Having had the pleasure of working with several talented interpreters who happened to be blind, the author can attest to the fact that this condition in no way inhibited their performance at either on-site or telephone interpreting. In fact, the author is familiar with at least one blind interpreter who gained certification as a court interpreter, and another who completed a Master's degree program in translation and interpretation at one of the leading graduate schools in the United States for interpreting and translation.

Telephone interpreters are essentially working in the absence of sight. Because they cannot process visual cues, professional telephone interpreters are specially trained to work in the absence of such cues. Telephone interpreters rely heavily on auditory information to pick up on many types of non-verbal cues and are trained specifically in listening skills and various techniques that are not covered in great depth by most training programs for on-site interpreters.

In one situation, a group of interpreters used to working in a visual environment attempted telephone interpreting themselves – most of them had no training in listening skills and techniques for working effectively as a telephone interpreter. The anecdotal evidence they shared from this experience included comments such as, 'I tried telephone interpreting, but I didn't interpret nearly as effectively because I couldn't see either party,' or 'Without visual cues, I felt that my performance was hindered.' Just as a seeing person wearing a blindfold would stumble around at first and feel uncomfortable in this new environment, an interpreter who is accustomed to seeing would also feel uncomfortable suddenly being subjected to a lack of visual cues in his or her work setting. This evidence also supports the need for specialized training before engaging in this profession.

Interestingly, telephone interpreters with no prior experience in the interpreting field often rapidly excel in the area of listening skills and techniques specific to telephone interpreting for this very reason. If they have no prior interpreting experience, they naturally compensate by using other senses, and they begin their interpreting career being fully accustomed to the lack of visual stimuli. In fact, many interpreters who work full-time over the phone and then work as on-site interpreters find the visual stimuli distracting. They report that they felt the need to close their eyes or look away from the speakers while listening and rendering the interpretation, because they were accustomed to working without visual cues. They do not typically report that they feel that they are able to interpret more accurately because they can suddenly see the speakers.

With interpreters who move from other interpreting settings into telephone interpreting, however, the opposite can be true. It is difficult for individuals with no prior training to learn to interpret in a new way, especially if for many years they have relied more heavily on visual cues.

However, this is not always the case. Some interpreters, even individuals with on-site experience, actually prefer the lack of visual stimuli for certain settings, because they feel that this enhances their interpreting abilities by enabling them to overcome certain challenges that are inherent to on-site interpreting. In the process of conducting research and interviews for this book, various views were captured from interpreters that reported some of the benefits provided to them through telephone interpreting:

- 'Because of my skin color and racial tensions in my native country, when I was an on-site interpreter, many people would second-guess my interpretation or simply try to speak broken English instead of allowing me to interpret. Since starting work as a telephone interpreter, I have not experienced those inconveniences, and I feel that I can provide better interpretation services as a result of the lack of tension surrounding my race. Over the phone, my race is essentially invisible to the other parties.'

- 'In my culture, it is not appropriate for a male to be present during a medical examination of a female, unless he is a close relative or spouse. For this reason, as a male medical interpreter, I was not able to interpret for a large number of in-person assignments, and nearly gave up my career as an interpreter due to a lack of work. Now that I work as a telephone interpreter, there are still certain situations in which a female interpreter is more appropriate, but I can be present over the phone without creating an uncomfortable environment for the patient or myself. This way, I can respect my culture and religion, while still working as an interpreter for health care organizations.'

- 'I live in an area where our ethnic community is very close-knit. When I worked as an in-person interpreter, I became aware of information that created conflicts of interest and difficulties for me. For example, if I knew that a man in our community had a sexually transmitted disease, he would live in fear that I might disclose this information, and I might be afraid if a friend or relative had a relationship with this person. As these instances became more commonplace for me, I became too compromised and resigned from my position. Later, I became a telephone interpreter, and it's a world of difference. Not having to worry about these issues gives me peace of mind and freedom from worry about my responsibilities to my community that I did not have as an on-site interpreter.

- 'As one of the only full-time interpreters in a local hospital, I often was called into the emergency room to interpret for victims of automobile accidents, burns, gunshot wounds, assaults, and other very gruesome injuries. Even though I tried not to look, on a couple of occasions, I actually began to feel faint and had to excuse myself due to the graphic nature of the injuries. I felt very guilty in those cases for leaving the patient without the ability to communicate for those precious minutes. When I interpret telephonically, the injuries do not impact my ability to interpret, because I cannot see them.'

- 'In my country, there are a lot of prejudices against people from a specific group, and they wear a certain type of dress and have features that makes them easy to recognize. We actually have had many conflicts with this group, and I had family members who were killed in battle, so it is hard for me to see them without feeling angry. While I worked as an on-site interpreter, I was aware of my own biases toward them and did not like it when I had to interpret for them. I worked as a telephone interpreter for several years, but it was only when I went back to on-site interpreting that I started to realize how seeing the speaker's identity again distorted my view of that person and was really making me change the way I interpreted for them. I am aware of it now and fighting against my own bias, but interpreting for them was much easier when I couldn't see their appearance.'

These comments highlight some of the real-life experiences faced by working interpreters. Often, critics of telephone interpreting ignore the potential benefits that are provided by a lack of visual cues. Many of these comments point out ethical issues and conflicts of interest that can have a dramatic impact on interpretation quality. While the available research does not prove that a lack of visual cues has a direct impact on interpretation quality, it is clear from the examples above that on-site interpreters do face many ethical issues that in m any cases can be avoided or diminished when visual elements could hinder effective interpreting are removed.

This is not to say that telephone interpreting is preferable to on-site interpreting. Indeed, both types of interpreting have pros and cons associated with them. However, when it comes to quality, current arguments against telephone interpreting are largely based on opinion. Proper research should be conducted in order to yield a fair assessment of the distinctions and preferable venues for on-site and telephone interpreting. Research could include studies in which interpretation is performed by interpreters with equal amounts of experience and training in both types of interpreting, and their performance is measured using the same criteria, with the only true variable being the lack or presence of visual cues.

Are there instances in which on-site interpreting is preferable to telephone interpreting? Absolutely. However, the reasons are related more to the needs of certain groups of speakers and equipment than to the telephonic medium itself.

Telephone interpreting should be avoided, when possible, for situations involving children, the elderly, the hard of hearing, and the mentally ill. All of these groups may have more difficulty understanding someone over the telephone, thereby affecting the quality of the communication.

Also, telephone interpreting is never ideal when the interpreter is placed on speaker phone – this may affect quality tremendously, because the voices are often distorted by background noise, and the interpreter's ability to hear both parties is compromised. Because of this, more requests for repetition are often needed, which makes the process more lengthy and cumbersome. For this reason, dual handset phone equipment is preferable.

Telephone interpreting is often not ideal when more than one speaker needs to hear the interpreter. For example, if a health educator is providing information to various patients who speak another language, it is better to have an on-site interpreter, or to have the interpreter available via video, so that all parties will be able to hear the interpreter at the same time. Finally, when small children or elderly parties are involved, it can often be less than optimal to use a telephone interpreter. Children may not be old enough to communicate effectively over the telephone, and the elderly often experience hearing loss that can create additional barriers to communication.

In the cases described above, the quality of the communication with telephone interpreting is less than optimal, so other types of interpreting, such as on-site or video interpreting, may be preferable. However, when language barriers are present, any interpreter is better than none. Quite often, telephone interpreting is used when other forms of interpreters are not available. While the communication process with telephone interpreting may not be ideal in the above situations, telephone interpreting can at least enable communication to take place.

Myth 2: No Screening of Interpreters
'Telephone interpreting companies will hire pretty much anyone to interpret.'

Taking into account that the vast majority of telephone interpretation is provided by the large, global companies, and given that these few companies have rigorous quality control and certification programs in place, it would be untrue to say that telephone interpreting companies will hire 'just anyone' to work as an interpreter.

Within the United States, quality assurance for interpreting – of all types, not just telephone interpreting – is widespread. For example, in some state courts, interpreters must attend an orientation session, in addition to passing a rigorous court interpretation test. However, in other state courts, untrained volunteer interpreters are still used, who in many cases are not required to provide any proof of language proficiency, interpreting skills or prior experience.

The same is true of health care interpreting, social services interpreting, educational interpreting, and community interpreting in general. Many organizations rely on volunteers or bilingual staff to provide interpreting services. While some volunteers and bilingual employees are trained and/or experienced, it is certainly common for organizations, out of sheer desperation owing to the lack of qualified interpreters in their areas, to accept anyone who volunteers, regardless of his or her professional background. Much of the reason for this problem lies with an uneducated market that takes enormous risks by hiring unqualified persons to perform as interpreters.

Just as it would not be fair to judge all court or community interpreters based on those unfortunate areas in which untrained, untested individuals are unscrupulously used as interpreters throughout the country, it is neither fair nor accurate to assume that this generalization could apply to all telephone interpreters.

The larger telephone interpreting providers have extensive screening and testing processes in place for their interpreters, who are subjected to language proficiency testing, interpretation skills testing, quizzes, and/or tests on ethical principles, and more. In addition, some companies have established a best practice for the field by subjecting each interpreter to criminal background checks and credit checks, as well as to drugs testing.

Myth 3: No Concern for Quality
'Telephone interpreting companies do not care about quality.'

On the contrary, some of the large telephone interpreting companies have programs in place with rigorous requirements that far exceed most quality programs for on-site interpreting. In fact, some programs are so comprehensive that, in addition to multiple training requirements, they include multiple testing requirements. There are some important differences between quality programs that apply to the majority of telephone interpreters and those used for the majority of on-site interpreters.

For example, the largest providers of telephone interpreting services have extensive on-the-job monitoring programs, in which interpreters are assigned a senior interpreter or mentor who specifically monitors on an ongoing basis them for quality and adherence to standards. This type of quality assurance process is extremely effective at improving and maintaining quality for interpreters. Yet, with certain exceptions, it is largely unheard of for interpreters to be subjected to such rigorous monitoring requirements outside of telephone interpreting. Certainly, there are no universal criteria for monitoring on-site interpreters.

Also, telephone interpreting companies often have programs in place to gather and analyze customer feedback. While customer feedback alone is not necessarily a valid indicator of quality, when used in conjunction with other information, such as monitoring scores, this can prove to be extremely valuable.

If a customer complains about a telephone interpreter's performance, a member of the company's quality assurance team is immediately alerted. If the company records calls for quality monitoring (which is common for some large providers), the company may retrieve the actual call in question to find out more details about the interpreter's performance and the customer's feedback. In some cases, the customer may have been complaining about an issue that was not related to the interpreter. For example, suppose a customer complains of a dog barking in the background. The quality assurance team may learn upon analysis of the call that the noise could not have come from the interpreter's background, because the interpreter was working in a call center environment, and that the noise probably came from the LEP caller's background.

However, if the complaint is a valid one, then, depending on the severity of the complaint, the interpreter will probably be put on an intensive monitoring program to ensure that the behavior is corrected. In some cases, especially if complaints recur, the interpreter may be dismissed.

Telephone interpreting companies also have the added pressure of knowing that, if quality is not maintained, they could lose the customer to a competitor. Therefore, telephone interpreting companies have an additional motivation for emphasizing quality, and for having processes for resolving complaints and for monitoring.

It is also rare for on-site interpreters to have opportunities for continuing education once they have received their initial training. In the telephone interpreting world, however, this is a standard practice in some of the largest companies, with training sessions being made available via telephone on a wide variety of topics for interpreters of many languages, often on a monthly or even weekly basis.

On the flip side, however, just as the on-site interpreting world is plagued with groups that put less emphasis on quality, many small telephone interpreting companies have sprung up in recent years, and some of these have been formed by individuals with little or no background in the language services industry. So it is difficult to say what kind of quality of services such companies are providing.

One thing is certain – some telephone interpreting companies do put a great deal of time, energy, and resources into their quality programs. Some go so far as to involve leading experts from academia in their programs on an ongoing basis.

Also, it is not necessarily the case that the smaller providers do not care about quality. It is more likely that their lack of experience and resources prevents them from developing processes and programs that ensure high-quality services. Or, perhaps their strategy is to pursue the low-hanging fruit: customers who do not care about quality and are motivated purely by price, or less sophisticated consumers, who do not require proof or quality assurance measures. The latter might be representative of a company that simply does not understand the importance of quality in the provision of telephone interpreting services. For a telephone interpreting company to survive and thrive, quality must be a top priority.

Myth 4: Desire to Replace On-Site interpreting

'Telephone interpreting providers are trying to replace the profession of on-site interpreting.'

In the chapter on the history and evolution of telephone interpreting earlier in this book, it was pointed out that telephone interpreting was created in response to specific needs. In Australia, it was born out of the need to provide interpreters for social services settings in spite of great distances. In the United States, it was created largely because companies and organizations sought to provide an ever-expanding array of services (such as 911 emergency services) via telephone to consumers and members of the public in populations with limited English proficiency.

In other words, the original intention behind telephone interpreting providers was not to replace on-site interpreters. Today, it is doubtful that telephone interpreting companies are seeking to replace on-site interpreters. However, providers of telephone interpreting services are responding to a demand that exists. In the case of public providers, they are responding to the need to provide LEP individuals with government services and benefits. In the case of private providers, they are responding to the market demand for services. If situations change and the demand decreases, so will the need for telephone interpreting.

In fact, it is likely that demand could decrease with time, or that the needs of the market will change. As more services are provided to consumers over the World Wide Web, interpreting services will more than likely be provided via VoIP (Voice over Internet Protocol) technology. Already, many large telephone interpreting companies have begun to provide interpretation services via video conferencing.

However, the costs of such technology are still prohibitive and the individuals who are most in need of interpreting services are often immigrant and/or marginalized minority-language populations with scarce financial resources. So it is uncertain at what point the cost of providing interpretation services through new technologies will enable the masses to experience these innovations. It will probably be a gradual process, but one that is dependent on economic stability, immigration patterns, language usage trends, technology developments, and other factors.

Eventually, if technology continues to progress along its current path, the notion of a telephone interpreter may be replaced by that of a remote interpreter. The end user will be able to control both video and audio feeds, thereby choosing to add visual cues when necessary, or perhaps eliminating them from certain scenarios if it seems that the disadvantages might outweigh the advantages. In fact, sight translation could be performed by the same remote interpreter through digital scanning and real-time text or instant messaging. With the support of emerging technology, there are many possibilities for revolutionizing access to language services.

Myth 5: Lack of Confidentiality

'Telephone interpreters routinely use cell phones, cordless phones, and other equipment subjecting client information to significant security risks.'

Most large telephone interpreting providers have interpreters in call center environments using landline telephones with headsets. Some companies have provisions in their employee contracts that stipulate that cordless and wireless devices may not be used at all, because of the risk of a line being intercepted.

With work-at-home employees, interpreting providers must have stringent guidelines in place to ensure that the interpreters understand and implement their internal standards for performance, which should include standards regarding equipment. In the case of some large providers, work-at-home employees are monitored with increased frequency and/or over longer periods of time, to ensure that the appropriate equipment is being used.

Even if all interpretation is one day provided via video or audio streaming over the Internet, and all interpretation is provided via call centers or from home-based offices, the debate about whether an interpreter should have access to visual cues or not and whether or not this affects the quality of the interpretation will probably remain a relevant issue of discussion many years from now.

In summary, all quality debates aside, remote interpreting is here to stay. As the field evolves in conjunction with technology improvements, it will be interesting to see what role telephone interpreting plays.

Part 3

Ethics and Standards

Chapter 9
Model Code of Ethics for Telephone Interpreting

There are numerous documents available that provide guidance related to ethical considerations for interpreters. Many national and local interpreting associations from various countries throughout the world have made efforts to define ethical responsibilities for interpreters, specifically as it pertains to their specific settings and types of interpreting (Bancroft, 2005).

In the case of medical and court interpreting associations, the codes of ethics are, quite naturally, tailored toward the specific skills and situations that interpreters will most likely need to consider, given the nature of their work in a given setting. Many codes of ethics and standards are more generalist in nature and could be applied to a number of settings.

Where telephone interpreting is concerned, there are additional ethical considerations to address, owing to the wide variety of settings in which telephone interpreting is utilized (e.g. health care, insurance, court, and emergency calls) and the types of interpreting performed.

Also, the fact that telephone interpreting is provided by private companies necessitates a customer service aspect of interpreting that may not be required in other settings. In legal interpreting, for example, providing a pleasant interaction and high level of customer satisfaction is not necessarily a consideration for the interpreter.

For this reason, many telephone interpreting companies find it necessary to either (a) provide their interpreters with a diverse array of codes of ethics, (b) provide their own, customized code of ethics for telephone interpreters, or (c) provide both. Many companies also have an internal code of ethics, which is distributed to interpreters and non-interpreters alike.

However, since many telephone interpreting companies supply interpreters for specific industries as well, these interpreters can benefit from familiarizing themselves with codes of ethics from a particular field.

Because there is no national association for telephone interpreting in the United States, no national code of ethics has been produced for the field. Therefore, in the interest of providing guidance and recommendations regarding the most important ethical considerations as they specifically relate to telephone interpreting, a model code of ethics for telephone interpreters prepared by the author is provided below.

Unlike a standards document, which often provides a great level of detail, a code of ethics usually serves to provide a foundation upon which standards can be built. It is typical in many professions for a set of ethical principles to guide behavioral practice of working professionals. The model code of ethics provides the ethical principles for the model standards found in Chapters 10 to 14.

Model Code of Ethics for Telephone Interpreters

The purpose of this Model Code of Ethics for Telephone Interpreters is to provide a general definition of the guiding ethical principles required of professional telephone interpreters. All interpreters employed by a telephone interpreting company are held accountable for adhering to these principles. Detailed standards that fall under each guiding principle and relate specifically to telephone interpreting are presented in the next chapter.

1. *Confidentiality:* The telephone interpreter maintains confidentiality of all information obtained throughout each call.
2. *Ethical Conduct:* The telephone interpreter avoids obtaining any personal advantage on any call and discloses any perceived conflicts of interest to both the client and the employer.
3. *Impartiality:* The telephone interpreter projects an impartial attitude and treats all parties in a manner that fosters trust and mutual respect.
4. *Accuracy and Completeness:* The telephone interpreter renders the information as accurately and completely as possible, conveying the information, as well as its original spirit and intent.
5. *Role Boundaries:* The telephone interpreter avoids personal involvement and respects the boundaries of the roles of all parties.
6. *Professional Conduct:* The telephone interpreter displays professional behavior at all times and uses language and tone of voice that displays a high level of customer service toward both parties.
7. *Professional Development:* The telephone interpreter continually seeks out opportunities to enhance his or her professional skills and knowledge.

Practical Applications

Now let us look a bit deeper into each ethical principle to provide more detail on the specific applications and unique aspects of these principles as they relate to telephone interpreting.

1. Confidentiality

The telephone interpreter maintains confidentiality of all information obtained throughout each call.

Unique aspects of confidentiality in telephone interpreting

Telephone interpreters are often in receipt of information that is highly confidential. In particular, some of the situations that are specific to telephone interpreting may present unique challenges when it comes to maintaining confidentiality. Unlike conference interpreting, in which the interpreted information is normally for an audience of multiple listeners, in telephone interpreting, the information is often being rendered for an audience of only one, and the end goal of the conversation is to complete a transaction of some sort, which is usually of a highly personal nature.

Confidentiality of financial information

Thousands of calls are interpreted via telephone each day that involve financial information, such as credit card numbers, social security numbers and bank account numbers. The transactions may involve taking out a loan from one's personal retirement account, transferring money to an overseas location, or setting up a payment arrangement for an overdue credit card balance.

Owing to the possibilities of identity theft and fraud, any financial information must be heavily guarded. In many countries, privacy of financial information is required by law. It is for this reason that many providers of financial services require interpreters to verbally confirm prior to beginning the interpretation that they will maintain confidentiality. In many cases, the provider will read a disclosure that the interpreter must render for the non-English-speaking customer, in order for the customer to approve the presence of a third party (the interpreter) throughout the duration of the conversation and/or transaction.

Privacy of health information

Another area where confidentiality takes on great importance is the health care industry. Because of regulations requiring privacy of patient information in health care, such as the Health Insurance Portability and Accountability Act of 1996 (HIPAA) in the United States, it is extremely important for all health care providers to be in compliance with this law. This includes their interactions with patients over the phone, or when a telephone interpreter is used for a live encounter.

An area of great concern related to confidentiality is that, in some communities, speakers of a certain language may be closely connected to one another. For example, in a small community where only 20 people speak Somali, it is very likely that the only person available in a live setting to interpret for the patient is someone who knows the patient on a personal level – perhaps even a family member. Obviously, this puts the interpreter in a potential ethical situation.

While having an in-person interpreter can be decidedly advantageous in certain situations, providing an interpreter over the phone can reduce or eliminate the possibility of this specific ethical dilemma when the number of speakers of a particular language group is small and the geographic pool from which interpreters are drawn is limited.

Disclosing information: How much is too much?

It is important for telephone interpreters to be able to speak about their work for many reasons. For example, they might need to request assistance and feedback regarding individual situations, to help mentor other telephone interpreters, to educate end users of telephone interpreting services, or to share information so as to benefit the interpreting community and society as a whole. In fact, many telephone interpreting companies require interpreters to participate in one or more of these activities as part of their ongoing professional development. Does this present a conflict of interests?

The answer to that question depends on the amount of information shared. As long as the telephone interpreter follows one basic rule of thumb, there should be no conflict of interests. The general guideline is this: When discussing actual telephone interpreting calls, the telephone interpreter should avoid revealing any identifying information that was disclosed during the call. In other words, the interpreter should avoid mentioning the names of any individuals or companies, or any geographic location or numerical information that would provide specific identification of a person, entity or place.

For example, if an interpreter needed to inquire about terminology during a mentoring session with a senior interpreter, the interpreter could phrase the inquiry while maintaining confidentiality of identifying information:

> Incorrect: When I was interpreting recently for Mary at A1 Services, she used the phrase 'budget billing', and I would like to know

the best way to interpret that phrase into Vietnamese.

Correct: When I was interpreting recently for a representative at a financial services company, she used the phrase 'budget billing', and I would like to know the best way to interpret that phrase into Vietnamese.

Finally, given the team-based nature of telephone interpreting, in which interpreters interact with each other in group training and coaching sessions, it is important for interpreters to remind each other of the importance of maintaining confidentiality and upholding this ethical principle, so that such practices become part of the organization's behavior and all interpreters are accountable for safeguarding information.

Obviously, there are times when certain identifying information must be shared, such as situations that require follow-up for customer service purposes, on the part of the telephone interpreting company. Also, in cases where client-specific training materials are provided, it is obvious that interpreters will need to refer to the client name for those situations. The overall goal, however, is that interpreters learn which settings are appropriate for sharing identifying information, and which settings are not appropriate.

Practice exercise

With a partner, discuss three telephone interpretation call scenarios, either real or hypothetical, without disclosing any identifying information. If any identifying information is accidentally shared, reinforce the fact that everyone is held accountable for safeguarding that information. Develop three optional appropriate phrases to talk about each call scenario.

2. Ethical Conduct

The telephone interpreter avoids obtaining any personal advantage on any call and discloses any perceived conflicts of interest to both the client and the employer.

Ethical issues in consumer situations

Because telephone interpreters often interpret for consumers, there is a large potential for exposure to information about new products, services, and rates. Given the competitive dynamic of the consumer marketplace, it makes sense that, as consumers, interpreters are also interested in the latest promotions and offers for personal use.

Suppose an interpreter receives a call to interpret for a long-distance telephone provider, in which the Spanish-speaking customer is offered a low promotional per-minute rate for her calls to a specific area of Mexico. The interpreter happens to use this telephone provider for her own home phone line, and is surprised that the rate being offered to the customer is lower than she herself is paying.

An obvious breach of ethical conduct would be for the interpreter to say, 'own home phone?' That is something that most interpreters would immediately realize constitutes a violation of their code of ethics, and professionally-trained interpreters would never even try such a thing. However, an interpreter might think, 'As soon as I finish work today, I'm going to call and request that my long distance calls be re-rated!' And, because the interpreter is not violating any ethical principles during the course of the call, it might seem to some interpreters that there is no violation of the code of ethics.

So, let's assume that the interpreter waits until after her workday has ended, and then places the call to the long distance phone provider:

INTERPRETER: Hello! I'm calling to enroll in the new promotional rate plan your company is offering for calls to Mexico. I'm currently paying 4 cents per minute more than the new rate.

REPRESENTATIVE: I'm sorry. You currently have the lowest per-minute rate plan for calls to Mexico.

INTERPRETER: But that can't be ... I just heard that your company is offering this new rate.

REPRESENTATIVE: No, ma'am. I'm sorry. There is no new rate.

INTERPRETER: I'm certain there is a new rate. May I speak to your supervisor please?

REPRESENTATIVE: Yes, Ma'am, but again, you have the lowest rate. Just one moment, and I'll get my supervisor on the line.

INTERPRETER: Yes, please do that!

SUPERVISOR: Thank you for calling. How may I help you?

INTERPRETER: Yes, your representative is claiming that I have the lowest possible rate for calls to Mexico, but I know that other customers are getting a better rate, and that is not fair! I want the new rate, which is 4 cents lower than my rate.

SUPERVISOR: Ma'am, you do have the lowest rate available for your area.

INTERPRETER: No, I don't! There are other people getting a much lower rate, and I want the lower rate too!

SUPERVISOR: Hmmm. We do have a promotional pilot program that we are offering to a test group of 200 customers in another state. However, that program just started today, and we have only enrolled a few individuals so far. It is not available here yet. Do you mind if I ask how you heard about the program?

As you can see, the interpreter has now entered into an even more difficult situation. If the interpreter responds to the supervisor's question by stating the truth, that she learned about the rate during a call she interpreted, it is very likely that the supervisor will call the telephone interpreting company to complain about the interpreter. For a violation such as this, most telephone interpreting companies would terminate the interpreter's employment. If the interpreter says anything other than the truth, the interpreter will be lying, and this could lead to a whole host of other problems.

In any case, this provides a clear example of why a telephone interpreter should not use any information obtained during the course of work for personal gain. The examples of potential situations are too numerous to list, and the fact that interpreters will often be exposed to information like this, which may create an opportunity for the interpreters to take advantage of the information, is simply a part of the telephone interpreter's daily work. Therefore, it is extremely important for telephone interpreters to be mentally prepared in advance for this type of situation to occur, and to be aware of the dangers of utilizing any information obtained for one's own personal advantage.

Obviously, there are many other examples of potential ethical dilemmas related to conduct, as is the case with any type of interpreting. However, because consumer situations are very common in telephone interpreting, they present challenges that are more likely to be experienced by telephone interpreters than by interpreters in other settings.

Practice Exercise

Think of three telephone-interpretation call scenarios, either real or hypothetical, in the following three categories: insurance, health care, and finance, that would present a temptation for the interpreter to use information for personal gain. What are the potentially dangerous or risky outcomes if the interpreter uses this information?

3. Impartiality

The telephone interpreter projects an impartial attitude and treats all parties in a manner that fosters trust and mutual respect.

Balancing customer service and impartiality

A telephone interpreter's job description is unique in that, in addition to maintaining impartiality, the interpreter must provide an exceptional level of customer service. At first glance, this may appear to present a conflict of interests. However, this is not the case, as long as the interpreter remembers that he/she should be providing good customer service to both parties.

More often than not, violations in impartiality for telephone interpreters tend to represent a bias toward the company client, perhaps in an interpreter's effort to provide good customer service. In other words, the interpreter may be more prone to 'take the side' of the client company representative, even though he or she has not been asked to do so in any way. This particular situation often occurs when the client company representative is having a difficult time obtaining the desired result or response from the LEP customer.

When monitoring telephone interpreters, experienced professionals in the industry make a distinction between what distinguishes a code of ethics violation under the category of impartiality from a violation in the category of role. Generally speaking, under the category of impartiality, an interpreter is expected not to favor one party over another and to treat all parties in the same manner.

Therefore, violations of impartiality may be more subtle and difficult to detect than violations of role, which are made obvious by an interpreter's words and/or actions. Over the phone, there are several common ways in which an interpreter may manifest a lack of impartiality.

Tone of voice/inflection

If the interpreter interprets for one party while using a tone of voice that audibly conveys a different level of respect or patience than is employed for the other party, this may be an indicator of a lack of impartiality. Also, if the interpreter changes the inflection, thereby altering the original intent, this may also indicate an interpreter's lack of impartiality. Obviously, a single instance of either of these may not be enough to determine that an interpreter is lacking impartiality. However, if they repeatedly occur, a pattern can be identified that may serve as a more reliable indicator.

Adding emphasis

The following is an example of how an interpreter's lack of impartiality might affect the interpreter's rendition by placing emphasis on words that did not have emphasis in the source utterance, thereby changing the inflection of speech:

CLIENT: We've asked you on multiple occasions to send your payment on time, but you are consistently paying 15 days behind schedule. This leaves us with no choice but to charge a late payment fee of $30.00 every time you pay late. Do you understand?

Assuming that the client representative stated this utterance in a very calm, business-like and neutral tone of voice, the interpreter should render it in the same way. However, let's assume that the interpreter renders it as follows, and that words written in all capital letters are given more emphasis by the interpreter:

INTERPRETER: We've asked you on MULTIPLE occasions to send your payment ON TIME, but you are CONSISTENTLY paying 15 days BEHIND SCHEDULE. This leaves us with no choice but to charge a late payment fee of $30.00 EVERY TIME you pay late. Do you understand?

The interpreter may be stressing these words in an effort to make it extremely clear to the LEP person that the company has already asked the LEP to send in the payment several times, but that again and again, the payment keeps arriving late, so the LEP is getting charged an additional $30.00 for each late payment. However, the interpreter's job is not 'to make it extremely clear', the interpreter's job is to render the information accurately.

At first glance, perhaps this does not seem like much of an issue. In fact, some might even say that the interpreter's lack of impartiality in this case is extremely minor and serves to support the goal of the client company in obtaining a timely payment from its customer.

However, what if the company has specifically trained its representatives to speak in a very calm and business-like tone of voice, without stressing or emphasizing any particular words, because the company has carried out studies that showed that such a tone of voice increased the likelihood that the customer will pay in a timely manner? In that case, the interpreter has defeated the purpose of the company's training techniques by altering the tone of voice.

Removing emphasis

Another situation that may also occur as a result of a lack of impartiality is for the interpreter to do the exact opposite of the above example. In this case, the interpreter removes emphasis that was originally intended by the speaker of the source utterance:

> **CLIENT:** We've asked you on MULTIPLE occasions to send your payment ON TIME, but you are CONSISTENTLY paying 15 days BEHIND SCHEDULE. This leaves us with no choice but to charge a late payment fee of $30.00 EVERY TIME you pay late. Do you understand?

What the interpreter renders is a watered-down version of the same statement. Technically, the interpreter leaves the words the same, but alters the meaning by changing the emphasis.

> **INTERPRETER:** We've asked you on multiple occasions to send your payment on time, but you are consistently paying 15 days behind schedule. This leaves us with no choice but to charge a late payment fee of $30.00 every time you pay late. Do you understand?

The interpreter may think that he or she is providing better customer service and improving the relationship between the two parties by changing the inflection slightly to make it sound less potentially offensive. However, let's stop to consider the potential consequences of this seemingly minor change.

If the interpretation is rendered with the source inflection intact, let's assume that the LEP customer (in this case a man) decides that he is tired of being charged a late fee, and because of his perception that the client is upset with him for making late payments, he decides to switch to a new credit card company. The customer finds a credit card company with a longer grace period, which means that he no longer has to pay late payment fees. However, if the interpreter 'tones down' the message, perhaps the customer will not switch companies, but will stay with this company. A few months later, because of the constant late fees, the account is sent to a collections agency.

While these examples may seem drastic, in reality an interpreter's inability to maintain impartiality can actually cause many 'ripple effects' that can affect the lives and businesses of the company clients and their customers. For this reason, it is best for telephone interpreters to focus on rendering the meaning accurately and completely, rather than worrying about the outcome or result of a telephone interaction.

Embellishment/repetition

Another common manifestation of an interpreter's lack of impartiality is the slight embellishment of the utterance, or repetition of certain words or phrases. For purposes of simplicity, we will build upon the previous example, in which the client had placed emphasis on certain words:

> **CLIENT:** We've asked you on MULTIPLE occasions to send your payment ON TIME, but you are CONSISTENTLY paying 15 days BEHIND SCHEDULE. This leaves us with no choice but to charge a late payment fee of $30.00 EVERY TIME you pay late. Do you understand?

It is not uncommon, especially when the client uses the above type of emphasis, for the interpreter to be tempted to take the message 'a step further' by adding additional emphasis through embellishment and/or repetition of certain words and phrases.

> **CLIENT:** It's very important that you realize that we've asked you on MULTIPLE occasions, over and over, to send your payment ON TIME instead of sending it late, but you are CONSISTENTLY paying 15 days BEHIND SCHEDULE. When you pay late like this, it leaves us with no choice but to charge a late payment fee of $30.00 EVERY TIME you pay late, which we have to keep doing again and again. Do you understand that if you keep paying late, you will be paying an extra $30.00 each time?

At first glance, perhaps it seems that the interpreter provided a rendition that was faithful for the most part. However, upon closer analysis, one can see that there was quite a bit of embellishment and repetition of ideas. Even if the embellishment and repetition did serve to support or reinforce the original intent behind the source utterance, it is important to recognize that this seemingly small change to the meaning may have an impact on the outcome that was not originally intended. Just as in the examples of inflection, there can be a ripple effect whenever a small change takes place.

> *Practice exercise*
>
> Write a sample phrase to be interpreted three different ways: (1) with no emphasis added, (2) with emphasis added, and (3) with slight embellishment/repetition added that reinforces the intended meaning Try writing phrases for various different

settings, such as education, telecommunications, and health care. Then, write down the potential impacts of rendering the utterance in these three different ways, and how it would affect both the client company and the LEP customer.

4. Accuracy and Completeness

The telephone interpreter renders the information as accurately and completely as possible, conveying the information as well as its original spirit and intent.

Offensive comments

When it comes to accuracy and completeness, one of the most common questions from interpreters is how to handle rude or offensive language. The very nature of the question is confusing, because what is considered 'rude' or 'offensive' varies substantially from one person to another, from one culture to another, and from one language to another. The answer to the question is that the interpreter's main duty is to render the information accurately and completely from one language to another.

In other words, the telephone interpreter should not simply 'leave things out' whenever there is a fear that the utterance might be regarded as rude or offensive. In order for a message to be regarded as accurate, it must be complete, and vice versa.

Let us take an example:

LEP: I just don't understand why my insurance doesn't cover me for this.

CLIENT: I've told you thirty times in the last two hours that you were not insured with us at the time of the accident! I don't know how many ways I have to explain it to you. You obviously aren't the sharpest knife in the drawer.

Although the client's comment may be regarded as very rude, the interpreter should simply render it as accurately as possible, regardless of concern over how it may be perceived. There are a variety of potential outcomes. Let us look at a few of them:

LEP: How dare you! I demand to speak to your supervisor!

In this case, the LEP caller may end up voicing his concern to the supervisor, and perhaps this was another incident of many that will cause the representative to be dismissed from the job. At the very least, the supervisor will probably coach the representative on this behavior, which means that the company benefits from this knowledge, and may retain the LEP as a customer.

> **LEP:** Well, I'm sorry, but I only made it to 2nd grade, and I never had insurance before in my home country, so I have a hard time understanding these concepts, but I am really trying my best.

The representative may then explain the coverage in a different way.

> **LEP:** I refuse to stand for this! I will pay the bill myself, and as of today, I am switching to a different company.

Only by interpreting this information accurately, could the interpreter give the LEP the chance to decide how to react to it. If the interpreter takes it upon him/herself to make an assumption about how this information might be perceived, the interpreter is taking on responsibility that falls, in most cases, outside of the role of the interpreter.

Profanity and racial slurs

In many cases, the context or industry for which the interpreter is interpreting will dictate how to handle profanity and/or racial slurs. If the setting is a public safety call or a domestic violence hotline, for example, this type of language should be faithfully and accurately rendered, just as if it were any other type of information. The same is true for legal and insurance scenarios.

In certain, rare scenarios where words or phrases are used that are undeniably offensive, such as highly profane language or racial slurs, and this language appears to be directed at one of the parties on the call, it may be advisable, depending on the context, for the telephone interpreter to provide a brief disclaimer to either party before interpreting phrases that may be perceived as exceedingly offensive.

In these cases, the telephone interpreter may provide a brief disclaimer prior to rendering the utterance, such as, 'This is the interpreter; the following is a verbatim interpretation and does not reflect the interpreter's personal opinion:' This disclaimer should be followed by a faithful interpretation.

Given the more customer-service-oriented nature of telephone interpreting, the chances of this happening outside of one of the contexts mentioned above, such as domestic violence or public safety, are minimal, but it may occur from time to time. Also, when highly sensitive terms, such as a racial epithet or extremely profane language, are used in a context in which these do not normally occur, it may be of extra importance to make it clear to the client company representative that the foul language or racial slur is not coming from the interpreter.

Cultural clarification

In certain situations, because of a cultural misunderstanding, it may be important for an interpreter to provide additional clarification. This is not necessarily to say that the interpreter would omit information or interpret with anything less than accuracy. However, at times, to alleviate a cultural barrier, an interpreter may need to provide a cultural explanation, such as in the following example:

> **CLIENT:** Can I get the last name, please?
> **INTERPRETER:** Can I get the last name, please?
> **LEP:** González López.
> **INTERPRETER:** González López.
> **CLIENT:** Which one is it? González or López? Why don't these people ever know their last name?
> **INTERPRETER:** This is the interpreter speaking. It is common for many Spanish speakers to use both the last name of the father and the mother's maiden name.
> **CLIENT:** Oh. I didn't know that. Thanks, interpreter. OK, Sir, I only have space for one last name on this form. Would you like me to use González or López?

By providing the client with this additional bit of cultural information, the interpreter was able to help overcome a barrier to communication. However, it is important that interpreters remember (1) to provide this type of clarification only when absolutely necessary, and (2) to refrain from making generalizations when clarifying.

As an example, it would not be appropriate to say, 'You need to rephrase that sentence, because in Vietnamese culture, you are not being polite,' or 'All speakers of Spanish use two last names'. These statements are too general and sweeping to really be accurate.

As with all guidelines and ethical principles, it is up to the individual telephone interpreting company to provide the interpreters with examples and training on how to provide cultural clarification. In fact, some companies may instruct interpreters to avoid this type of intervention. Much of it depends on the company's internal code of ethics and customer service guidelines.

Practice exercise

Write three sample scenarios in the categories of utilities, travel/ entertainment and social services in which either speaker directs a rude comment toward the other. How can the interpreter most effectively and appropriately handle the situation?

5. Role Boundaries

The telephone interpreter avoids personal involvement and respects the boundaries of the roles of all parties.

Health care interpreting

This book does not focus exclusively on health care interpreting, but it is extremely important to recognize that there are additional considerations for medical scenarios that may not necessarily apply to the situations and recommendations outlined in this chapter. Each telephone interpreting provider defines the roles of the interpreter in medical interpreting according to their specific training program for medical interpreters. In health care settings, it is not uncommon for the interpreter to focus more on cultural aspects of interpreting. Whether or not this constitutes an additional role, or an expanded definition of the role, for the interpreter may vary from one company to another.

Other telephone interpreting settings

While there are many possible examples of how an interpreter might step outside the role in non-health care settings, we will assume that most of a telephone interpreter's violations of this ethical principle stem from the fact that the interpreter has good intentions that sometimes get him or her into trouble. In other words, often in an effort to help, the interpreter may do something that falls outside of the scope of interpreting. Ironically, this is often an issue for experienced telephone interpreters as well as for novice interpreters. Let's look at the following example:

CLIENT: Thank you for calling A1 Services, may I have your account number please?

INTERPRETER: This is the interpreter. After getting the account number, would you like to verify the billing address and the seven-character password on the account, and then ask the reason for the call?

There are many reasons why the interpreter should not offer to 'take on' any additional responsibilities, such as obtaining all of the client's follow-up questions, even if the interpreter knows that this client normally asks questions in a specific order. However, for purposes of this example, let's assume that the interpreter gathers all of this information and then starts to render it back to the client.

INTERPRETER: The account number is 123456789. The billing address is ...

CLIENT: Actually, I can tell from that account number that this customer is in the wrong department. Let me transfer the customer to the correct office.

In this scenario, by stepping outside the role, the interpreter, in an effort to help, actually wasted the time of both parties. It was unnecessary for the interpreter to gather all of the additional information, and in doing so, the interpreter delayed the client's discovery of the fact that the customer was in the wrong department. In other words, even in an effort to help, it is not appropriate for the interpreter to step outside of the role.

In some cases, the interpreter may actually be requested to step outside of the role. For example, the client may say, 'Interpreter, can you explain to the customer the difference between long distance and local toll calls? If the interpreter is asked to do this, the interpreter can only state, 'The interpreter will defer to your expertise to provide an explanation, and the interpreter will be happy to interpret it for you.' The interpreter must not step outside of the role, no matter what requests are made by either party. If an individual is insistent in requesting that the interpreter steps outside of the role, the interpreter may say, 'The standards of practice for the profession dictate that this would fall outside of the interpreter's role.'

Practice exercise

Write three examples of how a telephone interpreter's desire to help may result in the interpreter stepping outside of the role within the legal, insurance, and telecommunications industries. What is the impact of this on the other two parties?

6. Professional Conduct

The telephone interpreter displays professional behavior at all times and uses language and tone of voice that displays a high level of customer service toward both parties.

Professional conduct refers to a great number of things, such as focusing solely on the task of interpreting, behaving in a professional manner and using a tone of voice and language that are appropriate for the setting.

However, the reference to tone of voice and customer service toward both refers to the interpreter's professional behavior when speaking as the interpreter. Unlike tone of voice in the context of impartiality, in which the interpreter is not to alter or enhance the inflection and tone conveyed in the source utterance, here tone of voice refers to the tone of voice used by the interpreter when the interpreter is interacting with the client company representative or the LEP customer.

In other words, the interactions in which the interpreter will be judged on professional behavior are probably very limited, but they are important nonetheless, especially as they display a telephone interpreter's level of customer service.

Examples of an interpreter's level of professionalism and customer service when requesting a repetition is given below. These range from (a), which exhibits a very poor level of customer service and professionalism, to (j), in which the interpreter would be in observance of this particular ethical principle.

(a) 'Repeat that.'
(b) 'Repetition, please.'
(c) 'Can you repeat that?'
(d) 'Can you repeat that, please?'
(e) 'The interpreter needs a repetition.'
(e) 'The interpreter requests a repetition."
(f) 'May the interpreter have a repetition?'
(g) 'May the interpreter have a repetition, please?'
(h) 'Would you mind repeating that for the interpreter, please?'
(i) 'May the interpreter kindly request a repetition, please?'
(j) 'Sir/Madam, may the interpreter kindly request a repetition, please?'

Obviously, the poorest customer service tactic is to give the client an order, such as, 'Repeat that.' As the phrases improve along the scale of customer service from (a) to (j), the interpreter is increasingly polite and respectful toward the client.

Practice exercise

During a telephone interpretation call, the interpreter needs to verify the payment amount given by the client to ensure accuracy. Write a list of at least seven different ways to express the request for a verification of the payment amount. Which are the most appropriate in terms of professionalism and customer service?

7. Professional Development

The telephone interpreter continually seeks out opportunities to enhance his/her professional skills and knowledge.

The traditional definition of professional development for interpreters usually includes continuing education through courses, membership in professional associations, and mentoring other interpreters. While all those things are equally important for telephone interpreters, numerous additional opportunities wait around every corner.

To learn new terminology that may come up in a call, the telephone interpreter might simply review the language used in advertisements, such as the financial disclosures and terms in fine print on one of the many credit card offers. Instead of tossing out the insert on the new money-saving offer that is enclosed with the monthly gas bill, the savvy telephone interpreter will scan the information for new terminology and make a mental note of any phrases that are repeated. When calling to request a price quote for auto insurance, a telephone interpreter mentally interprets all the phrases being used throughout the quote process.

Telephone interpreters can find terminology that is useful in their everyday lives, and there is never a shortage of new terminology and new scenarios, especially given the customer service relationship that is typically found in many telephone interpreting calls. In addition to terminology, however, telephone interpreters are constantly experiencing new challenges, diverse situations, and fresh experiences.

An added feature of telephone interpreting is the fact that so many different industries are encompassed within the job description. This makes telephone interpreters uniquely likely to join various organizations and professional associations across many different types of interpreting, in order to gain as much information as possible about all areas that the telephone interpreter might encounter.

When interpreters fail to take charge of their professional development, this usually results in a lack of enthusiasm for the job, and therefore, decreased performance and quality. For this reason, many telephone interpreting companies provide training programs and learning opportunities, to ensure that the job is kept fun and exciting, which increases employee retention and boosts quality of service. Also, this allows interpreters to benefit by learning from each other and sharing information to enable experienced interpreters' strengths to shine.

Practice exercise

Write a list of ways in which an interpreter might advance his or her professional development by utilizing professional associations, training programs of interest to telephone interpreters, books, and educational conferences, as well as 'everyday learning opportunities' that may enhance one's skills as a telephone interpreter. List the resource, the action or involvement the interpreter can take and the benefit that he or she would receive.

Chapter 10
Model Standards of Practice for Telephone Interpreting

Background

This chapter presents Model Standards of Practice for Telephone Interpreters developed by the author in order to foster high standards of ethical and professional practice in the delivery of telephone interpreting services through recognized standards that assure the competency of telephone interpreters. The Model Standards of Practice were developed to ensure that working telephone interpreters are aware of the existence of high standards of practice for the profession and are committed to upholding those standards.

Also, the Model Standards of Practice are meant to assist members of the general public, including consumers, with understanding the duties and responsibilities of telephone interpreters. The Standards are a reflection of existing best practice and prevailing standards in the industry. It is hoped that they will be adopted more formally – by providers, customers, and the interpreting community at large – so that they can be enforced. This will help to ensure that the necessary levels of quality in telephone interpreting can be maintained.

Finally, these standards serve to provide telephone interpreters with a clear statement of the expectations of professional conduct and level of practice afforded to the public in the following areas: professionalism, ethical requirements, confidentiality, interpreting practices, roles, and boundaries, and customer service.

As in many other areas of professional practice, a Model Code of Ethics provides guiding principles by which individuals conduct their day-to-day work. Within the field of interpreting, the idea of providing model standards of practice that link to guiding ethical principles is one that has been successfully pioneered by the National Council on Interpreting in

Health Care.

In the context of telephone interpreting, the Standards build on this foundation by providing specific guidelines and applications of the principles. Through the Standards, the telephone interpreting community may establish and uphold the highest levels of quality for the profession of telephone interpreting.

The Standards are statements of enforceable guidelines for professional conduct, are stated in observable and measurable terms and are intended as minimum levels of practice to which each telephone interpreter is held accountable. In order to work as a professional telephone interpreter, each individual should agree to uphold and abide by the Code of Ethics, Standards, and applicable policies.

A telephone interpreter's failure to comply with the Code of Ethics and the Standards would constitute professional misconduct and would result in sanctions, or other appropriate disciplinary actions, including the suspension or termination of employment.

The Standards reflect clear commitment to making sure that telephone interpreters provide an optimal level of service, and strive for excellence. This includes remaining in good standing with a telephone interpreting provider, making a commitment, without limitation, to continued personal and professional development through self-study, self-assessment, and continuing education, seeking support from peers and experienced professionals to provide optimal service, serving as a mentor, and understanding that a telephone interpreter's actions are a reflection of the integrity of the entire profession. For this reason, telephone interpreters and end users of interpreting services should report unethical behavior and violations of the Code of Ethics and Standards when observed.

Each telephone interpreter is responsible for showing and maintaining professional compliance with the Standards. As the profession of telephone interpreting evolves, so, too, will the Standards. Therefore, the Standards do not encompass every single situation that an interpreter may encounter, and are subject to revision in keeping with the changing demands and expectations of the telephone interpreting profession. Finally, to provide coherence and consistency between the Code of Ethics and the Standards, each guiding principle from the Code of Ethics (Chapter 9) is stated below following its corresponding number, and the Standards that relate to each guiding principle are listed immediately below it with a corresponding letter.

MODEL STANDARDS OF PRACTICE

1. Confidentiality

The telephone interpreter maintains confidentiality of all information obtained throughout each call.

1(a) The telephone interpreter protects confidentiality at all times and indefinitely. The telephone interpreter avoids discussing or revealing any information obtained from an interpreted call. There is no limit or expiration to this standard; confidentiality extends for an indefinite period.

1(b) The telephone interpreter eliminates written records of confidential information. The telephone interpreter destroys and disposes of all information and call notes recorded in any format, at the end of each call.

1(c) The telephone interpreter maintains confidentiality with colleagues. The telephone interpreter exercises confidentiality when speaking with colleagues, in order to protect the privacy and confidential nature of information. During training and group mentoring sessions, the telephone interpreter refrains from revealing identifying details that compromise confidentiality. The telephone interpreter encourages colleagues to adhere to this standard.

2. Ethical Conduct

The telephone interpreter avoids obtaining any personal advantage on any call and discloses any perceived conflicts of interest to both the client and the employer.

2(a) The telephone interpreter avoids obtaining personal advantage. The telephone interpreter avoids actively using any information revealed in the course of a call to obtain personal gain or benefit.

2(b) The telephone interpreter discloses conflicts of interest. If a telephone interpreter perceives a conflict of interest, he/she discloses this information to both parties and asks to withdraw from the interpreted session.

2(c) The telephone interpreter declines to accept gifts and/or gratuities. In the case that a client or LEP person offers to provide the telephone interpreter with any additional compensation, in the form of any object, service or bonus whatsoever, the telephone interpreter declines to accept it.

2(d) The telephone interpreter withdraws from scenarios for which he/she is not qualified. If the telephone interpreter is found in a scenario for which the telephone interpreter lacks the knowledge and/or skills to successfully complete the interpretation, the telephone interpreter respectfully withdraws from the call.

3. Impartiality

The telephone interpreter projects an impartial attitude and treats all parties in a manner that fosters trust and mutual respect.

3(a) The telephone interpreter maintains neutrality at all times. The telephone interpreter strives to constantly maintain a neutral attitude toward both parties. The telephone interpreter refrains from 'taking sides' with either party.

3(b) The telephone interpreter refrains from providing opinions, even when solicited. When asked for an opinion, the telephone interpreter politely refrains from giving one. The telephone interpreter does not volunteer opinions to either party at any time.

3(c) The telephone interpreter prevents feelings and beliefs from affecting the interpretation. The telephone interpreter's emotions, feelings, and beliefs are in no way reflected in his/her tone, inflection, volume or choice of terminology.

3(d) The telephone interpreter avoids engaging in side conversations. Even when the telephone interpreter is left alone with either party, the telephone interpreter refrains from becoming involved in conversations with that party.

3(e) The telephone interpreter avoids disclosing personal contact information. The telephone interpreter does not share personal contact information, such as full name, telephone number, and address, with either party.

3(f) The telephone interpreter refrains from exerting influence on either party. The telephone interpreter does not influence the parties' communication in any way.

4. Accuracy and Completeness

The telephone interpreter renders the information as accurately and completely as possible, conveying the information as well as its original spirit and intent.

4(a) The telephone interpreter is accurate and faithful to meaning. The telephone interpreter strives to provide an interpretation that is accurate and faithful at all times, using appropriate linguistic equivalents, grammatical structure, tone of voice, and inflection.

4(b) The telephone interpreter refrains from adding, omitting or modifying. The telephone interpreter renders the interpretation without embellishing or eliminating anything, and avoids changing the original meaning.

4(c) The telephone interpreter renders all interpretation in the first person. To ensure utmost accuracy and completeness, the telephone interpreter renders all interpretation directly in the first person, and avoids using reported speech (i.e. 'he said', 'she is saying ...') at all times.

4(d) The telephone interpreter uses good judgment when interpreting offensive language. For most customer service settings, the telephone interpreter provides a reminder that everything said will be interpreted. For legal settings, the telephone interpreter renders the offensive language accurately without any reminder.

4(e) The telephone interpreter preserves the source tone of voice, hesitations, and interjections. In addition to rendering equivalent meaning, the telephone interpreter renders the interpretation using equivalent tone of voice, hesitations, interjections, and other audible clues that help provide a more accurate sense of the original meaning. The telephone interpreter does this in a way that will not be perceived as offensive or mocking to either party.

4(f) The telephone interpreter accurately renders apparent untruths. In cases where the speaker may be saying things that are not true (e.g. in psychiatric interviews), the telephone interpreter refrains from correcting or qualifying these statements, and simply renders them accurately in the target language.

4(g) The telephone interpreter uses paraphrasing when there is a lack of linguistic equivalents in the target language. In situations where there is no linguistic equivalent, the telephone interpreter provides a brief and concise definition or paraphrase in the target language.

4(h) The telephone interpreter requests repetitions and clarification when needed. If the telephone interpreter has any doubt regarding the meaning or proper understanding of a specific term or phrase, the telephone interpreter requests repetitions and clarification as necessary.

4(i) The telephone interpreter uses appropriate register. The telephone interpreter strives to retain the source language register whenever possible. If retaining the same register presents a difficulty in understanding, the telephone interpreter should use his/her best judgment to adjust the register accordingly.

4(j) The telephone interpreter renders 'uninterpretable' words appropriately.

When the source utterance contains a word or phrase that is impossible to identify, the telephone interpreter should attempt to transliterate the word or phrase (i.e. 'repeat it as you hear it'). This allows the other party to request clarification from the original speaker through the telephone interpreter. In the case of proper names, the other speaker may be able to identify the term from the telephone interpreter's transliteration.

4(k) The telephone interpreter promptly discloses and rectifies errors. If the telephone interpreter discovers that an error was made earlier on in the call or learns new information that would change the way a term or phrase should be rendered, the telephone interpreter promptly discloses this to both parties and rectifies the error.

(4l) The telephone interpreter favors meaning-based interpretation over word-for-word interpretation. Without sacrificing accuracy or completeness, the telephone interpreter refrains from providing interpretation on a word-by-word basis, since this often prohibits understanding and communication because of differences in phrases and grammatical structure between languages. Instead, the telephone interpreter strives to produce a highly accurate and complete meaning-based rendition.

4(m) The telephone interpreter requests manageable segments of speech as needed. To ensure accuracy, the telephone interpreter requests pauses and adjustments of segment length when necessary, from either party.

5. Role Boundaries

The telephone interpreter avoids personal involvement and respects the boundaries of the roles of all parties.

5(a) The telephone interpreter provides a pre-session to both parties. In order to ensure that all parties understand the telephone interpreter's role, at the beginning of the call. the telephone interpreter identifies him/herself to both parties as the telephone interpreter. If the client is a novice user of interpreting services, the telephone interpreter may direct the client to use the first person and speak directly to the LEP person.

5(b) The telephone interpreter maintains the least invasive role possible. Unless special circumstances arise that require clarification because of linguistic or cultural issues that have a direct impact on the parties' ability to communicate, the telephone interpreter remains in a noninvasive role, interpreting only the utterances spoken, and refraining from providing additional information.

5(c) The telephone interpreter refers questions to the other party. When one party asks telephone interpreter a question, the telephone interpreter refers the question to the other party, rather than answering the question directly.

5(d) The telephone interpreter intervenes when necessary to clarify linguistic misunderstandings. If the telephone interpreter perceives that a certain linguistic aspect of the interpretation (such as a specific word or phrase) has been misunderstood, he/she intervenes to clarify the issue. However, the telephone interpreter refrains from explaining in-depth concepts and limits him/herself to interpreting.

5(e) The telephone interpreter intervenes when necessary to clarify cultural issues. If the telephone interpreter is made aware that communication is prohibited because of cultural misunderstandings or differences, the telephone interpreter provides a limited clarification that will permit understanding of the specific issue at hand within a cultural framework. When providing such clarification, the telephone interpreter is extremely careful at all times to avoid stereotyping or generalizing.

6. Professional Conduct

The telephone interpreter displays professional behavior at all times and uses language and tone of voice that displays a high level of customer service toward both parties.

6(a) The telephone interpreter exhibits professional behavior. The telephone interpreter displays a demeanor and attitude that are appropriate to the setting of the interpreted session, and are reflected in all aspects of the interpreter's actions.

6(b) The telephone interpreter is prompt, expedient, and time-efficient. The telephone interpreter is prompt to answer the phone, and delivers the interpretation in the most time-efficient and expedient manner possible.

6(c) The telephone interpreter provides good customer service to all parties. The telephone interpreter treats all individuals with respect and courtesy, using polite forms of address (i.e. Sir, Ma'am) and professional displays of respect and courtesy whenever possible with both parties.

6(d) The telephone interpreter refrains from interrupting other parties. The telephone interpreter attempts to actively listen for pauses as a cue to begin the interpretation, and refrains from interrupting other parties whenever possible.

6(e) The telephone interpreter demonstrates knowledge of code of ethics and standards. The telephone interpreter actively implements all standards, as well as the guiding principles in the code of ethics.

6(f) The telephone interpreter exercises good judgment when unusual situations arise. When a telephone interpreter encounters a situation for which no standard would directly apply, the telephone interpreter uses his/her best judgment to come up with the best solution for all parties.

6(g) The telephone interpreter is prepared to interpret the call. The telephone interpreter demonstrates professional preparedness in terms of the knowledge, skills, and tools needed for a specific call. Tools include proper phone equipment, dictionaries, glossaries, and note-taking utensils.

6(h) The telephone interpreter withdraws from a call only with just cause. The telephone interpreter attempts to interpret each call and handles challenges related to knowledge and skills in a professional manner. In extreme cases, if a highly specialized scenario exceeds a telephone interpreter's competency level, he/she politely withdraws from the call.

6(i) The telephone interpreter recognizes his/her personal threshold for fatigue. If a telephone interpreter's performance is affected by fatigue, he/she recognizes this and avoids working excessive/over-time hours in order to uphold maximum performance standards.

6(j) If withdrawing from a call, the telephone interpreter reports this. If a telephone interpreter withdraws from a call, he or she immediately reports this to the company.

6(k) The telephone interpreter is accountable for decision-making. The telephone interpreter recognizes his/her accountability with relation to all decisions made regarding how to handle any and all circumstances that may occur within the interpreted session for which no clear standard of practice exists. The telephone interpreter makes decisions in the best interest of the communication needs of all parties.

6(l) The telephone interpreter remains on the line until dismissed. The telephone interpreter stays on the line until dismissed, with the exception of withdrawing from a call. If the client has not made it clear whether or not the telephone interpreter should hold on the line, the telephone interpreter verifies with the client prior to disconnecting.

6(m) The telephone interpreter honors brief requests for assistance with written words or phrases. When the telephone interpreter is asked to assist a client in providing written instructions in another language (e.g. instructions for taking a medication), the interpreter works to the best of his or her ability to provide some assistance. However, for documents of more than a few short sentences or phrases in length, the telephone interpreter instructs the client to contact the translation department. If the company does not have a translation department, the telephone interpreter recommends that the client contact a translation agency.

6(n) The telephone interpreter avoids self-promotion. The telephone interpreter refrains from speaking about his/her qualifications and professional accomplishments, unless specifically requested to do so by a client for purposes of establishing the telephone interpreter's qualifications.

6(o) The telephone interpreter provides information on policies, when appropriate. If a circumstance arises in which a client requests information on company policies, the telephone interpreter provides information, as deemed appropriate by the company.

6(p) The telephone interpreter expresses respect for colleagues. Both during and outside working hours, the telephone interpreter treats all other members of the interpreting community (court interpreters, conference interpreters, health care interpreters, other telephone interpreters, etc.) with the highest level of professionalism and respect, in both word and action.

6(q) The telephone interpreter seeks counseling after traumatic events. If a telephone interpreter encounters an extreme situation that provokes high levels of stress or emotional reaction, he or she seeks counseling through a company-designated counselor.

7. Professional Development

The telephone interpreter continually seeks out opportunities to enhance his/her professional skills and knowledge.

(7a) The telephone interpreter demonstrates familiarity with training materials. The telephone interpreter reviews and becomes familiar with all printed information, manuals, and multimedia materials distributed by the telephone interpretation provider.

7(b) The telephone interpreter remains active with both languages. To ensure continual proficiency, the telephone interpreter constantly seeks out opportunities to improve and enhance his/her knowledge of both languages.

7(c) The telephone interpreter is active within the interpreting community. The telephone interpreter constantly seeks out professional organizations, conferences, and training opportunities to enhance his/her professional skills.

7(d) The telephone interpreter constantly increases terminology knowledge. The telephone interpreter has a system for organizing new words or phrases and researching new terminology challenges.

7(e) The telephone interpreter builds note-taking and memory skills. The telephone interpreter becomes more efficient with note-taking and improves memory skills with active practice.

7(f) The telephone interpreter supports peers. In all interactions with colleagues, the telephone interpreter demonstrates a willingness to help others improve their skills and knowledge.

Chapter 11
Interpreting the Standards: Explanations and Exceptions

Now that the rules of the road for telephone interpreting have been set out, how should they be put into practice? As we all know, reading about driving a vehicle is a far different thing from actually being behind the wheel. In this chapter, we will look at each of the standards in more detail, to provide a fuller vision of the requirements of a professional telephone interpreter.

It is important to note that there are no exceptions to the overall guiding principles outlined in the code of ethics. Such principles are largely philosophical in nature, serving to describe overarching ethical ideals. It is also worth noting that these principles, in some form or another, are commonly found in codes of ethics throughout the global interpreting community.

However, where standards of practice are concerned, there is an exception to nearly every rule and the rules that apply to telephone interpreting (which spans a broad array of industries) have considerably more exceptions than do standards of practice for other types of interpreting owing to the diversity of settings encompassed.

With regard to the model Standards of Practice provided in the previous chapter, the situations that could arise to challenge each standard are numerous and varied. Each telephone interpreting company must provide interpreters with examples and specific guidelines that detail explicitly how to proceed in certain commonly-occurring situations.

However, it would be impossible to detail every possible situation in writing. Therefore, some interpreting companies provide interpreters with basic examples, instructing interpreters to default to the guiding principles in the Code of Ethics and use their best judgment in situations for which a specific guideline might not exist.

In addition, some telephone interpreting companies often offer a variety of support mechanisms to interpreters. Often, a telephone interpreter will report to a senior interpreter mentor or quality manager, and the interpreter may address questions and issues related to standards of practice with this individual. Also, some telephone interpreting companies provide newsletters, conference call sessions, and web forums, so that their interpreters may pose questions and receive guidance regarding situations that may not specifically be outlined in the company's internal Standards of Practice.

This chapter includes an outline of explanations of the standards and the possible exceptions to them. For each standard of practice, additional detail will be provided and circumstances will be discussed that might necessitate a modification of or deviation from the standard. Not every standard will necessarily have an exception listed. The focus of the telephone interpreter should always be to follow the Standards of Practice. However, because no one document can encompass all behaviors, and because of the ever-changing markets and industries served by telephone interpreters, some flexibility will always be necessary. Also, it is important to note that different industry settings may require certain exceptions and adaptations of the standards. This will be covered separately in later sections in this chapter.

1. Confidentiality

Standard 1(a)

The telephone interpreter protects confidentiality at all times and indefinitely. The telephone interpreter avoids discussing or revealing any information obtained from an interpreted call. There is no limit or expiration to this standard; confidentiality extends for an indefinite period.

Explanation

Telephone interpreters constantly receive extremely confidential information, including sensitive financial information and health care information. In the United States, telephone interpreting companies are required to comply with certain laws protecting confidential information, such as the Health Insurance Portability and Accountability Act of 1996 (HIPAA) and the Financial Services Modernization Act of 1999, known as the Gramm-Leach-Bliley Act (GLBA) within the United States. Therefore, it is of utmost importance that all interpreters adhere strictly to this standard.

Exception

If an interpreter is called to provide testimony for purposes of a legal proceeding, the interpreter must answer all questions asked by the court to the best of his/her knowledge and ability. If the interpreter is able to recall details from the call, the interpreter should share those details when ordered to do so under oath, to the best of his or her ability.

Standard 1(b)

The telephone interpreter eliminates written records of confidential information. The telephone interpreter destroys and disposes of all information and call notes recorded in any format, at the end of each call.

Explanation

Telephone interpreters are constantly taking notes, many of which would be indiscernible to anyone but the actual interpreter. Usually, notes are taken with regular pencil and paper, because the sound of keystrokes on a computer could interfere with the sound quality and detract from the interpreter's active listening. The interpreter must always destroy and dispose of call notes. Telephone interpreters in call center environments are provided with a company shredder, into which they must deposit call notes. Interpreters who work from home are required to sign a document agreeing to destroy all call notes upon completion of the call. Most home office interpreters employ a shredder for this purpose.

Exception

It is important for interpreters to write down key terminology, especially new and/or client-specific terms and phrases that the interpreter may wish to research further in order to provide a better interpretation for the next call. This is an important part of each interpreter's ongoing development. For this reason, telephone interpreters are encouraged to have a place to record terms that require further investigation and questions that may require further discussion. A simple notebook will do.

It is highly recommended that, before destroying call notes, interpreters scan the notes for any key words, phrases or situations and transfer them to this separate, dedicated location. In addition, interpreters should write down questions related to call-handling procedures, so that in the next interaction with a senior interpreter mentor, the interpreter can request the appropriate guidance.

Furthermore, if an interpreter realizes that the overall quality of service to the client could be enhanced through the development of a client-specific glossary and/or training tool, the interpreter may contact the quality control department to suggest this. In doing so, the interpreter may need to share details regarding the client and/or calls handled for that particular client, including any company-specific terminology. The telephone interpreting company would need to keep the client informed of any client-specific materials developed internally, and only the necessary information (client-specific terminology and phrases) would be utilized.

Standard 1(c)

The telephone interpreter maintains confidentiality with colleagues. The telephone interpreter exercises confidentiality when speaking with colleagues, in order to protect the privacy and confidential nature of information. During training and group mentoring sessions, the telephone interpreter refrains from revealing identifying details that compromise confidentiality. The telephone interpreter encourages colleagues to adhere to this standard.

Explanation

Telephone interpreters, especially those working for large companies, are often grouped into teams, and the various team members are provided with numerous opportunities to interact with one another, be it in person at local events, over the phone, via e-mail, or some other forum. Normally, this interaction takes place with the supervision or facilitation of a more senior interpreter, team leader or moderator, who ensures that confidentiality is maintained throughout the interactions. However, interpreters might also have the ability to interact with each other, or with other company employees, in a one-on-one format, and for these types of interactions especially, when no other company representative might be present, it is extremely important that the interpreter maintains utmost confidentiality when speaking about information obtained during the course of work.

Exception

If a customer complains to the company about an interpreter's behavior, it may be necessary for the telephone interpreting company's customer service representative to contact the interpreter to ascertain and/or verify certain facts regarding the complaint. When this happens, the interpreter is able to speak openly to the customer service representative to ensure that the customer complaint is handled appropriately. However, the interpreter should continue to protect proprietary and/or confidential information by revealing only what is necessary to address the customer service issue. In addition, the customer service representative would also be bound by the company code of ethics relating to confidentiality of information obtained for the individual's job duties.

2. Ethical Conduct

Standard 2(a)

The telephone interpreter avoids obtaining personal advantage. The telephone interpreter avoids actively using any information revealed in the course of a call to obtain personal gain or benefit.

Explanation

Telephone interpreters are exposed to a wealth of information regarding numerous subjects. Given that many of the calls received by telephone interpreters deal with everyday, practical issues, such as paying a gas bill, enrolling in an insurance plan or applying for a loan, telephone interpreters, by virtue of this work, often accumulate a great deal of knowledge in these subjects. As defined in this standard, it is important that an interpreter never make a conscious effort to use specific pieces of information to obtain a personal benefit.

Exception

Obviously, an interpreter may not be able to prevent certain knowledge from seeping into his or her brain. For example, an interpreter who has interpreted an insurance claims process on hundreds of occasions, will probably be more informed about this subject when needing to make a claim in his or her personal life. Likewise, an interpreter who has interpreted for numerous question-and-answer sessions between diabetic patients and health educators may have less of a learning curve if he or she becomes diabetic, by virtue of being exposed to the same information, time and time again. This is an example of how information obtained in a call (or in multiple calls) might actually work to an interpreter's benefit. Obviously, this is not considered a violation of the standard, but shows that an interpreter should use common sense when interpreting the standards, and always refer back to the code of ethics for general guidance.

Standard 2(b)

The telephone interpreter discloses conflicts of interest. If a telephone interpreter perceives a conflict of interest, he/she discloses this information to both parties and requests to withdraw from the interpreted session.

Explanation

The levels and degrees of a 'conflict of interest' may vary. In fact, the definition of the very notion of a 'conflict of interest' can be highly subjective. For example, a telephone interpreter who recently lost a brother to AIDS might receive a call in which the interpreter has to convey to an LEP patient that he has been diagnosed with AIDS. Depending on the scenario, the interpreter may feel that his or her ability to interpret in a detached manner would be compromised by his or her emotional attachment and recent negative experience with the subject matter in his or her personal life.

This could definitely affect his or her neutrality and impartiality when interpreting. Therefore, if the interpreter's neutrality is affected, the most ethical behavior for the interpreter would be to politely disqualify him or herself from the call, and request that the client call and request a different interpreter.

However, for certain rare languages, the telephone interpreting company might have only a limited number of interpreters available. If that is the case, should the interpreter disqualify him or herself from the call? In such a situation, the telephone interpreter should briefly disclose the conflict of interests and allow the client to make the decision as to how to proceed. The interpreter should also explain that there are a limited number of interpreters available for the language in question. The client may elect to proceed with the call.

However, if the interpreter feels that he or she absolutely cannot proceed with the interpretation, he or she must make this clear to the client. In some cases, there may not be another choice (e.g. there may be no other interpreter available for a given languages). If this happens, the interpreter may have no other alternative than to go ahead and interpret if at all possible. There is a difference between feeling uncomfortable regarding a scenario and not being able to interpret due to emotional distress. Obviously, in the latter of the two cases, the interpreter should disqualify him or herself from the call.

In certain situations, however, such as in an emergency situation, the interpreter may not have the opportunity to disclose such information. When a person's life is at stake, the interpreter may not be afforded the luxury of the seconds necessary to provide such a disclosure, let alone the time it would take to connect to a back-up interpreter. In the rare cases in which this may occur, the interpreter would need to proceed with interpreting the call. For this reason, most large telephone interpretation providers offer stress debriefing or counseling services for interpreters who might experience challenges of this nature.

Exception

As mentioned earlier, in many cases, the interpreter will have to use his or her best judgment to ensure that the company's ethical principles are observed while still providing the best possible telephone interpretation service to the client. From the interpreter's perspective, it is important to avoid extremes when applying certain guidelines. For example, if an interpreter is interpreting a call for a utility company where the customer is calling in to dispute a high bill, it would not be appropriate for the interpreter to say, 'The interpreter's neutrality is compromised due to the fact that the interpreter currently is receiving high electricity bills as well'.

There are limits and exceptions to every rule, and many telephone interpreting companies would expect interpreters to exercise some degree of common sense when asking themselves the question, 'Is my ability to maintain an impartial attitude truly compromised by this situation?' If the answer is yes, the interpreter should make a disclosure.

Large providers of interpreting services often have strategies in place to help interpreters deal with these issues. In addition to the stress debriefing and counseling services mentioned earlier, which help the interpreter after such an event has already occurred, some companies may allow interpreters to proactively prevent conflicts of interest from occurring.

For example, an interpreter might request to his or her manager, 'I recently suffered a loss in my family, so I'd prefer not to receive any emergency or health care calls for the next while'. Then, the manager can change the interpreter's profile to ensure that such calls are temporarily not routed to that individual interpreter. This serves to help prevent stressful situations for the interpreter, and the manager can check back with the interpreter to see when the interpreter is ready to add those calls to his or her profile again.

Standard 2(c)

The telephone interpreter declines to accept gifts and/or gratuities. If a client or LEP person offers to provide the telephone interpreter with any additional compensation, in the form of any object, service or bonus whatsoever, the telephone interpreter declines to accept it.

Explanation

Thankfully, perhaps owing to the telephone interpreter's anonymity (interpreters are usually identified to the client by ID number and first name only), the opportunities for an interpreter to be approached by an LEP person or client for a gift or gratuity are extremely infrequent. Also, since the telephone interpreter is employed by a company, the usual expressions of gratitude and appreciation are normally routed through the client services department.

One situation that may occur from time to time is that a client may ask an interpreter to provide translation of a written material. Since the interpreter is unable to do this over the phone, the client will sometimes ask if he or she may fax or mail the document directly to the interpreter and offer the interpreter a monetary amount in exchange for the service. Fortunately, many large telephone interpreting companies have full-scale translation departments, or they may partner with an outside agency. Therefore, in this example, the telephone interpreter's company guidelines would instruct the interpreter to provide the appropriate contact information for the translation department or agency, rather than accepting a job offer directly.

Exception

For some of the less commonly requested languages, or in rare instances for even major languages, if the telephone interpreter is also a qualified and/or certified translator who also does freelance translation work, an interpreter may receive a request for translation as described above. Then, when the job is referred to the appropriate department or agency, the translation vendor chosen might actually end up being the same interpreter who took the call and referred the client to the translation department.

With large organizations, these occurrences would be extremely rare, since the translation department acts completely independently of the telephone interpreting services, with separate procedures for vendor recruiting and management. However, it is a possibility. If it were to occur, the original telephone interpreter would, in fact, receive additional compensation as a result of his/her work, which would at first glance appear to be a violation of this standard. Few companies would see this as a violation, so long as internal company protocols for appropriate channels of communication and referral were observed by the telephone interpreter. This depends on each company's unique set of guidelines.

Standard 2(d)

The telephone interpreter withdraws from scenarios for which he/she is not qualified.

If the telephone interpreter is found in a scenario for which the telephone interpreter lacks the knowledge and/or skills to successfully complete the interpretation, the telephone interpreter respectfully withdraws from the call.

Explanation

Telephone interpreting companies should thoroughly prepare interpreters for specific industries and scenarios before allowing them to interpret, to prevent at all costs a situation in which an interpreter taking a given call is under-qualified to interpret. The very definition of what constitutes a high-quality telephone interpretation has, until the writing of this book, been somewhat difficult to pinpoint, owing to the lack of standards for the profession of telephone interpreting.

Normally, large telephone interpreting companies provide interpreters with sufficient training, testing, and monitoring to ensure quality of interpretation. The assessments and training are often tailored to specific industries and situations. In addition, as described earlier, call routing systems used by larger companies can prevent this situation from happening by routing the call to an interpreter with a profile that matches the client's requirements. Therefore, in theory, it is unlikely that an interpreter would lack the skills or knowledge to provide the interpretation. However, in practice, it is possible for this to occur.

Some situations are beyond the control of the telephone interpreting company. For example, suppose that a long-distance telephone company commonly uses a telephone interpreting service, and the calls normally deal with billing issues, service inquiries, and the sale of new products and services. However, 0.01% of the time, the company's the technical support department might need to call an engineer in another country to discuss technical issues.

Let's assume that the company's quality control department was not forewarned by the customer that a call with this subject matter was even a remote possibility. Unless the telephone interpreting company has specifically provided the necessary training, testing, and monitoring to ensure the interpreter's expertise in this subject matter, an interpreter could find him or herself feeling unprepared for this type of call.

How the interpreter should proceed in this case depends greatly on the individual. Is the interpreter able to request clarification on specific problematic terminology? If so, the interpreter should continue with the call. Or, is the terminology so unfamiliar to the interpreter that he or she cannot grasp the meaning of the utterances? In that case, the interpreter should disqualify him or herself from the call.

Exception

In an ideal world, there would be enough qualified telephone interpreters available for every possible scenario and at any given time. For many commonly requested languages, this is often the case. However, for certain, less common languages, this may not always be possible. For some languages, there might be only a given number of interpreters available at a certain time. When that happens, and no other interpreter is available, the interpreter may have no choice but to continue with the call and interpret to his/her best ability. Obviously, if this is completely impossible due to highly specialized terminology used throughout the call, the interpreter would have no choice but to decline the call. Then, the telephone interpreting company might offer to return the call to the client with another interpreter for that language.

It is important to realize that telephone interpreting carries a high degree of variation in terminology, even within the same industry. Therefore, telephone interpreters will, without a doubt, come across terminology that is new and unfamiliar, sometimes on a daily basis. A recent example from the United States is when the Immigration and Naturalization Services changed their name to the Department of Homeland Security. In addition, numerous other standard terms were changed, such as the term 'deportation', which was replaced by the term 'removal'. Practically overnight, interpreters who had interpreted these terms with their well-known translations for many years found themselves facing these new linguistic challenges.

Obviously, telephone interpreters cannot suddenly disqualify themselves from interpreting every time they face a new or unfamiliar term, because every telephone interpreter might be in the exact same situation, depending on the term in question. In addition, if interpreters were to disqualify themselves too often, they would more than likely miss out on excellent opportunities for professional growth. Therefore, it is important for each interpreter to use his or her judgment and common sense with regard to this standard. A general question when trying to determine whether or not a situation warrants disqualification would be to ask, 'Am I able to do a good job in this situation?' If response is a confident 'yes', then the interpreter can proceed. If the answer is 'no', the interpreter should disqualify him/herself.

3. Impartiality

Standard 3(a)

The telephone interpreter maintains neutrality at all times. The telephone interpreter strives to constantly maintain a neutral attitude toward both parties. The telephone interpreter refrains from 'taking sides' with either party.

Explanation

Telephone interpreters are required to maintain an impartial and neutral attitude, but this is often easier said than done. Ultimately, the client is the payer of the interpreting services, but this does not mean that the interpreter should 'take sides' with the client or favor the client over the LEP caller. The interpreter is accountable for providing a high-quality interpretation to both parties, and this responsibility is not weighted toward one side, otherwise it would inhibit the interpreter from interpreting accurately, completely and in an impartial and neutral manner.

Exception

It is important to remember that, normally, the English-speaking end user represents a place of business, and is therefore bound by certain professional requirements and expectations. However, this is not normally the case for the LEP individual, and this is why certain situations may arise more commonly with the LEP caller than with the client. For example, suppose an LEP person calls up his insurance plan to register a complaint. If the complaint is not resolved, he may begin to use profanity out of his frustration.

In infrequent and extreme cases, some callers have been known to insult the interpreter directly, using profanity and sometimes even threatening language. In these cases, the interpreter is normally advised to defer to the client to determine what to do in response to this type of behavior. In certain rare instances, if the caller is completely unreasonable, screaming and yelling and not allowing the interpreter to speak, the client may advise the interpreter to disconnect the call along with the client. In these cases, the caller's behavior does not really leave the interpreter with much choice.

Also, as the payer of the services, the client does have the ultimate authority to decide when to end the interpreted session. However, it is important to recognize that the interpreter in this case is not attempting to 'take sides' with the client by hanging up the phone on the caller. In such a case, the interpreter's actions would merely be out of necessity and the inability to proceed any further with the interpretation.

Standard 3(b)

The telephone interpreter refrains from providing opinions, even when these are solicited. When asked for an opinion, the telephone interpreter politely refrains from providing any. The telephone interpreter does not volunteer opinions to either party at any time.

Explanation

Owing to a lack of education among end users of interpreting services, telephone interpreters are sometimes asked for their personal opinions. While most trained telephone interpreters would not dream of providing an opinion of their own accord, some interpreters feel that, if the client asks for their opinion, they are obliged to provide it. This is not the case. If an interpreter provides an opinion, it could influence the client's words or actions, and the interpreter should not exert any influence over either party at any time during the call.

For example, if an LEP person calls the police and is not speaking in full sentences or responding to the officer's questions, the client might assume that the caller is under the influence of drugs and ask, 'Interpreter, do you think the caller is on drugs?' If the interpreter says, 'Yes, he sounds completely out of it', the officer might make a judgment call regarding the need to dispatch help to the individual. However, what if this individual has a mental illness? The interpreter should NEVER make an assumption based on what he or she hears.

However, the interpreter is encouraged to provide auditory observations – information perceived by the interpreter that may not be apparent to the client because of the language barrier. Therefore, while an interpreter may not say, 'Yes, he sounds completely out of it', the interpreter may (and should) report, 'He is not speaking in complete sentences, and his pronunciation is slurred.' This may provide valuable information to the client that would otherwise be unobtainable, while preventing the sharing of any personal opinions. If pressed for an opinion, the telephone interpreter should politely state that their standards of practice require that interpreters do not reveal any personal opinions.

Exception

There are certain situations in which an interpreter might need to share an opinion. However, these are usually issues related to service, not issues related to the interpretation itself. For example, if the client says, 'Interpreter, I have a person here who says he speaks Spanish, but his passport says he's from Brazil. What should I do?', the interpreter might offer a suggestion, such as, 'Would you like the interpreter to try speaking to him in Spanish to see if he understands well enough to continue, and if he does not, we can get you a Portuguese interpreter?' The phrasing of this is of utmost importance for customer service reasons. If the interpreter says, 'The interpreter will speak to him in Spanish', it could come across as sounding rude or not very helpful to the client. For this reason, telephone interpreters should always pose suggestions regarding call-handling questions from the client as questions back to the client.

This specific example is based on a request from the client for advice from the interpreter, which could be construed as a request for the interpreter's opinion. However, let's take another example, in which the interpreter is directly asked for an opinion, related to linguistic issues. Suppose the client says, 'Interpreter, he does not seem to be understanding the concept of "deductible". Do you think I should find another way to explain it? What's your opinion?' In this case, depending on the language, the interpreter might know that this particular concept is unfamiliar to many LEP callers.

Depending on what has transpired in the call thus far, the interpreter might reply with any number of suggestions, such as, 'There appeared to be some confusion earlier regarding the difference between the 'deductible' and 'copayment'. Would you like the interpreter to ask Mr Jimenez if he would like clarification on these two concepts?', or 'The concept of a 'deductible' is not common in [language], and there is not a specific term for this, so the interpreter is rendering it as, "the amount you must pay before your insurance begins to pay."Would you like the interpreter to ask Mr. Jimenez if he understands this phrase?'

In other words, whenever the interpreter is asked for an opinion, even regarding issues that deal with call-handling practices and techniques, the interpreter should always refer the question back to the client, to allow the client to make the ultimate decision regarding how to proceed. This returns the interpreter to a position of neutrality and ensures that he or she does not make decisions that could influence the call in any way.

Standard 3(c)

The telephone interpreter prevents feelings and beliefs from affecting the interpretation. The telephone interpreter's emotions, feelings, and beliefs are in no way reflected in his/her tone, inflection, volume or choice of terminology.

Explanation

It is easy to imagine a host of scenarios in which the interpreter might feel pulled in a certain direction. Many interpreters might find themselves interpreting for someone, particularly an LEP caller, who not only speaks a common language, but might have a similar background, a regional dialect, or even an accent that make it easy for the interpreter to feel a common bond. This might make an interpreter feel as if he or she has a greater responsibility to this individual than normal, especially when the situation is going to affect the person negatively.

For example, an interpreter might be able to tell from a caller's accent that he or she is from the same village as the interpreter in their mutual country of origin. Owing to linguistic similarities, the interpretation might even be less challenging than normal for the interpreter. Let us assume that the caller is having financial trouble and finding it hard to meet his payments, and is calling to work out a financial arrangement.

However, the company representative says, 'We are unable to help create a payment plan because the account is so overdue. You have paid late for the last 6 months, Ma'am.' The interpreter feels terrible that no one can help the caller, and changes the inflection a little and alters the words slightly. The interpreter renders it as, 'We are very sorry, Ma'am, but the account is past due and the payments have arrived late recently, so we unfortunately cannot make a payment plan for you at this time, but we apologize.'

This is an example of how an interpreter might attempt to 'soften' a statement that he or she perceives as harsh. While at first glance this might not seem extremely problematic, there are many other considerations. What if the caller actually has the money to pay, but is taking advantage of the company? What if the company has made payment plans for the caller in the past, but she has not met her payments? What if the account representative is purposely trying to sound harsh, to let the customer know that this is a serious situation? If any of those situations is the correct one, then the interpreter is directly interfering with the client's desires. And, even if they are not the case, the interpreter is influencing the call, no matter how small the influence.

Standard 3(d)

The telephone interpreter avoids engaging in side conversations. Even when the telephone interpreter is left alone with either party, the telephone interpreter refrains from becoming involved in conversations with that party.

Explanation

The telephone interpreter should avoid 'side talk' with either party. From time to time, an interpreter may need to verify something with one of the speakers. In this case, the interpreter should alert the other party regarding the need to ask for clarification. For example, if the interpreter wants to verify something with the caller, the interpreter should state to the client, 'This is the interpreter speaking. May the interpreter verify the name of the medication with Mr Chen?' If the verification is needed from the client, the interpreter should ask the client directly for the verification, 'This is the interpreter speaking. Could you please repeat the name of the medication?'

Interpreters who question the reason for avoiding side talk need only to step temporarily into the shoes of the client or caller. When either party does not understand both languages, they are putting full faith in the interpreter to interpret everything that is spoken. When the interpreter does not do this, it will likely evoke feelings of mistrust and/or doubt on the side of the party not engaged in the side talk.

A common example would be the interpreter who requires several exchanges with the LEP caller to verify an address. What sounds like a long conversation to the client might only be rendered as '51 North Main'. The client knows that more than this has been spoken, but is left wondering what was actually said. It is of utmost importance to keep everyone apprised of what is being stated at all times, by all parties, to the interpreter's best ability.

Exception

Exceptions to this standard will vary from one company to another depending on specific circumstances. For example, some providers may train interpreters to verify all numbers and addresses without requesting permission. In this case, the interpreter should retroactively inform either party that the information was confirmed, so that the other party understands the nature of the side talk. Obviously, certain situations, such as emergencies, would require an exception to this rule as well.

Standard 3(e)

The telephone interpreter avoids disclosing personal contact information. The telephone interpreter does not share personal contact information, such as full name, telephone number, and address, with either party.

Explanation

The telephone interpreter should never volunteer this information. Telephone interpreting companies normally assign interpreters a numerical ID code, which can be used to identify the interpreter in necessary situations. Also, while it may be tempting for an interpreter to exchange contact details with someone the interpreter meets via phone in the course of a call, this is prohibited by most telephone interpreting companies.

Exception

When interpreting for a legal proceeding, a judge or other officer of the court may require this information of the interpreter. Only in this situation is the interpreter required to provide this.

Standard 3(f)

The telephone interpreter refrains from exerting influence on either party. The telephone interpreter does not influence the parties' communication in any way.

Explanation

The interpreter should never attempt to control or manage the call in any way. This includes the interpreter making suggestions and recommendations of his or her own accord. Some interpreters, particularly after working within a given industry or with a specific client, begin to feel that they are experts in a particular field. At no time should an interpreter assume responsibility for handling the call.

Exception

There are exceptions in certain cases, such as emergency situations. See Chapter 12 for more details.

4. Accuracy and Completeness

Standard 4(a)

The telephone interpreter is accurate and faithful to meaning. The telephone interpreter strives to provide an interpretation that is accurate and faithful at all times, using appropriate linguistic equivalents, grammatical structure, tone of voice, and inflection.

Explanation

This is the essence of the telephone interpreter's work, and the main criteria used when assessing an interpreter's job performance. The interpreter must constantly strive to convey the most accurate and complete rendition possible.

Only through on-the-job monitoring can an interpreter truly demonstrate that this standard is being met consistently. While customer feedback is important, telephone interpreting companies rely most heavily on internal monitoring, as well as tracking this data and using to identify trends, in order to assess overall quality.

Exception

When conveying the inflection and tone of voice, it is important for the interpreter not to copy or mimic any individual's voice, as this could appear to be done in an antagonistic or mocking manner. Rather, the interpreter should provide a rendition that carries the source meaning, spirit, and intent.

Standard 4(b)

The telephone interpreter refrains from adding, omitting or modifying. The telephone interpreter renders the interpretation without embellishing or eliminating anything, and avoids changing the original meaning.

Explanation

Most interpreters who are guilty of violating this standard are not aware of it until they are monitored and their behavior is pointed out to them. Therefore, monitoring is extremely important for enabling an interpreter to understand their individual success in adhering to this important standard. Sometimes, an interpreter's omissions or embellishments can be so subtle, that only highly experienced, senior interpreters would be able to catch them. While an omission or embellishment may be small, it may also be a critical part of the message.

Exception

For emergency calls, telephone interpreters may be required to temporarily omit information, using specific techniques, such as prioritization and summarization, in order to expedite getting help to an individual in a critical situation. This is explained in further detail in Chapter 9, in the section on Cultural clarification.

Standard 4(c)

The telephone interpreter renders all interpretation in the first person. To ensure utmost accuracy and completeness, the telephone interpreter renders all interpretation directly in the first person, and avoids using reported speech (i.e. 'he said', 'she is saying ...') at all times.

Explanation

First person interpretation is mandatory for telephone interpreters. Reported speech is a form of interpreting that is rarely found in the professional interpreting world. Normally, reported speech is used only by untrained or inexperienced interpreters, as it often leads to confusion regarding the speaker, and can lead to inaccuracies, errors, and omissions.

When the interpreter needs to clarify or speak as the interpreter (as opposed to interpreting something stated by another party), the interpreter must at all times refer to him or herself in the third person. This is not to be confused with using reported speech. For example, the interpreter should not say, 'I need a repetition', because it may be unclear to the listener who is requesting the repetition – the interpreter, or the other party. The interpreter should say, 'May the interpreter please ask for a repetition?' or 'This is the interpreter; would you mind repeating that question?'

It is extremely important that the interpreter never use the words 'I' or 'me' to refer to him or herself, even when prefaced by the phrase, 'This is the interpreter'. This is especially important in a telephonic setting. If the listener does not hear the phrase 'This is the interpreter', the use of 'I' or 'me' to refer to the interpreter could still leave the door open for confusion regarding who is speaking. For this reason, it is extremely important for telephone interpreters to become very comfortable requesting clarification in this manner.

Exception

In a few cultures, it may be considered impolite for the interpreter to speak to the caller directly, owing to the nature of the relationship between the interpreter and the caller. In these rare cases, the interpreter may render the interpretation in first person to the client, while using a form of indirect interpretation to the LEP individual.

Standard 4(d)

The telephone interpreter uses good judgment when interpreting offensive language.

For legal settings, the telephone interpreter renders offensive language directly without providing any explanation. For customer service settings, the telephone interpreter may add a clarification. The interpreter then proceeds to render the interpretation.

Explanation

Offensive language is something that most telephone interpreters find challenging. Given that most relationships in an over-the-phone setting are collaborative, it is rare to encounter profanity, racial epithets, and other offensive language in a telephone interpreting setting. However, when it does occur, normally because a caller is unhappy with a product or service or because the client believes that he or she is talking directly to the interpreter, the interpreter must deal with it appropriately. In some cases, the interpreter will provide a reminder to the party that everything that is stated must be interpreted. In other cases, especially when the phone is being passed back and forth, it may be appropriate for the interpreter to preface an extremely offensive utterance by explaining that these words are not coming from the interpreter, but rather, from the speaker. The offensive language must then be interpreted exactly as stated. In legal settings, no explanation is required.

Exception

It is important to remember that the level of offensiveness of a specific term may change drastically from one location to the next. A word that is so inoffensive that it is used in diaper commercials in Spain might never be spoken in public in Mexico. For this reason, it is extremely important for the interpreter to understand the intent of the statement, and for the interpreter to be highly aware of regional variance in meaning. In other words, while an interpreter may at first find a certain offensive word quite shocking, it may be that, given the source, the word was not meant to offend. Therefore, it is important to keep this in mind when interpreting offensive language.

In certain settings, such as customer service settings where offensive language would not normally occur, the telephone interpreter may provide a brief disclaimer before rendering the utterance. For example, the interpreter might say, 'This is the interpreter; the following is a verbatim interpretation and does not reflect the interpreter's personal opinion:' This disclaimer should be followed by a faithful interpretation.

Standard 4(e)

The telephone interpreter preserves the source tone of voice, hesitations, and interjections. In addition to rendering equivalent meaning, the telephone interpreter renders the interpretation using equivalent tone of voice, hesitations, interjections, and other audible clues that help provide a more accurate sense of the original meaning. The telephone interpreter does this in a way that will not be perceived as offensive or mocking to either party.

Explanation

It is extremely important for the interpreter to convey, not just the general meaning, but all aspects of the utterance that will help the listener to best understand the original spirit, intent, and meaning.

Exception

If the speaker has impaired speech and is slurring, mumbling or stuttering, this need not be conveyed through the interpreter's rendition.

However, the interpreter may report this to the other party as an auditory observation.

Standard 4(f)

The telephone interpreter accurately renders apparent untruths. In cases where the speaker may be saying things that are not true (e.g. in psychiatric interviews), the telephone interpreter refrains from correcting or qualifying these statements, and simply renders them accurately in the target language.

Explanation

In certain settings, particularly in mental health, it is not uncommon for the speaker to state things that are untrue. When these remarks are made, the interpreter should simply render them as stated.

Exception

If the interpreter becomes aware that a speaker is purposely being deceptive, the interpreter should relay this. For example, if the caller were to say to the client, 'I don't know why you're bothering me with this; I already mailed the payment two weeks ago', but then whispers to a child in the background, 'Go put this in the mail, because I told them I sent it two weeks ago', the interpreter is required to interpret both the untrue statement, as well as the whispered statement that was overheard in the background.

Standard 4(g)

The telephone interpreter uses paraphrasing when there is a lack of linguistic equivalents in the target language. In situations where there is no linguistic equivalent, the telephone interpreter provides a brief and concise definition or paraphrase in the target language.

Explanation

For many terms, there may not be a linguistic equivalent in the target language. When this occurs, the interpreter may provide a short definition or paraphrase instead. For example, the term 'Primary Care Physician', which is common in the United States, may not have an equivalent in other languages. For this reason, it would be acceptable to interpret a short paraphrase, such as 'your primary doctor', or 'your main doctor', in this case.

Exception

While some terms come up so often that the interpreter will have a standard way of paraphrasing it, it is important that an interpreter defers to the client's expertise when there are any doubts whatsoever, especially regarding terms that may be unique to a particular client. The interpreter should request clarification, to ensure that the definition or paraphrase provided to the other party is accurate.

Standard 4(h)

The telephone interpreter requests repetitions and clarification when needed. If the telephone interpreter has any doubt regarding the meaning or proper understanding of a specific term or phrase, the telephone interpreter requests repetitions and clarification as necessary.

Explanation

Too often, interpreters feel embarrassed about requesting a repetition or clarification, because they are afraid it may make them look inexperienced, or as if they are not doing a good job. Quite to the contrary, requesting repetitions and clarifications proves that the interpreter is dedicated to ensuring that the interpretation is of the highest quality.

Exception

While an interpreter should definitely clarify and request repetitions when needed, there is such a thing as excess. An interpreter who requests too many clarifications and repetitions may actually have difficulties with note-taking, concentration or memory retention. The source of the excessive requests can be verified through ongoing monitoring. As indicated in Standard 2(d), the interpreter should disqualify him or herself from a call in which he or she lacks the ability or knowledge to interpret correctly.

Standard 4(i)

The telephone interpreter uses appropriate register. The telephone interpreter strives to retain the source language register whenever possible. If retaining the same register presents a difficulty in understanding, the telephone interpreter should use his/her best judgment to adjust the register accordingly.

Explanation

The interpreter's job is primarily to render the information accurately and completely, and this includes register. If the listener has difficulty understanding the information in one register, the interpreter should interpret this back to the other speaker, thereby making him or her aware of the difficulty. This will allow the original speaker to restate the information in a different way. However, in certain situations, there may not be a linguistic equivalent for the lower-register term. When this happens, the interpreter should exercise good judgment in using alternatives for conveying the same message, and keep the client informed.

Exception

In certain settings, the client might request that the interpreter adjust the register. For the most part, it is still the client's responsibility to adjust his or her own register. However, within the bounds of good judgment, the interpreter should do his or her best to facilitate communication between the two parties.

Standard 4(j)

The telephone interpreter renders 'uninterpretable' words appropriately. When the source utterance contains a word or phrase that is impossible to identify, the telephone interpreter should attempt to transliterate the word or phrase (i.e. 'repeat it as you hear it'). This allows the other party to request clarification from the original speaker through the telephone interpreter. In the case of proper names, the other speaker may be able to identify the name from the telephone interpreter's transliteration.

Explanation

Speakers of another language may often be required to pronounce words in English, particularly street names, cities, and other place names. This can prove very difficult for the interpreter to understand, especially if the call originates in a state, province or country that the interpreter may not be familiar with. When this happens, the interpreter should provide a transliteration, also known as a phonetic repetition. In the case of place names, the client will often be more familiar with these proper nouns, and therefore, might more readily identify the words.

Exception

The interpreter should use good judgment to ensure that, in providing a transliteration, it does not appear that the interpreter is attempting to mock the speaker. If the interpreter is incapable of transliterating the unintelligible speech, the interpreter may request a repetition with permission from the client.

Standard 4(k)

The telephone interpreter promptly discloses and rectifies errors. If the telephone interpreter discovers that an error was made earlier on in the call or learns new information that would change the way a term or phrase should be rendered, the telephone interpreter promptly discloses this to both parties and rectifies the error.

Explanation

It is important for the interpreter to be completely honest regarding any mistakes that may have been made in the course of the interpretation. The interpreter is encouraged to disclose and rectify any errors in a professional and helpful manner. For example, the interpreter might state, 'The interpreter previously rendered a term used by Mr Lopez as a "credit", but given the newest comments, the interpreter has realized that Mr Lopez was referring to a "loan" instead of a "credit".' In many cases, especially when a term has multiple meanings, the interpreter is not to be blamed for the error, but should immediately report and rectify it.

Exception

If the interpreter realizes that an error was made only after the call has ended, he or she should still make a report. Depending on the company guidelines, the interpreter might report this to the Client Services department, or the Quality Control department. The method and mechanism for reporting such errors will vary from company to company.

Standard 4(l)

The telephone interpreter favors meaning-based interpretation over word-for-word interpretation. Without sacrificing accuracy or completeness, the telephone interpreter refrains from providing interpretation on a word-by-word basis, since this often prohibits understanding and communication because of differences in phrases and grammatical structure among languages. Instead, the telephone interpreter strives to produce a highly accurate and complete meaning-based rendition.

Explanation

The concept of word-for-word interpretation, to the layperson, simply means an interpretation that is accurate and complete. However, within the interpreting world, this term conjures the image of an interpretation that may focus too much on each individual word, as opposed to an interpretation that takes into account the full context and overall spirit and intent of the message. For this reason, telephone interpreters must strive to provide a meaning-based interpretation.

Standard 4(m)

The telephone interpreter requests manageable segments of speech as needed. To ensure accuracy, the telephone interpreter requests pauses and adjustments of segment length when necessary, from either party.

Explanation

The telephone interpreter should always ensure that the utterances are neither too short nor too long. Some end users of telephone interpreting services might not be familiar with an interpreter's ideal segment length, and provide only a few words at a time. Since, in most language pairs, it is impossible to interpret just a few words of a sentence at a time, the interpreter should request that the speaker provides an utterance of at least one full sentence. Normally, the ideal segment will consist of several sentences at a time; however, this varies drastically depending on the number of words in each sentence.

For interpreters who are just starting out, utterances may at first appear too lengthy, thereby compromising the interpreter's ability to produce an accurate and complete rendition. In this case, the interpreter may need to employ various techniques (such as listening for breathing patterns and pauses in speech) to begin interpreting expediently at the first available opportunity. Note taking is also extremely important.

In general, the length of utterance an interpreter finds manageable will increase with the amount of practice the interpreter has obtained at consecutive interpreting. Telephone interpreters often find that their short-term memory skills increase dramatically with time. For this reason, it is also important for interpreters to recognize that, even if their memory allows them to take long segments of information and render them accurately, it is still important to render the interpretation more rather than less frequently, because the other party may feel uncomfortable being isolated from the conversation for long periods of time.

Since a telephone interpreter does not have the ability to make a gesture to the other parties to indicate when the interpreter needs to interpret, the interpreter should use techniques that reflect the auditory nature of telephone interpreting, such as slightly inhaling to indicate that the interpretation will begin, or beginning the interpretation when the other party stops for a breath or completes a thought. Active listening skills are extremely important to ensure success in adhering to this standard.

5. Role Boundaries

Standard 5(a)

The telephone interpreter provides a pre-session to both parties. In order to ensure that all parties understand the telephone interpreter's role, the telephone interpreter identifies him/herself as the telephone interpreter to both parties at the beginning of the call. If the client is a novice user of interpreting services, the telephone interpreter may direct the client to use the first person and speak directly to the LEP person.

Explanation

Particularly in an over-the-phone setting, it is very important for the interpreter to provide a pre-session, or introduction, to both parties. Otherwise, there could be considerable confusion regarding who is performing what role throughout the call. Most providers of telephone interpreting services provide ample training to clients on how to work with an interpreter; however, it is always of benefit for the interpreter to explain that he or she will speak in the first person, to ensure accurate communication.

Exception

Obviously, in emergency settings, there is not much time for a pre-session. However, the interpreter should at the very least provide a brief introduction, such as 'I am your interpreter', to both parties.

Standard 5(b)

The telephone interpreter maintains the least invasive role possible. Unless special circumstances arise that require clarification because of linguistic or cultural issues that have a direct impact on the parties' ability to communicate, the telephone interpreter remains in a non-invasive role, interpreting only the utterances spoken, and refraining from providing additional information.

Explanation

It is important for the interpreter to stay in a non-invasive role, allowing both parties to interact with each other free of any influence or interference on the part of the interpreter. The interpreter must maintain an attitude of professionalism at all times, and this should be reflected in neutral and hands-off behavior on the part of the interpreter.

Exception

In emergency settings, the interpreter may be required to act on behalf of the client. More information is provided in Chapter 12.

Standard 5(c)

The telephone interpreter refers questions to the other party. When one party asks telephone interpreter a question, the telephone interpreter refers the question to the other party, rather than answering the question directly.

Explanation

If an interpreter is asked a question by one party, such as, 'Interpreter, what do you advise?', the interpreter should alert the other party, stating, 'This is the interpreter; Mr Gonzalez is asking for the interpreter's advice.' Then, the client may determine how to proceed. Likewise, if the client says, 'Interpreter, I'm not sure Mr Gonzalez is understanding.', the interpreter may say to the client, 'Would you like the interpreter to ask if Mr Gonzalez understands?'

Exception

If the telephone interpreter is asked a question regarding call-handling procedures, such as, 'Interpreter, would you like me to stop now so that you can interpret?', the interpreter can obviously respond to the question directly. The interpreter should exercise common sense with regard to this and all other standards of practice.

Standard 5(d)

The telephone interpreter intervenes when necessary to clarify linguistic misunderstandings. If the telephone interpreter perceives that a certain linguistic aspect of the interpretation (such as a specific word or phrase) has been misunderstood, he/she intervenes to clarify the issue. However, the telephone interpreter refrains from explaining in-depth concepts and limits him/herself to interpreting.

Explanation

It is extremely important for telephone interpreters to provide clarification for linguistic reasons, but the interpreter may be tempted to provide additional detail above and beyond what is necessary for linguistic clarification. For this reason, it is important for the interpreter to clarify in a manner that is succinct and concise.

There are no exceptions.

Standard 5(e)

The telephone interpreter intervenes when necessary to clarify cultural nuances. If the telephone interpreter is made aware that communication is prohibited because of cultural misunderstandings or differences, the telephone interpreter provides a limited clarification that will permit understanding of the specific issue at hand within a cultural framework. When providing such clarification, the telephone interpreter is extremely careful at all times to avoid stereotyping or generalizing.

Explanation

The line between cultural and linguistic clarification is often blurred. A cultural practice might be expressed with a single word in one language, yet require a lengthy description in another language. At other times, a cultural issue may be summarized in one short sentence. When providing cultural clarification, it is extremely important that the interpreter does not generalize or make assumptions about a specific culture. For example, rather than saying, 'speakers of [language] use this traditional healing method', the interpreter might say, 'in some places where [language] is spoken, this traditional healing method is sometimes used.' Please see the 'Cultural clarification' section in Chapter 9 for additional information and an example.

There are no exceptions.

6. Professional Conduct

Standard 6(a)

The telephone interpreter exhibits professional behavior. The telephone interpreter displays a professional demeanor that is reflected in all aspects of the interpreted session.

Explanation

The telephone interpreter must always keep in mind that his or her interactions with both parties are a reflection of the company's image. For this reason, telephone interpreters must behave in the most polite and professional manner possible, throughout the duration of each interaction. While professional appearance is obviously not a factor when the interpreter cannot be seen, the interpreter should make every effort to convey a pleasant and professional telephone demeanor, using speech, vocabulary, and tone of voice that is appropriate for a professional setting.

Of particular importance in telephone interpreting are the opening and closing of the call. These are two of the interpreter's only chances to interact with the parties on behalf of the company. For this reason, it is important that the interpreter convey an attitude of helpfulness and friendliness when the opportunity arises.

Standard 6(b)

The telephone interpreter is prompt, expedient, and time-efficient. The telephone interpreter is prompt to answer the phone, and delivers an interpretation in the most time-efficient and expedient manner possible.

Explanation

When calling a telephone interpreting company, the client requires interpreting services immediately. When the telephone interpreter's phone rings, the client is already on the line. Telephone interpreters are required to answer the phone immediately, in most cases, on the first ring. If the interpreter does not answer the phone promptly, the company will most likely dial another interpreter and record the attempt as a failure to answer on the part of the interpreter.

Once on the call, the interpreter must interpret in the most expedient and time-efficient manner possible. In other words, the pauses between the end of an utterance and the start of the interpretation should be minimal. In addition, the interpreter's rate of speech should be time-efficient.

Exception

The interpreter should never speak so quickly that it would inhibit understanding. Every effort must be made to enunciate clearly, to ensure that the interpretation can be readily understood.

Standard 6(c)

The telephone interpreter provides good customer service to all parties. The telephone interpreter treats all individuals with respect and courtesy, using polite forms of address (i.e. Sir, Ma'am) and professional displays of respect and courtesy whenever possible with both parties.

Explanation

Given the customer service nature of telephone interpreting, the interpreter should use every possible opportunity to use polite forms of address when interacting with both parties. In addition, polite phrases, such as 'please', 'thank you', and 'you're welcome', should be used whenever the interpreter is speaking as the interpreter.

Exception

The interpreter should avoid adding polite phrases to the actual interpretation.This may 'soften' or distort the spirit and intent of the original meaning. The interpreter is limited to using such polite forms of address and phrases when interacting directly with either party as the interpreter (requests for clarification, opening and closing, etc.)

Standard 6(d)

The telephone interpreter refrains from interrupting other parties. The telephone interpreter attempts to actively listen for pauses as a cue to begin the interpretation, and refrains from interrupting other parties whenever possible.

Explanation

To exercise good customer service, the interpreter should try not to interrupt either speaker, but should wait for the utterance to be completed. To facilitate this, the interpreter should listen closely to breath patterns and pauses, and may try other techniques, such as audibly to indicate that he or she is ready to begin.

Exception

In many cases, the interpreter may have no choice but to interrupt. A polite way of doing so may be to say a quick, 'thank you' to the speaker, or 'may the interpreter proceed?' in either language. It is important for the interpreter to show professionalism and politeness when interrupting either speaker.

Standard 6(e)

The telephone interpreter demonstrates knowledge of code of ethics and standards. The telephone interpreter actively implements all standards, as well as the guiding principles in the code of ethics.

Explanation

In all aspects of the telephone interpreter's work, his or her behavior should demonstrate a complete familiarity with the code of ethics and standards of practice. This is not limited to the interpreter's actions while interpreting, but should occur in all job-related activities, such as training sessions, testing, monitoring, mentoring, and any and all team meetings.

There are no exceptions.

Standard 6(f)

The telephone interpreter exercises good judgment when unusual situations arise. When a telephone interpreter encounters a situation for which no standard would directly apply, the telephone interpreter uses his/her best judgment to come up with the best solution for all parties.

Explanation

There is always a possibility that unforeseen situations will arise. When this happens, the interpreter should do his or her best to apply the guiding principles of the code of ethics and the standards of practice. The interpreter should also document the question and share it with his/her manager or mentor, so that a company guideline can be written to aid interpreters who encounter that situation in the future.

There are no exceptions.

Standard 6(g)

The telephone interpreter is prepared to interpret the call. The telephone interpreter demonstrates professional preparedness in terms of the knowledge, skills, and tools needed for a specific call. Tools include proper phone equipment, dictionaries, glossaries, and note-taking utensils.

Explanation

The telephone interpreting company should always prepare the interpreter to receive calls from a specific industry or setting. However, the interpreter must also be prepared. The interpreter must have appropriate utensils on hand for note-taking and adequate phone equipment (if not supplied by the employer), and must also continue to ensure preparedness by consulting dictionaries, glossaries, and other resources when necessary.

There are no exceptions.

Standard 6(h)

The telephone interpreter withdraws from a call only with just cause. The telephone interpreter attempts to interpret each call and handles challenges related to knowledge and skills in a professional manner. In extreme cases, if a highly specialized scenario proves to exceed a telephone interpreter's competency level, he/she politely withdraws from the call.

Explanation

A telephone interpreter might also need to withdraw from a call because of a personal emergency. The number of such personal emergencies should be limited.

There are no exceptions.

Standard 6(i)

The telephone interpreter recognizes his/her personal threshold for fatigue. If a telephone interpreter's performance is affected by fatigue, he/she recognizes this and avoids working excessive/over-time hours to uphold maximum performance standards.

Explanation

Some telephone interpreters are able to work long shifts and many overtime hours each day, while others find this to be extremely taxing. To ensure high quality for all calls, each interpreter must recognize his or her limits, and should avoid working excessively.

Some large telephone interpreting companies have carried out sufficient data analysis over the years to determine correlations between an interpreter's utilization ratio and levels of quality. Beyond a certain point, the average telephone interpreter's ability to interpret accurately is compromised. For this reason, most companies strive to keep the ratio of interpreter utilization well below this level.

There are no exceptions.

Standard 6(j)

If withdrawing from a call, the telephone interpreter reports this. If a telephone interpreter withdraws from a call, the telephone interpreter immediately reports this to the company.

Explanation

The telephone interpreter should immediately report any occasion in which he or she needed to withdraw from a call. In most cases, the client services team would act to make sure that the customer's needs were addressed and that another interpreter was immediately available.

There are no exceptions.

Standard 6(k)

The telephone interpreter is accountable for decision-making. The telephone interpreter recognizes his/her accountability with relation to all decision made during an interpreted session. The telephone interpreter makes decisions in the best interest of the communication needs of all parties.

Explanation

The telephone interpreter should take full responsibility for any decisions made while interpreting. All decisions must be made in conjunction with the code of ethics and standards of practice.

There are no exceptions.

Standard 6(l)

The telephone interpreter remains on the line until dismissed. The telephone interpreter stays on the line until dismissed, with the exception of withdrawing from a call. If the client has not made it clear whether or not the telephone interpreter should hold on the line, the telephone interpreter verifies with the client before disconnecting.

Explanation

It is not uncommon for telephone interpreters to be placed on hold, normally by the client. The interpreter should never, under any circumstance, drop the call without first alerting the client and verifying that this is the client's desire. When the interpreter does drop off without the client being present, the interpreter should report the incident to the company.

Exception

If the interpreter has been placed on hold for an unreasonable length of time or the interpreter suspects that the client has accidentally disconnected, the interpreter may then disconnect from the call, but only after advising the LEP, for example, by saying, 'This is the interpreter speaking. It appears that A1 Services is no longer on the line with us. Please call back and request another interpreter.' The length of time may vary from one company to another, and from one client to another, but many companies recommend that if the interpreter is placed on hold for more than 5–10 minutes, the interpreter should disconnect and report the incident to the telephone interpreting company. The client services team will then make a record of the event and follow up with the client.

Standard 6(m)

The telephone interpreter honors brief requests for assistance with written words or phrases. When the telephone interpreter is asked to assist a client in providing written instructions in another language (e.g. instructions for taking a medication), the telephone interpreter works to the best of his or her ability to provide some assistance. However, for documents of more than a few short sentences or phrases in length, the telephone interpreter instructs the client to contact the translation department.

Explanation

Just as on-site interpreters are sometimes asked to perform sight translation, telephone interpreters are sometimes requested to perform 'auditory translation'. This occurs when the client has something in writing that needs to be converted to the other language. If the request is brief, such as a few words, phrases or sentences, the interpreter may take down the information, word by word, and then provide the translation back to the client, one word at a time, spelling each word clearly.

Providing auditory translation is not ideal, for many reasons. However, in some cases, it is the only option available to the client. Some common examples of auditory translation requests would be when a physician needs to write 'take with food' on a prescription, or a social worker needs to translate a short list of required documents that the LEP individual will need to bring into a local office for acceptance into a program, such as 'rent receipt, income verification and social security card'.

Exception

If the request is for more than a few phrases or sentences, the interpreter should direct the client to contact the translation department or agency.

Standard 6(n)

The telephone interpreter avoids self-promotion. The telephone interpreter refrains from speaking about his/her qualifications and professional accomplishments, unless specifically requested to do so by a client for purposes of establishing the telephone interpreter's qualifications.

Explanation

The interpreter should never self-promote to a client or LEP individual.

There are very few situations in which this would be necessary. If a client has questions regarding the telephone interpreting company's quality control processes, these questions should be directed back to the Client Services department.

Exception

In a court setting, an interpreter may often be asked questions regarding his or her experience as part of the process commonly used in court settings by which the judge establishes the interpreter's qualifications. In this case, it is acceptable for the interpreter to answer questions regarding his or her qualifications.

Standard 6(o)

The telephone interpreter provides information on policies, when appropriate. If a circumstance arises in which a client requests information on company policies, the telephone interpreter provides information, as deemed appropriate by the company.

Explanation

The telephone interpreter should be provided with all the information needed to respond to standard requests for information from clients. The interpreter should respond to requests accordingly. When the interpreter does not have the information necessary to respond, the interpreter should direct the client to the appropriate party.

Exception

If an interpreter is contacted by a member of the press, the interpreter should refer the inquiring party directly to the appropriate person or department within the company. Since many magazines, newspapers, and television stations may use a telephone interpreting company's services, it is possible that a call might come in to an interpreter from a reporter without the interpreter initially realizing the purpose of the call.

Standard 6(p)

The telephone interpreter expresses respect for colleagues. Both during and outside working hours, the telephone interpreter treats all other members of the interpreting community (court interpreters, conference interpreters, health care interpreters, other telephone interpreters, etc.) with the highest level of professionalism and respect, in both word and action.

Explanation

The telephone interpreter should always strive to build up, support, and mentor all peers in the interpreting community, both within the company and in the community at large. The telephone interpreter should always hold all practitioners of his or her profession in the highest regard and work to create a nurturing and respectful environment.

There are no exceptions.

Standard 6(q)

The telephone interpreter seeks counseling after traumatic events. If a telephone interpreter encounters an extreme situation that provokes high levels of stress or emotional reaction, he or she seeks counseling through a company-designated counselor.

Explanation

Telephone interpreters may be exposed to traumatic or extreme scenarios, such as child abuse, sexual assault, domestic violence, medical trauma, and numerous types of public safety issues. Whenever the interpreter has experienced such an event, he or she should contact the appropriate parties to request counseling and/or stress debriefing. Often, the interpreter may not realize that there is a need to debrief until a session is requested. For this reason, the interpreter should request this support whenever such a situation has been encountered.

There are no exceptions.

7. Professional Development

Standard 7(a)

The telephone interpreter demonstrates familiarity with training materials. The telephone interpreter reviews and becomes familiar with all printed information, manuals, and multimedia materials distributed by the telephone interpretation provider.

Explanation

Telephone interpreting companies often go to great lengths to develop and administer training in an array of industries and settings. In addition, many companies provide ongoing updates, notices, and news related to quality and training resources. As part of the interpreter's job requirements, the interpreter should be thoroughly familiar with these materials.

Standard 7(b)

The telephone interpreter remains active with both languages. To ensure continual proficiency, the telephone interpreter constantly seeks out opportunities to improve and enhance his/her knowledge of both languages.

Explanation

By virtue of the interpreter's work, he or she will constantly be using both languages. However, it may be important for the interpreter to brush up on a specific regional variety of the language. Also, since languages are constantly evolving and telephone interpreting calls are often highly reflective of these changes, the telephone interpreter should strive to constantly seek out news sources, books, television, and any other media in both languages.

Standard 7(c)

The telephone interpreter is active within the interpreting community. The telephone interpreter seeks out professional organizations, conferences, and training opportunities to enhance his/her professional skills.

Explanation

At the time of writing, no organization exists specifically for telephone interpreters. However, other professional interpreting organizations abound. Therefore, the telephone interpreter should try to remain as active as possible within the interpreting community, attending conferences and training events, keeping up to date on the profession, and in the case of highly experienced telephone interpreters, acting as a mentor and educator to novice telephone interpreters.

Standard 7(d)

The telephone interpreter constantly increases terminology knowledge. The telephone interpreter has a system for organizing new words or phrases and researching new terminology challenges.

Explanation

Since terminology knowledge is an essential part of the job, many telephone interpreting companies supply interpreters with dictionaries (both hard copy and web-based), to enable them to increase terminology knowledge. Telephone interpreters should also track new and unfamiliar terms, in an attempt to constantly increase their vocabulary.

Standard 7(e)

The telephone interpreter builds note-taking and memory skills. The telephone interpreter becomes more efficient with note-taking and improves memory skills with active practice.

Explanation

By virtue of working as an interpreter over the phone, the telephone interpreter will usually gain improved memory skills with practice. However, specific memory exercises may also be used from time to time to ensure good memory skills. For most telephone interpreters, note taking is an essential skill. Interpreter's techniques and personal preferences for note taking vary, and in-depth, book-length resources are available that provide substantial amounts of information (see Gillies, 2005; Rozan, 1956). Although, note-taking systems are often unique to each interpreter, the interpreter should frequently evaluate his or her own system and seek to improve it.

Standard 7(f)

The telephone interpreter supports peers. In all interactions with colleagues, the telephone interpreter demonstrates a willingness to help others improve their skills and knowledge.

Explanation

The telephone interpreter should seek out opportunities to help other colleagues excel in the profession. By using such opportunities, the interpreter can help others to improve, while improving the interpreter's own skills as a senior telephone interpreter and mentor.

Chapter 12
Model Standards of Practice: Emergency Situations

When a caller's life could depend upon the interpreter's actions, the expectations of the interpreter's performance are necessarily different from the expectations implicit in normal standards of practice. At the time of writing, no standards of practice exist for interpreting services in emergency settings, let alone for telephone interpreting in emergency settings. Because of these special considerations, this chapter examines additional recommended standards of practice that would apply to emergency situations only.

What constitutes an emergency situation? For the most part, an emergency call is determined by the type of client initiating the call to the telephone interpreting provider. In the United States, calls originating from city, county, and state 911 call centers, for example, would be considered sources of emergency calls. And, while not all calls placed to these locations are 'real emergencies' (for example, many are misdials and hang-up calls), every call originating from one of these client types should be considered a true emergency until it is otherwise determined by the dispatcher (the person who takes the emergency call and dispatches appropriate help to the scene) . It is the responsibility of the telephone interpreting provider to make all telephone interpreters aware of which calls should be treated as emergencies, and which calls should not.

The standards that follow use a continuation of the same numbering system used in the Model Standards of Practice (Chapter 10), so that they may be used as a supplement to the primary set of standards. When a standard in this chapter appears to directly contradict a standard previously described in the general standards of practice for telephone interpreting, the standard in this chapter should override the general standard in question, due to the nature of emergency situations.

It is also important for all standards of practice to refer back to a guiding principle in the Code of Ethics. Therefore, all behavior for emergency settings should be directed by the guiding principal that follows:

8. Emergency Settings

The telephone interpreter strives to interpret in such a manner that the person taking the emergency call will obtain the same outcome for an LEP caller that would be obtained for a non-LEP caller.

As interpreters refer to this guiding principle for emergency settings, it is important to keep in mind the spirit and intent of the principle, while still striving to uphold all of the previously defined ethical principles as well. It is obvious that, when an interpreter is involved, the same outcome might not be possible for all LEP callers. Also, with an interpreter, the call will obviously take longer than an identical call with a non-LEP caller where no interpreter is needed. However, the standards of practice that follow are meant to assist telephone interpreters in upholding this guiding principle.

Also, it is important to remember that telephone interpreting for emergency settings is not for novices – it is best left to only the most experienced telephone interpreters with the best possible listening skills, in addition to specialized training in interpreting emergency calls. Often, the subject matter is stressful, which can greatly impair one's ability to interpret. In addition, since time is critical there is little, if any, opportunity to request repetitions and clarification.

Standard 8(a)

When rendering information provided by the LEP, the telephone interpreter prioritizes the information, using his or her best judgment. The telephone interpreter provides the most essential information to the emergency call handler as quickly as possible, and then proceeds to interpret the rest of the information, even if this changes the actual order in which the information was provided.

Explanation

Professional emergency dispatchers are well trained in call protocols, and know exactly what information is needed to dispatch the appropriate emergency services to the location. Often, due to high stress and life-threatening scenarios, the caller may not provide the information in the order that will be most helpful to the dispatcher in sending out the appropriate type of help.

For this reason, telephone interpreters should listen carefully to the questions being asked by the dispatcher, in order to organize the information provided in accordance with its relevance to the question asked. Most commonly, the dispatcher will request the location of the emergency first, then the type of emergency, and then ask a series of follow-up questions while help is being dispatched.

The following scenario depicts an acceptable example of how to appropriately observe this standard while interpreting in an emergency (911) setting.

DISPATCHER: 911. Where is the emergency?

LEP CALLER: [*in non-English language*] They're outside, and I'm in the living room looking out at them. They are across the street from me. There are six of them, and they've been out there for the past 3 hours. I am here at 26 Cedar Way, but I don't know their address.

INTERPRETER: I am here at 26 Cedar Way, and they are across the street from me, outside, but I don't know their address. There are six of them, and they've been out there for the past 3 hours. I'm in the living room looking out at them.

Without omitting any of the information provided, the interpreter reorganized it according to the priorities implied in the dispatcher's question. The interpreter first provided the address, which enabled the dispatcher to confirm the location and begin dispatching help to that address immediately. After this was completed, the interpreter rendered the other information provided.

Had the interpreter organized this information in the same way that it was originally rendered, valuable seconds would have been lost, and the outcome might not have been so similar to the outcome for a non-LEP caller.

Standard 8(b)

The interpreter uses summary interpretation when necessary. The interpreter occasionally omits certain, non-essential information, such as interjections and incomplete phrases. The following scenario depicts an acceptable example of how to appropriately observe this standard while interpreting in an emergency setting.

DISPATCHER: Did you say you're at 523 North Yates? I need to verify the address.

INTERPRETER: [*in non-English language*] Did you say you're at 523 North Yates? I need to verify the address.

LEP CALLER: [*in non-English language*] I think I ... whoa, hold on ... I ... I believe it's ... yes, it's 523. Yes, that's it. 523 North Yates, that's where I'm at.
INTERPRETER: Yes, it's 523 North Yates.

It is important to remember at all times that the interpreter should resort to using summary interpretation only when absolutely necessary, such as at the beginning of the call when the location and nature of the emergency are being determined. In this case, the interpreter is basically rendering the most important information quickly and omitting any information that is obviously not critical (such as the incomplete phrases and interjections) so that the dispatcher can continue asking questions according to his or her protocols.

This standard enables the interpreter to improve the likelihood of an outcome for the LEP caller that would mirror the outcome for a non-LEP caller, thereby helping to reduce the disparity between service provision to the two types of callers. However, it is important for the interpreter to remember at all times that summary interpretation should only be used occasionally in emergency calls – not throughout the entire duration of the call, but only when there is really a necessity.

Standard 8(c)

The interpreter assists the dispatcher in ascertaining and verifying critical pieces of information. When a certain piece of information is critical, the interpreter requests repetition and/or repeats the information to verify accuracy. The following is an example of an acceptable implementation of this standard.

DISPATCHER: This is extremely important. I need to verify the characters of the car's license plate number. Can you see it well enough to read it to me?
INTERPRETER: [*in non-English language*] This is extremely important. I need to verify the characters of the car's license plate number. Can you see it well enough to read it to me?
LEP CALLER: [*in non-English language*] It looks like a B, and then a W ... and then I see what looks like a 7. Then it's an M, I guess... and then 22.
INTERPRETER: [*in non-English language*] To verify, is that B as in Boy, W as in William, 7, M as in Mary, and the number 22?
LEP CALLER: [*in non-English language*] Yes, that's right.
INTERPRETER: The number is B-W-7-M-2-2.

In this case, the interpreter knew that it was important for the dispatcher to obtain the license plate number correctly. In a non-emergency call, the telephone interpreter would seek permission from the client before verifying the number. However, in an emergency setting, verifying without first seeking permission is sometimes acceptable, such as in the example. This helps to make the experience more similar to that of a non-LEP caller. Normally, a dispatcher would verify this type of information automatically with a non-LEP caller.

However, because of the language barrier, the dispatcher may sometimes rely on the interpreter to ensure that the information is accurate. It is not to say that the interpreter should verify or repeat each piece of information. This would take up valuable moments and further delay the dispatching of help. However, the interpreter should use his or her best judgment to determine when verification and repetition are needed to ensure accuracy.

Standard 8(d)

The interpreter projects a tone of voice that is appropriate for the situation. The interpreter uses a tone of voice that will neither amplify nor diminish the nature of the emergency.

Explanation

When interpreting the caller's statements to the dispatcher, it is important that the interpreter is not over-dramatic in conveying the source tone and inflection. The dispatcher listens carefully to the caller's voice, and will easily be able to recognize the sounds of someone crying, or the sound of someone yelling, so in those cases the interpreter does not need to replicate the source tone.

On the other hand, it is very important for the interpreter to replicate the tone of the dispatcher as closely as possible. Professional dispatchers are trained to use a calming tone of voice in certain scenarios, and a harsher tone in other settings. Therefore, the telephone interpreter must do everything possible to replicate the source tone, in order to provide the best possible outcome for the LEP caller.

The LEP caller will often not even be listening to what the English speaker says because he or she cannot understand the language, and because an emergency is transpiring, so the only voice the LEP caller actually 'hears' is the voice of the interpreter. For this reason, the interpreter must project the appropriate tone of voice by mirroring the dispatcher's original tone.

This standard relates to the guiding ethical principle in that, replicating the dispatcher's source tone, gives the LEP caller has an experience similar to that of a non-LEP caller in the same circumstances and with the sane dispatcher.

Standard 8(e)

The interpreter uses the fastest rate of speech possible, without sacrificing the listener's comprehension quality.

Explanation

Again, this standard serves to make the LEP caller experience as similar as possible to that of a non-LEP caller experience. Decreasing the amount of time used to interpret enables the conversation to take place quickly so that help can be dispatched as soon as possible. It is essential for the interpreter to speak quickly, without sacrificing clarity of pronunciation. If a choice must be made between the two, the interpreter should always err on the side of pronouncing clearly rather than to speaking too quickly, so that as few repetitions are requested as possible. However, whenever possible, the interpreter should provide the best of both worlds: speech that is rapid and clear.

Standard 8(f)

The interpreter interrupts the LEP speaker when necessary. Let us take a look at how a scenario that requires an interruption might play out when all parties speak English:

DISPATCHER: 911. Where is the emergency?
CALLER: My husband is threatening to kill me ... he has a gun and he just went outside ... he's ....
[*Caller is interrupted by dispatcher.*]
DISPATCHER: Ma'am, are you at 121 West Park, Apartment C?
CALLER: Yes ...

Now, let us take a look at how the same emergency call might progress if the caller speaks another language, and if the interpreter follows the general standards of practice for telephone interpreting, as defined in the previous chapters.

DISPATCHER: 911. Where is the emergency?
LEP CALLER: [*in non-English language*] My husband is threatening to kill me ... he has a gun and he just went outside ... he's on the porch now, and he has been drinking all night. He always does this when he gets drunk, and I never should have married him,

oh my God, what was I thinking? Please send someone to take him away from me and my son, I am afraid he'll hurt my son. My son is only 3 years old, and I don't want him to grow up thinking that all men are like this and this is his only role model. Please, send someone, please help me! I don't know what I'm going to do if you don't send someone!

[*The interpreter reaches the manageable segment length, politely waits for the caller to stop speaking, and proceeds to interpret ...*]

INTERPRETER: [*in non-English language*] My husband is threatening to kill me ... he has a gun and he just went outside ... he's on the porch now, and he has been drinking all night. He always does this when he gets drunk, and I never should have married him, oh my God, what was I thinking? Please send someone to take him away from me and my son, I am afraid he'll hurt my son. My son is only 3 years old, and I don't want him to grow up thinking that all men are like this and this is his only role model. Please, send someone, please help me! I don't know what I'm going to do if you don't send someone!

DISPATCHER: Ma'am, are you at 121 West Park, Apartment C?

INTERPRETER: [*in non-English language*] Ma'am, are you at 121 West Park, Apartment C?

LEP CALLER: [*in non-English language*] Yes ...

Obviously, by adhering to the normal standards of practice for telephone interpreting, many precious seconds, if not minutes, are spent listening to and conveying information that is probably not essential to dispatching help to the location. Now, let's take a look at a scenario in which the interpreter adheres to the standard of practice that is recommended for emergency calls.

DISPATCHER: 911. Where is the emergency?

LEP CALLER: [*in non-English language*] My husband is threatening to kill me ... he has a gun and he just went outside ... he's ...

[*Interpreter interrupts the caller.*]

INTERPRETER: [*in non-English language*] My husband is threatening to kill me ... he has a gun and he just went outside ... he's ...

DISPATCHER: Ma'am, are you at 121 West Park, Apartment C?

INTERPRETER: [*in non-English language*] Ma'am, are you at 121 West Park, Apartment C?

CALLER: Yes ...

It is clear that the last scenario most closely mirrors the experience of the non-LEP caller in the first scenario. In the second scenario, the interpreter's failure to interrupt could actually lead to a person's death. Therefore, it is extremely important that interpreters maintain this standard of practice and interrupt when necessary.

At the opposite end of the spectrum, it is necessary to provide a word of caution here. While the telephone interpreter must sometimes interrupt in emergency settings to enable the LEP caller to have the best possible outcome, the telephone interpreter should never take over the dispatcher's role. It is a fine line for an interpreter, and one that could be easily crossed even with the best intentions.

The best rule of thumb for interpreters is to refer back to the general standards regarding avoiding side conversations and maintaining appropriate role boundaries. The interpreter should always revert back to a conduit role and allow the communication to go through the interpreter. When an interruption must take place, it should be brief, and for a very specific purpose.

Immediately after the interruption, the interpreter should revert back to the normal role of the interpreter, observing the general standards.

Standard 8(g)

The interpreter uses reported speech when necessary. When the caller's identity could be confused with another LEP individual on the line, such as someone else who is on another phone within the LEP caller's home, the interpreter may resort to using reported speech to clarify the identities of the speakers.

Explanation

Reported speech consists of converting the pronouns in the utterance from first person ('I') to third person ('he', 'she'). Normally, telephone interpreters should use first person exclusively. However, emergency settings require a special exception to this general rule.

Also sometimes referred to as 'third person' interpretation, reported speech is to be strictly avoided by all professional telephone interpreters, except for very specific settings, such as this. Many professional interpreting associations, while not making specific reference to telephone interpreting, prohibit reported speech from being used in professional interpreting practice, and for very valid reasons. Reported speech not only distorts the message, but it leads to numerous issues regarding role boundaries and neutrality. For this reason, telephone interpreters should use reported speech only when absolutely necessary. These instances will occur very infrequently, if ever, in a telephone interpreter's professional career.

Like all other standards for emergency settings, this standard should be exercised with caution, and implemented only when absolutely necessary. Sometimes, especially when other voices are heard in the background or directly on the phone, it can become difficult or confusing for the interpreter to render the information in first person, thereby delaying the process of dispatching help to the scene.

In cases when the normal turn-taking process in the call is disrupted by additional speakers, the interpreter may need to use reported speech to clarify the identity of each speaker in a quick and clear manner. The following example may best illustrate an appropriate example of this standard put into practice.

LEP CALLER: [*in non-English language*] I don't know what color his shirt was. I think it's black. Maria, do you know what color his shirt was?

2ND LEP VOICE: [*in non-English language*] No, I think it's brown.

INTERPRETER: The original caller thinks that the shirt was black. Another person on the line, Maria, thinks it was brown. In non-emergency settings, the interpreter could rectify this problem as follows:

INTERPRETER: This is the interpreter speaking. The first speaker stated, 'I don't know what color his shirt was. I think it's black. Maria, do you know what color his shirt was?' The second speaker then stated, 'No, I think it's brown.'

However, in emergency settings, this may not always be realistic because providing such an explanation uses up precious seconds. Also, this option could become problematic in emergency calls, especially when the speakers have more than one exchange between them.

Another option would have been for the interpreter to render the utterances in first person, by saying, 'I don't know what color his shirt was. I think it's black. Maria, do you know what color his shirt was? No, I think it's brown.' However, what if the dispatcher did not understand that there were two speakers on the line? This can be quite common, since it is often harder to distinguish between two voices in an unfamiliar language. In order to avoid confusion, the best solution may be, in certain, limited emergency scenarios, for the interpreter to resort to using reported speech.

Standard 8(h)

The interpreter reports any auditory observations that may be of assistance to the dispatcher. The interpreter listens attentively and conveys factual observations that may be of use to the dispatcher.

Explanation

When a non-LEP caller is in an emergency setting, the dispatcher can often use auditory observations to gain a better understanding of the caller's situation. However, when an LEP caller is on the line, this may not be possible for the dispatcher.

For example, an emergency call comes in from an LEP caller, and the dispatcher hears a child screaming in the background in another language. The dispatcher does not know why the child is screaming, or what the child is screaming about, and assumes there is an emergency involving the child.

However, the interpreter hears something different. The interpreter hears the child screaming, 'Mommy, I want my dolly back. He won't give me back my dolly!' and realizes that the child may be simply having a temper tantrum. Therefore, the interpreter can state, 'This is the interpreter – a child in the background is screaming that she wants her dolly back.' This will immediately convey to the dispatcher that the child's reason for screaming is probably not related to the caller's reason for calling.

What is important to remember here is that the interpreter may never, in any instance, ever say, 'This is the interpreter – a child in the background is having a temper tantrum'. That would be an assumption on the part of the interpreter, as opposed to a factual statement that was actually observed.

In summary, the nature of emergency calls requires slight revisions to the general standards of practice. The main reason for the revisions is the fact that the dispatcher's ability to send help during an emergency situation is hampered greatly by a language barrier and the increased length of time required for communication. However, by following the standards identified in this section, telephone interpreters can dramatically help to decrease disparities between the level of service provided to LEP callers and the level provided to non-LEP callers.

Chapter 13
Model Standards of Practice: Health Care Settings

In 2005, the National Council on Interpreting in Health Care made an important step toward the professionalization of the field of health care interpreting with the publication of the National Standards of Practice for Interpreters in Health Care. These standards were endorsed by many organizations and associations throughout the United States. It is recommended that all interpreters working in the health care field, including telephone interpreters, become familiar with the standards issued by the National Council as their foremost source of guidance for interpreting work in the health care field.

The model standards of practice in this chapter are provided by the author to assist the telephone interpreting community, and are not intended to replace the work of the National Council or similar associations in other countries. On the contrary, telephone interpreters around the world are encouraged to become members of organizations such as the Council and to become intimately familiar with their work. However, since the standards of practice issued by such organizations do not normally address telephone interpreting specifically, here we will examine some recommended standards of practice that would apply primarily to telephone interpreters when working in health care settings. These standards serve as a compliment to the general standards.

All standards of practice should refer to an ethical principle in the code of ethics. The standards in this chapter are based on the following guiding principle:

9. Health Care Settings

The telephone interpreter strives to interpret in such a manner that will assist the health care provider in obtaining the best possible outcome for the LEP patient.

You may notice that this guiding principle is very similar to the guiding principle for emergency settings. The difference is in how the interpreter should go about seeking to uphold that principle, because the settings are often very different. This is made evident in the standards that follow.

Standard 9(a)

The telephone interpreter checks to ensure that the LEP patient has understood the information and instructions given by the provider. To ensure proper understanding of the information being communicated, the interpreter requests permission periodically to check for understanding on the part of the LEP patient.

Explanation

Sometimes, because the nature of the communication process is altered and extended when an interpreter is present, the LEP patient may be less likely to interrupt the process or ask for clarification, even when important information has not been properly understood. Also, there may be hesitation or reluctance to ask clarifying questions, as this is considered inappropriate or disrespectful among certain cultures and segments of society.

Some health care providers might assume that, if there is any lack of understanding on the patient's part, the interpreter will somehow be able to alert them of this. To some degree, the interpreter could be a better judge of an LEP patient's understanding than the provider is. This is because the interpreter hears the speaker's original rendition and may be able to pick up on certain nuances that can be difficult to convey when transferring the information into another language.

To the best of his or her ability, the interpreter should attempt to convey the original tone, inflection and meaning of the source utterance, so that these details are clear to the provider. However, this is not always possible, even for the most highly skilled interpreter. In addition, sometimes even when the interpreter attempts to render such subtleties, they might not necessarily be understood clearly by the provider.

There are times when the interpreter perceives that there is confusion or lack of understanding but the interpreter cannot be certain of this. Just as an on-site interpreter is not allowed to state opinions based on observations of the LEP patient's gestures or facial expressions, the telephone interpreter is not allowed to share opinions that were arrived at based on a person's tone of voice, hesitations, and breath or speech patterns.

For this reason, rather than wait until such cues are provided to indicate a lack of understanding, it is best for the interpreter to periodically and proactively ask the provider for permission to verify that the patient has understood the information that has been communicated thus far. This way, the patient's understanding of the information is consistently and frequently verified, regardless of whether or not the interpreter has perceived a lack of understanding. When the interpreter verifies understanding periodically as opposed to whenever the interpreter perceives a lack of understanding, the understanding of all parties becomes less dependent on the interpreter's observations (or lack thereof), and more dependent on the interpreter's ability to adhere to this standard of practice.

To check for understanding, the interpreter might say, 'This is the interpreter speaking. May we check to see if Mr. Yamashita understood the instructions regarding how to take his medication?' or, 'This is the interpreter speaking. With your permission, the interpreter will check to see if Mrs. Sharma has understood these instructions.'

With regard to how often to request permission to check for understanding, a general guideline is to do this each time dosage or treatment information is given and whenever numbers and times of day are involved. In addition, any time a series of instructions is given, the patient's understanding should also be verified. Whenever the communication involves training or teaching of any kind, the patient's understanding should also be verified frequently.

Standard 9(b)

When providing clarification regarding cultural issues, the telephone interpreter avoids stereotyping or generalizing. The telephone interpreter provides clarification in an objective manner, without making sweeping references to all speakers of a given language or members of a specific cultural group, ethnicity or nationality.

Explanation

While it is important for telephone interpreters to uphold this standard in all settings, cultural issues often come up more frequently in health care settings. An example of an interpreter upholding this standard would be as follows:

> **PROVIDER:** How have you tried to treat your daughter's symptoms so far?
>
> **INTERPRETER:** [*in non-English language*] How have you tried to treat your daughter's symptoms so far?
>
> **LEP PATIENT:** [*in non-English language*] I did what anyone would do

when their daughter is afflicted with the evil eye. I wrapped my daughter in blankets and turned up the heat so that she would sweat it all out. She did get better, but I must not have done it right, because she still has the same symptoms.

INTERPRETER: This is the interpreter speaking. The patient believes her daughter was afflicted with the evil eye. This is a common belief in some places, and there are many different folk remedies for treating this. The patient stated the following, 'I did what anyone would do when their daughter is afflicted with the evil eye. I wrapped my daughter in blankets and turned up the heat so that she would sweat it all out. She did get better, but I must not have done it right, because she still has the same symptoms.

By providing a clarification, the interpreter is preparing the provider by laying down a context in which to take in the LEP patient's remarks. Without the clarification, the LEP patient's comment might have come as somewhat of a surprise, especially if the provider is unfamiliar with this cultural framework for understanding certain ailments and symptoms. For contrast, here is an example of an inappropriate way of providing clarification:

INTERPRETER: I did what anyone would do when their daughter is afflicted with the evil eye. I wrapped my daughter in blankets and turned up the heat so that she would sweat it all out. She did get better, but I must not have done it right, because she still has the same symptoms. This is the interpreter speaking. By the way, people who speak [*language*] believe that these symptoms are caused by the evil eye.

This clarification was inappropriate because the interpreter made a generalization regarding all speakers of a language, which can lead to the provider stereotyping in the future. The provider may often see the interpreter as the 'subject matter expert' in terms of cultural healing practices, so the interpreter must be very careful not to contribute to any generalizations or stereotypes about a particular language group. Also, the interpreter's statement was untrue. A common language is no indication of a common adherence to a specific concept or belief-practice. In most cultures that have an 'evil eye' concept, there are individuals who believe more fervently in it than others, and there are those who do not believe in it at all.

In summary, the interpreter should avoid generalizing or stereotyping at all times when giving the provider a background or context with which to understand a specific cultural practice.

Standard 9(c)

When left on hold with the patient, the interpreter politely refrains from engaging in personal conversation. If the interpreter is placed on hold and left alone on the line with the patient, the interpreter should politely decline to make conversation with the patient.

Explanation

The provider may put the interpreter on hold for a variety of reasons. The provider may need to go down the hall to retrieve a patient brochure for the patient, or perhaps the provider needs to make a call to another department to verify something on behalf of the patient. Whatever the reason, the telephone interpreter can be left on hold with the patient.

When this happens, the patient will often try to make conversation with the interpreter. To prevent this from happening, many telephone interpreters put on the 'mute' button so that the LEP patient is not tempted to engage in conversation. If this is not an option, or if the LEP patient insists on making conversation, the interpreter may say, for example, 'My apologies, but the interpreter is not allowed to speak with you while the provider is off-line', or 'This is the interpreter speaking. The interpreter cannot have a private conversation with you; please hold your comments until the provider returns.'

Some readers may think that this guideline is too rigid, and that no harm can result in a few minutes' worth of conversation with a fellow speaker of a common language. Let's look at some examples of situations that are likely to occur when the interpreter engages in 'harmless' small talk with the LEP patient.

Example 1

PATIENT: Where are you from, Ma'am?

INTERPRETER: [*Country*]. Where are you from?

PATIENT: Yes, I thought you were from [*Country*]. I could tell by your accent. You pronounce words incorrectly and your grammar is terrible. I just hope your English is not as bad.

Example 2

PATIENT: How are you today?

INTERPRETER: Fine, and you?

PATIENT: Well, don't tell the doctor this – he thinks I am fine – but

I've actually been having blood in my urine for several months now. But he is so proud of me and my progress has been so good that I don't want him to know about this.

Example 3

PATIENT: How many years have you been interpreting?

INTERPRETER: Seven years.

PATIENT: Oh, since you have a lot of experience, maybe you can tell me what to do about another problem. I don't want to bring this up to the doctor – he seems to be in a hurry today – but my son started to cough up blood. What do you think I should do?

Example 4

PATIENT: What was the doctor's name again?

INTERPRETER: Dr Jones.

PATIENT: Yes, that's it. I don't feel like Dr. Jones is doing a good job listening to me. He doesn't seem to want to hear me talk. Do you think I should switch to another doctor? In each of these examples, if the interpreter had initially responded by letting the LEP patient know that he or she is unable to participate in conversation without the provider being present instead of engaging in conversation, these difficult situations are unlikely to have arisen. For this reason, the interpreter should decline any requests or attempts to engage in personal conversation with the LEP patient.

Chapter 14
Model Standards of Practice: Legal Settings

In 1995, a Code of Professional Responsibility for Judiciary Interpreters was published in for interpreters working in state courts within the United States (Hewitt, 1995). The majority of the consortium-member states have adopted these ethical principles, and in recent years, some states have developed enforcement procedures in order to oversee their implementation. Many of these states also offer certification for interpreters. However, the criteria to become certified, as well as the costs associated with obtaining certification, vary somewhat from one state to another. What is common to the consortium member states is that they all require interpreters to pass an exam in order to become certified.

In the above-mentioned publication, Hewitt devotes an entire chapter to telephone interpreting, and the chapter includes a discussion of both the limitations and potential benefits of telephone interpreting. The majority of the limitations and concerns mentioned in the publication relate to the issue of quality.

Although Hewitt's book is now more than a decade old, many of the concerns outlined are still extremely valid. For this reason, the standards that are outlined here will also focus primarily on quality. In fact, some of the standards in this chapter merely serve to reiterate standards that are included in the general section (Chapter 10), but they are reinforced here for added emphasis. The standards are based on the following guiding ethical principle.

10. Legal Settings

When interpreting for legal settings, the telephone interpreter strives to provide the most accurate and fair interpretation possible, while upholding the existing principles and standards of practice for the judiciary interpreting profession. Interpreters should look to the codes of ethics and standards of practice provided by professional associations.

For example, in the United States, interpreters may wish to defer to the ethical principles issued by the National Association of Judiciary Interpreters and Translators (NAJIT). In practice, in courtrooms across the United States, there is still a lack of uniformity with regard to standards for court interpreting. While experts in the field agree that there is a need for uniform standards for the profession, this is a goal that has not yet been reached.

Because of this lack of consensus regarding national standards, it may be even more difficult to determine what the standards of practice should be for telephone interpreting in court settings. Therefore, the ethical principle above is broader in scope, and the standards that apply to it below are also general.

Standard 10(a)

The telephone interpreter disqualifies him or herself from legal interpreting assignments for which he or she is unqualified. If the interpreter receives a call for a legal setting and realizes that he or she is not qualified to interpret for this setting, the interpreter promptly discloses this to the court personnel.

Explanation

To provide an accurate interpretation, the interpreter must have received specialized training in judiciary interpreting and legal terminology knowledge, and/or must have passed a test for legal interpreting to prove his or her level of skill. If the interpreter does not meet this requirement, he or she should not accept legal interpreting calls.

Interpreters working in any legal setting, including interpreters who providing services telephonically, should hold a certification from a court-approved entity. If the interpreter is providing services in a language pair for which no certification exists, the interpreter should meet certain minimum criteria, such as receiving an advanced rating on a language proficiency test and interpretation skills test, as well as having successfully completed one or more court interpreter training programs.

Standard 10(b)

The telephone interpreter renders all legal interpretation in first person, with no exceptions whatsoever. At all times, the interpreter performs first person (direct speech) interpretation, and does not slip into indirect speech.

Explanation

Using direct speech is important for telephone interpreters in all other settings as well. However, in other settings, a slip into indirect speech is less likely to have a dramatic impact on the outcome of the interpreted session. In legal settings, direct speech takes on an enhanced importance, and it is imperative for the interpreter to avoid indirect speech at all costs.

Standard 10(c)

If the telephone interpreter makes a mistake in the interpretation, he or she informs the court immediately. If the interpreter realizes that an error was made, such as a mistranslation or an omission, he or she rectifies the error for the record.

Explanation

In contrast to other settings, in legal settings the call is likely to be transcribed and analyzed by a legal team. In the case of court appearances the interpreter is providing sworn testimony subject to the same time allotment as each witness giving testimony on the stand, since the trial is assigned a predetermined amount of time. Since all testimony is given at one time, it will not be possible for the interpreter or the provider to 'call back'. For this reason, the interpreter must immediately alert the court of any possible errors, and when necessary, request permission from the judge to have the question or response repeated. Such requests are spoken in the third person, for example, 'The interpreter requests of the court to have the question repeated.'

Standard 10(d)

The telephone interpreter provides services in the appropriate interpretation mode for the legal setting in question. In nearly all cases, this means that the telephone interpreter should use the consecutive interpretation mode.

Explanation

As a reminder, consecutive interpreting is when information is interpreted a portion at a time, with speakers pausing to allow the interpreter to render the interpretation. With simultaneous interpreting, the interpreter is listening while simultaneously interpreting the speech. There are two conditions that must exist in order for a telephone interpreter to provide accurate and complete interpretation in simultaneous mode: facilitating technology and specialized training. The specialized training in simultaneous mode heightens the auditory skills and accuracy in transferring information from one language to another while simultaneously producing speech and listening to the speaker. These skills must be perfected in order to maintain the integrity of the communications of the attorney, the judge and all witnesses.

Unless the contracting court is currently kitted out with this technology, and unless the interpreter has received training and been evaluated in the simultaneous mode, telephone interpreters should only interpret for situations that require consecutive interpreting.

Part 4

Practice Scenarios

Chapter 15
How to Use the Practice Scenarios

Each of the next 8 chapters contains industry-specific practice scenarios. The scenarios include sample segments that are commonly spoken either by the LEP customer or the client representative. All the segments are written in English, so that they may be used for all language pairs. All the scenarios include terminology that is representative of calls and situations that are common in the United States. To make these scenarios most useful, readers from other countries may wish to replace this terminology with words and phrases that are more commonly used in the reader's own country of origin.

To get the most out of the practice scenarios, it is best to work with a partner. A partner can give you insight and feedback that you might not be able to obtain on your own. In addition, working with a partner helps you to get accustomed to receiving feedback from others, which is a standard part of working in a telephone interpreting company.

With a Partner

Find a fellow student of telephone interpreting who shares a common language pair with you. Divide the scenarios between yourself and your partner, so that each person is assigned two scenarios.

Take your assigned scenarios and translate the LEP caller's segments into your other working language. As you translate, be especially careful to make sure that your translations sound like something that someone would speak naturally in a free-flowing conversation, as opposed to something that someone would write. The dialogue should reflect natural, informal speech. Once you and your partner have finished translating the LEP caller segments for all of the industry-specific setting in Chapters 16 to 23, you should have a total of 26 bilingual practice scenarios.

Next, schedule a time to have a telephone call with your partner so that you can use the practice scenarios over the phone. Since you are attempting to gain practice at telephone interpreting, there is no replacement for actually interpreting over the phone. It does not matter whether you use a cell phone, analog phone, headset or audio conference-calling software on the computer for this exercise. What matters is that you are replicating an over-the-phone experience and gaining practice at actually interpreting real-world scenarios common to the telephone interpreting profession.

If you are not able to arrange for practice over the phone, be creative and try your best to replicate an over-the-phone experience. For example, in order to begin gaining a heightened sense of auditory awareness, make sure that you cannot see the other party while you are practicing. For best results, plan to record the scenarios using digital or analog recording equipment. This will enable you to play the scenarios back in order to analyze your performance. Make sure you are familiar with any laws related to recording telephone conversations, and read the appropriate disclosures to each other over the phone to gain the necessary permission from each other to record the sessions.

Now, decide which one of you will be first at practicing as the telephone interpreter. The person reading the scenario will act out the parts of both the LEP caller and the client representative. The other person will interpret the segments from both parties. In other words, the two of you will take turns being the reader and the interpreter.

Initial Rules of Engagement

When you first begin to use the exercises with a partner, it is important to observe these general guidelines.

For the Reader:

1. Speak clearly and pronounce accurately. Do not slur your words. Practice reading the segments out loud before you begin your practice sessions.
2. Use appropriate intonation and inflection. Do your best to act out the parts of both speakers.
3. Stay in character. Even if the person interpreting makes mistakes or starts laughing due to nervousness or frustration, just go with the flow and continue reading the segments.
4. Honor requests for repetitions and clarification. The person interpreting may ask for as many repetitions as he or she needs. Each time a request is made, politely repeat the entire segment. If your partner asks you to clarify something, do your best to honor the request.
5. Do not correct your partner. If you hear your partner interpret something

incorrectly, resist the temptation to point it out. You may make a note on the page for discussion later, but continue reading the segments, and focus on doing the best possible job reading the segments.

For the Interpreter:

1. Ask for repetitions if necessary. Before beginning your practice sessions, you may wish to write out a sample request for a repetition, such as, 'May the interpreter have a repetition, please?', in order to have it near you for reference until you are more comfortable using such phrases. In fact, you should sometimes request a repetition even if you do not need one, just to gain practice at doing so.
2. Paraphrase when necessary. If you do not know the exact rendition of a specific term, but you know what it means, do your best to render it by using your own words.
3. Ask for clarification when necessary. If you do not know what a given term means, ask for clarification. Your partner will attempt to clarify the term for you, so that you can interpret it using his or her clarification.
4. If you make a mistake, correct yourself. Make sure that you correct yourself if you make a mistake. Please refer to Standard 4(k) (in Chapter 10) for additional details on how to proceed.
5. Relax. Interpreting can be extremely difficult, and it does not come naturally to most people. Now is the time to make mistakes, while you are just practicing. Just go with the flow, and remember that the scenarios are designed to help you improve your skills.

Post-Practice Discussion

After using each scenario, discuss the performance with your partner. Ask the following questions, and discuss them with your partner:

- What did I do well when interpreting this scenario?
- What would I do differently, if I were to interpret the same scenario again?
- Did I have difficulties with any terminology? If so, which terms gave me trouble?
- Did I have difficulty upholding any of the standards of practice? If so, which ones?
- How could I improve my performance?

Enhanced Practice

Once you have used all the scenarios a few times and are familiar with their content, you should be able to interpret them with ease. Once you have reached that goal, to make your practice more challenging, you can modify the scenarios by doing the following:

- *Make the segments longer.* Add words or sentences to the segments to test your ideal segment length and note-taking skills. Include at least one segment that is so long that it should require your partner who is performing the role of the interpreter to request a pause from the speaker in order to interpret.
- *Include challenging regional terms in the language of the LEP caller.* Research some terms that are likely to be unknown by your partner and insert them into the dialogue. This will require your partner to ask for permission to clarify the term with the LEP caller.
- *Include more place names and proper nouns in English.* Of particular importance are names of cities, towns, counties, states, neighborhoods, and landmarks, such as stores, restaurants, statues and government buildings.
- *Insert numbers wherever possible.* Make up some amounts, phone numbers, account numbers, etc. and put them into the dialogue to make the segments more heavily saturated with information that would require note taking.
- *Place an ethical challenge into the dialogue.* Review the Code of Ethics (Chapter 9) and find a creative way to include a situation in the dialogue that would put the interpreter in an ethical dilemma in the midst of the scenario. For example, ask the interpreter to give you advice on a specific matter, offer to compensate the interpreter, or confide something in the interpreter, but ask him or her not to interpret it. In addition, make sure you have a suggested way of handling the ethical issue ready for your post-practice discussion.
- *Increase your rate of speech.* Speak quickly, to see if your partner mirrors your rate of speech and is able to 'keep up' with the increased pace.
- *Change your tone and inflection.* State some of the segments with an angry or forceful tone, and others with a shy or faint tone. See if your partner mirrors the tone and inflection.
- *Slur your words.* Run some of your words together to see if this requires your partner who is performing the role of the interpreter to request clarification or repetition. This will enable your partner to get used to individuals who might mumble or slur their words together.
- *Turn down your volume.* In the real world, sound quality might not always be optimum because of faulty equipment on the LEP caller or client's side. To replicate this, practice with older equipment or with

your phone volume turned down significantly.

- *Breathe into the phone.* Exhale while the interpreter is interpreting to see if this distracts the interpreter's focus. This is a very realistic scenario that telephone interpreters deal with in the real world.
- *Create background noise.* Often, the LEP caller is calling from a home phone, and there may be noise in the background from a television, radio, running water, etc. Replicate some of these background noises to see if it distracts your partner who is performing the role of the interpreter.
- *Build in some surprises.* The telephone interpreter never knows what will happen on a call. Be creative and use your imagination to script unusual segments to keep an element of surprise in store for your partner. For example, build in unexpected events, such as sneezing or coughing, starting a sentence and stopping halfway through, stuttering and mumbling, speaking too softly for the interpreter to hear you, sobbing or crying while speaking, yelling and/or using profanity and pretending not to understand something by asking for a repetition several times in a row regarding the same thing.
- *Write your own scenarios.* Working on what you've learned from other scenarios and, perhaps by doing additional research, write some sample scenarios of your own and practice using them. Even if your scenarios are not realistic examples of real-world telephone interpreting, they will still be useful for practice. The more you practice, the more prepared you will be to enter the real world of telephone interpreting.

English-Only Partners

If you do not have a partner who speaks both your working languages, it may be important for you to refer to Standard 7(c). It is extremely important for interpreters to be members of professional associations in order to network with and interact with peers. However, if you live in a remote location or speak a language that is very rare in your country of residence and cannot find a partner even within local associations, you may still be able to use the practice scenarios if you can locate a partner who also speaks English. In this case, you can both practice interpreting all of the segments from English into the other language (unidirectional interpreting).

This is not meant to give you practice interpreting from your other language into English, but will help you develop many of the nonlinguistic skills that are required for success as a telephone interpreter. If you can work with a partner to do English-only versions of the exercises, you can enhance the scenarios later by using many of the methods described above. It is recommended that you use the self-study adaptation of the exercises, as described below.

Self-Study

Perhaps you do not wish to work with a partner, or perhaps you do not have a partner available. Whatever the reason, you can still benefit from all of the practice scenarios included in the following chapters.

Have a friend or colleague translate the LEP caller's segments into your other working language. If you do not have anyone who can translate them for you, and you have to translate them yourself, you risk becoming familiar with the segments before hearing them. Either way, you can still benefit from the scenarios. Once the LEP caller's segments are translated, either have a friend record the segments, or record them yourself. Then, play the segments back and practice interpreting them. You may also record yourself interpreting the segments, so that you can later go back and review your performance.

You can also use nearly all of the methods described above for enhanced practice at telephone interpreting. As you improve and become more proficient with interpreting the scenarios, adapt them as you see fit. You can record the segments again each time you make modifications, and practice interpreting the segments as usual. Then, when you review your performance, ask yourself the same questions that you would ask for post-practice discussion with a partner.

Chapter 16
Practice Scenarios: Utilities

These scenarios represent calls and situations that are common in the United States. To make them most useful, readers from other countries may wish to replace some of the terminology with words and phrases that are more commonly used in the reader's own country of origin or are more reflective of everyday language in the country where interpreting will be provided.

Utility Scenario 1: Budget Billing Plan

GAS COMPANY: Thank you for calling Premium Gas Company. How may I help you?

LEP CALLER: Yes, I'm calling because my neighbor told me she pays the same amount every month, and I don't think that's fair, because my bill is much higher in the winter.

GAS COMPANY: Oh, well it sounds like your neighbor might be on our budget billing plan, in which you pay the same amount every month.

LEP CALLER: I don't know what plan she is on, but I want to pay the same amount every month.

GAS COMPANY: OK, let me explain how it works. If you want to enroll in the plan, first we look at the last year of your gas bills. Then, we estimate how much you will be paying in the next 12 months.

LEP CALLER: But I've only been in this apartment for six months.

GAS COMPANY: Then, we look at the usage of the previous tenant.

LEP CALLER: OK. So what would my payment be?

GAS COMPANY: Well, before I can tell you that, I need to continue explaining the program, and if you still want to sign up, I can help you enroll over the phone.

LEP CALLER: OK, what else?

GAS COMPANY: Well, once we estimate your payment amount, you pay that for the next 11 months. Then, we figure out the actual billed usage versus what we estimated.

LEP CALLER: What if I pay too much?

GAS COMPANY: We pay you back the money in the form of a refund, or we can credit your account, whichever you prefer.

LEP CALLER: I think I'd prefer you to credit my account.

GAS COMPANY: Well, you would decide that when and if it actually happens. Also, if you paid too little, then we bill you for the balance.

LEP CALLER: Wait a minute – if you are estimating the amount, how do you figure out what my actual usage is?

GAS COMPANY: We continue to read your meter each month, just like we always do, to determine your actual usage. In fact, we show you the actual usage each month when we bill you for the estimated payment.

LEP CALLER: Would it cost me anything extra to do it this way?

GAS COMPANY: No, there is no fee to enroll in the program.

LEP CALLER: OK, so what would my estimated payment be?

GAS COMPANY: Just one second and I'll calculate that for you ... it looks you're your estimated monthly payment would be $118.56.

LEP CALLER: What? $118.56? But my bill last month was only around 80 bucks! Why would I want to pay so much more? I'm not paying that!

GAS COMPANY: Yes, your bill was lower last month because it's the summer, and your bill is normally higher in the winter. Your bills in the summer are lower, but one of the bills last winter was for more than $200. So, if you enroll in the program, you'll have a lower monthly payment in the winter months.

LEP CALLER: Well, I wasn't here last winter, so maybe my bill will be less than that. Maybe the previous residents were not as smart with their gas usage, but I am pretty frugal.

GAS COMPANY: Well, it's your choice, Ma'am. You don't have to enroll in this plan unless you want to.

LEP CALLER: Wait a minute, but why is my neighbor paying so little? I am paying a lot more than she is, and our houses are the same size.

GAS COMPANY: There are a lot of reasons. It could have something to do with the appliances, the usage ... even the location of the apartments in the building. So then, do you want to enroll in this program or not, Ma'am?

LEP CALLER: No way. I'm not going to pay more. Only a fool would do something like that. And I'm no fool!

GAS COMPANY: Well, actually, some people call in during the winter months, when their bill is high, to enroll in the program, because it lowers their bill during those months.

LEP CALLER: OK, but I don't think it makes much sense for me right now. I don't want to enroll.

GAS COMPANY: OK, that's no problem at all, Ma'am. Is there anything else I can help you with today?

LEP CALLER: No, that's all. But I'm going over to my neighbor's house to find out what appliances she has and to see why her bill is so much lower than mine.

GAS COMPANY: That's fine, Ma'am. Thank you for calling Premium Gas Company, and have a great day.

LEP CALLER: Thank you too. Goodbye!

Utility Scenario 2: Meter Reading

GAS COMPANY: Thank you for calling Premium Gas Company. How may I help you?

LEP CALLER: Yes, I think I just missed the meter reader. I had to step out for a minute to pick up my daughter at school, and when I came back, I saw the gas company's van pulling out of my driveway, but I couldn't catch them in time.

GAS COMPANY: OK, well that's no problem, ma'am. We'll just send you a bill for an estimated reading.

LEP CALLER: Oh, but I hate it when they do that. I'd much rather pay exactly what I owe. I wish I had remembered to leave my gate unlocked!

GAS COMPANY: Well, if you can read the meter for me over the phone, I can enter it for you. Are you on a cordless phone?

LEP CALLER: Yes. I'm walking toward the meter right now.

GAS COMPANY: OK, when you get there, can you tell me how many dials it has on it?

LEP CALLER: Sure, I am looking at it, and it has seven dials.

GAS COMPANY: You're looking at the water meter. Do you know where the gas meter is located?

LEP CALLER: Oh, it must be the other one. OK, this one has five dials on it.

GAS COMPANY: That's your electric meter. The Gas meter should have three dials on it.

LEP CALLER: That one is on the other side of the house. OK, just give me a second.

GAS COMPANY: OK, when you get there, can you confirm for me that it has three dials?

LEP CALLER: Yes, let me see ... yes, it has three dials.

GAS COMPANY: Great! Do you see that the first dial on the right has single digits? That one rotates clockwise.

LEP CALLER: Yes, I see it.

GAS COMPANY: OK, where is the pointer? What number is it pointing at?

LEP CALLER: It's between the 6 and the 7.

GAS COMPANY: OK, we read the lower number, which is 6.

LEP CALLER: Yes, so the next dial is going in the other direction.

GAS COMPANY: Yes, you're looking at the right one. It should be going counterclockwise.

LEP CALLER: That's right, and it says 3.

GAS COMPANY: Perfect. Can you tell me what the last dial says?

LEP CALLER: The pointer is right on the 8.

GAS COMPANY: Excellent, you've just read your meter. If you ever miss the readers again, just call in and you can read it to us over the phone.

LEP CALLER: I didn't realize it was so easy. Thank you. So my bill will show the amount I really owe?

GAS COMPANY: Yes, you will be billed for the actual usage.

LEP CALLER: Great, thank you so much.

GAS COMPANY: Thank you for calling Premium Gas Company, and have a great day.

Utility Scenario 3: Gas Leak

GAS COMPANY: Thank you for calling Premium Gas Company's Gas Emergency Line. Are you calling to report a gas leak?

LEP CALLER: Yes, but I'm not sure if it's really a leak or not. I just barely smell it.

GAS COMPANY: Are your range burners turned off?

LEP CALLER: We have an electric range.

GAS COMPANY: Is the smell still faint?

LEP CALLER: Yes.

GAS COMPANY: Do you hear any hissing sound?

LEP CALLER: No, but now I think the smell is getting a little stronger.

GAS COMPANY: I need you to get everyone out of the house, and leave the doors and windows open. Don't turn on any light switches, phones or anything else that could generate a spark on your way out. And don't turn on your car ignition.

LEP CALLER: OK, I am already outside. I am walking into the neighbor's yard.

GAS COMPANY: OK, just stay there until one of our on-site representatives arrives.

LEP CALLER: So, once the representative arrives, can I go back in with him? I forgot to get some things from inside.

GAS COMPANY: Don't go back inside until the representative says it is safe to do so. Just stay in your neighbor's yard until the representative tells you it's safe to go inside.

LEP CALLER: Fine, I'll wait here then.

GAS COMPANY: OK, he will be there shortly. Would you like me to stay on the line with you until he arrives?

LEP CALLER: No, I think I'll be OK here.

GAS COMPANY: OK, and remember, do not go back inside until the representative tells you it is safe to do so.

LEP CALLER: Fine, thank you.

GAS COMPANY: OK, thank you for calling the Premium Gas Company Gas Emergency Line.

LEP CALLER: Thank you.

Utility Scenario 4: New Residential Water Service

WATER DEPT: Water Department, how may I help you?

LEP CALLER: Hello! I'm calling to find out how to set up an account and get water services in my new location.

WATER DEPT: Is this for a residential or a commercial account?

LEP CALLER: It's for my house.

WATER DEPT: OK, when would you like to have the service put into your name?

LEP CALLER: Today, if possible.

WATER DEPT: We need at least 3 days advance notice over the phone, but you can come into the office and we might be able to process the request in less time.

LEP CALLER: OK, where do I go?

WATER DEPT: You'll need to go to 16 Monroe Boulevard, next to the fire department.

LEP CALLER: What do I need to bring with me?

WATER DEPT: You'll need to bring the full service address, your full name, social security number, driver's license number and state, your home and work telephone numbers, and your mailing address, if it is different from the service address.

LEP CALLER: Wait a minute, let me write this down. You said I need to bring my social security number, driver's license... ?

WATER DEPT: Yes, and your home and work telephone numbers, full service address and mailing address. You'll also need to bring a deposit in the amount of $60.00.

LEP CALLER: After I go to the office and pay my deposit, when will they connect the service?

WATER DEPT: The work orders for water connections are completed between 8:00am and 4:30pm, Monday through Saturday. You do not have to be present when the meter is turned on, but you need to make sure that all taps and appliances that use water are turned completely off.

LEP CALLER: OK, can I make an appointment? I'm not sure if I'll be able to stay home from work the entire day.

WATER DEPT: You don't have to be home, but yes, you can make an appointment if you prefer. But, if you're in a hurry to have the service connected, it might be better not to make an appointment. That way, if the work crew gets a cancellation, they can go and connect your service.

LEP CALLER: I'm not sure I understand. Why would I cancel?

WATER DEPT: No, if another customer cancels, then the work crew might be able to connect your service sooner than if you make an appointment.

LEP CALLER: Oh, I understand. OK, then I will go to the office and pay now.

WATER DEPT: Before you go, you need to know that once you pay the deposit, it will be returned to you after 12 months as long as you pay on time each month. If you do not pay on time, we will keep holding your deposit until you have paid on time for 12 consecutive months.

LEP CALLER: OK, that's fine. I'm going to go to the office now.

WATER DEPT: Thank you for calling the Water Department. Have a nice day.

Chapter 17
Practice Scenarios: Travel and Entertainment

Travel and Entertainment Scenario 1: Flight Reservation

AIRLINE: Thank you for calling Worldwide Airlines. May I have your departure city, please?

LEP CALLER: Yes, it's New York City.

AIRLINE: Thank you, Sir/Ma'am. And what is your destination city, please?

LEP CALLER: San Antonio, Texas.

AIRLINE: What are your departure and return dates, please?

LEP CALLER: Departing on May 7th, and returning on May 24th.

AIRLINE: Are those dates flexible by any chance?

LEP CALLER: No, unfortunately those are the only dates I can travel, because I already requested my vacation time for those days.

AIRLINE: Thank you. When you leave out of New York, which airport do you prefer?

LEP CALLER: JFK, please.

AIRLINE: Would you like me to compare surrounding airports for both your departure and arrival cities, in order to give you the best possible fare for multiple locations?

LEP CALLER: No thank you. I would prefer to leave from New York and arrive in San Antonio.

AIRLINE: And how many passengers will be traveling in your party?

LEP CALLER: Three.

AIRLINE: Are all three passengers adults, or are there any children traveling with you?

LEP CALLER: Two adults, and one child.

AIRLINE: What is the age of the child?

LEP CALLER: Two years old.

AIRLINE: OK, children under three fly for free, so we will only need to book two tickets for you. Please hold while I search for available flights.

LEP CALLER: OK.

AIRLINE: Do you prefer your departure flight to leave in the morning, afternoon or evening?

LEP CALLER: The late afternoon, please.

AIRLINE: OK, and for your return flight, would you prefer to arrive in the morning afternoon or evening?

LEP CALLER: Evening.

AIRLINE: Fine, let me just pull up these flights for you and see what I have available.

LEP CALLER: Very well.

AIRLINE: OK, Sir/Ma'am, I have Flight 1420 departing from New York's JFK airport at 4:25pm on May 7th, arriving in San Antonio at 10:05pm, with a layover in Houston, giving you a total travel time of 6 hours and 40 minutes.

LEP CALLER: OK.

AIRLINE: For the return, I have you on Flight 1626 departing from San Antonio at 5:12pm on May 24th. That flight also connects in Houston and will get you into New York at 11:33pm. Total travel time is 5 hours and 21 minutes.

LEP CALLER: How much is it?

AIRLINE: The total fare for the round-trip ticket is $367 per person, which includes all taxes and fees.

LEP CALLER: I'm a member of your frequent flyer program. Do I get any type of discount?

AIRLINE: Unfortunately, no. With our frequent flyer program, you can accumulate points each time you travel, and you can redeem your points for free and discounted flights, as well as other offers, but you would not receive a discount on flight purchases with us.

LEP CALLER: If I purchase through you, will you send me a printed ticket in the mail?

AIRLINE: No, Sir/Ma'am. We only issue e-tickets at this reservation line. If you want paper tickets, you would need to either go into one of our reservation centers or purchase your ticket on our web site and choose the paper ticket option. However, there is an issuance fee of $9.95 for paper tickets.

LEP CALLER: How many bags can I bring?

AIRLINE: The checked baggage allowance is limited to two pieces per passenger. Each bag can have a total maximum weight of 70 pounds or 32 kilograms. The total dimensions of the bag cannot exceed 62 inches or 158 centimeters when adding up the height, width and length of the bag.

LEP CALLER: That doesn't include items that I bring onto the plane with me, right?

AIRLINE: You are allowed one carry-on item and one personal item. The carry-on must fit into the overhead compartment, and the personal item must fit underneath the seat in front of you.

LEP CALLER: Do you serve any meals on the flights?

AIRLINE: No, we have eliminated our standard meal service, but we do have complimentary beverages available, as well as snack boxes and alcoholic beverages for purchase.

LEP CALLER: I may want to use my computer during the flight. Do your seats have power ports?

AIRLINE: We do have a limited number of seats with power ports. Hold on, and let me check what seats are available. I'm assuming you would want both seats together, right?

LEP CALLER: Yes, please.

AIRLINE: Well, looking here it doesn't appear that we have any seats available with power ports. Only the first ten rows of the plane have power ports, but there is no space available in those rows. I can put you in row 12, but you would not have a power port.

LEP CALLER: I will really need to have a power port, because I am meeting a colleague of mine for work, and I will need to do some work on the plane.

AIRLINE: I'm sorry, Sir/Ma'am, but we really don't have any seats with power ports available.

LEP CALLER: OK, I'm going to check with some other airlines, and if I want to reserve the flight, I'll call you back.

AIRLINE: That's fine, Sir/Ma'am, but I want to let you know that the fare I quoted to you is only valid for the duration of this call, and the fare is subject to change.

LEP CALLER: I understand that. Thank you for your time.

AIRLINE: Thank you for calling Worldwide Airlines, and we hope you'll fly with us soon.

LEP CALLER: Thank you, goodbye.

Travel and Entertainment Scenario 2: Hotel Reservation

HOTEL: Thank you for calling Luxury Brand Hotels. May I have your reservation code, please?

LEP CALLER: I'm not sure where to find the reservation code. I have a paper in front of me with my booking details. How long is the number?

HOTEL: It's an alphanumeric number that usually begins with the letter 'W', 'C' or 'K'.

LEP CALLER: I don't see a number like that here, but I have a confirmation number. Will that work?

HOTEL: Let's give it a try.

LEP CALLER: The confirmation number is X45 ... 368 ...1246.

HOTEL: OK, I'm searching under that number now. Just one second.

LEP CALLER: OK.

HOTEL: I've searched under the number X453681246, and I don't see anything coming up.

LEP CALLER: You have the number wrong. The number I gave you was X45 ... 378 ... 1246.

HOTEL: My apologies, Sir/Ma'am. Let me try that number instead.

LEP CALLER: Yes, please.

HOTEL: OK, I'm not finding it under that number either. Let me confirm the number with you. Is it X453781246?

LEP CALLER: Yes, that's correct.

HOTEL: OK, perhaps I can find it under your name. Can you please give me your first and last names, with the spelling of each name?

LEP CALLER: Fine, the first name is Mario/Maria, m-a-r-i-o / m-a-r-i-a, and the last name is Silva, s-i-l-v-a.

HOTEL: Aha, I found it. It looks like you will be arriving on October 24th, and checking out on October 27th. Is that correct?

LEP CALLER: Actually, that's why I'm calling. I'm going to need to extend my stay by an extra day.

HOTEL: OK, that's no problem, Sir/Ma'am. I see you made this reservation under a group booking code for a trade show that is taking place at the hotel. Unfortunately, the group discount is not available for the extra night.

LEP CALLER: That's fine. Please just charge me the regular rate.

HOTEL: Fine, that will be $129.95 instead of $99.95.

LEP CALLER: OK, is that all I need to do?

HOTEL: Let me give you your reservation code for this night's stay. It's K2486672.

LEP CALLER: K2486762?

HOTEL: No, it's K2486672.

LEP CALLER: K2486672.

HOTEL: That's correct.

LEP CALLER: OK, thank you very much.

HOTEL: Thank you for calling Luxury Brand Hotels, and have an enjoyable stay.

Travel and Entertainment Scenario 3: Hotel Check-Out

HOTEL: Good morning, Mr/Mrs Chen. You've dialed the front desk. How may I help you?

LEP CALLER: Yes, I'd like to check out over the phone please.

HOTEL: OK, certainly. We can bill the entire amount to the card we have on file here.

LEP CALLER: Sure. What is the total amount?

HOTEL: Just one second ... the total amount is $798.37.

LEP CALLER: What? I don't understand. Why is it so high?

HOTEL: Well, the majority of the charges here, aside from the nightly rate, are for room service, mini-bar and pay-per-view fees.

LEP CALLER: The mini-bar?

HOTEL: Yes, it appears that the mini-bar was accessed every day for the duration of your stay. Let's see here ... all of the items taken were candy and soda.

LEP CALLER: [in background] Children, did you take anything from the mini-bar?

[pause]

LEP CALLER: It appears my children must have been accessing the mini-bar without me knowing.

HOTEL: It wouldn't be the first time that has happened at our hotel, Sir/Ma'am.

LEP CALLER: OK, I'll go ahead and close out my bill.

HOTEL: Would you like us to use the same card we have on file, the one you gave us for incidentals?

LEP CALLER: Yes, that is fine.

HOTEL: OK, the full amount of $798.37 will be billed to your Mastercard ending in 2184. Thank you very much, Mr/Mrs Chen. Can I help you with anything else today?

LEP CALLER: No, that's all I needed.

HOTEL: Thank you!

LEP CALLER: Thank you. Goodbye.

HOTEL: Goodbye.

Travel and Entertainment Scenario 4: Cruise Line

CRUISE LINE: Thank you for calling Coastal Cruise Line's Reservation Center.

LEP CALLER: I received a brochure in the mail regarding your cruises to the Caribbean, and I am interested in taking my wife/husband on one of these cruises for our anniversary.

CRUISE LINE: Great! I'll be happy to help you, Sir/Ma'am. Did you have a particular cruise in mind?

LEP CALLER: Yes, the cruise that costs $449.00.

CRUISE LINE: OK, if you're referring to the cruise I believe you would like to book, it departs from Galveston and has three ports of call: Ocho Rios, Jamaica, George Town, Grand Cayman and Cozumel, Mexico.

LEP CALLER: Yes, that's the one.

CRUISE LINE: OK, well the prices do start at $449.00 for an interior stateroom.

LEP CALLER: My wife/husband gets claustrophobic in those rooms. What are the prices of other rooms?

CRUISE LINE: We can give you an ocean view stateroom starting at $599.00.

LEP CALLER: OK, that sounds good.

CRUISE LINE: OK, I see that there are various upcoming departures for that cruise. It leaves every Wednesday and returns the following Tuesday. Did you have a particular date in mind?

LEP CALLER: Yes, November 21st.

CRUISE LINE: OK, let me make sure I have an ocean view available.

LEP CALLER: OK.

CRUISE LINE: We do have one available. Have you ever sailed with us before?

LEP CALLER: Yes, I did two years ago.

CRUISE LINE: Do you have your membership number on hand?

LEP CALLER: Yes, I do. It has a little symbol on it, and then some numbers and letters.

CRUISE LINE: OK, after the anchor, can you read me the first ten numbers and letters?

LEP CALLER: Sure, it's EJ749H25X2.

CRUISE LINE: Fine, I see you in the system. Since you're a member and you're celebrating your anniversary, I'm going to put a request in the system to see if you can be upgraded to a deluxe stateroom. There is no guarantee that we'll have any available, but it might be worth trying.

LEP CALLER: Thank you, I appreciate that.

CRUISE LINE: Included in the price of the cruise are your shipboard accommodations, ocean transportation, some beverages, most meals, and most onboard entertainment. Specialty restaurant fees, gratuities and service fees, land excursions and other services are billed separately.

LEP CALLER: That's fine.
CRUISE LINE: With taxes and fees, the cost for you and your spouse will be $1487.56. Would you like to use the Visa card on file with the expiration date of 12/09?
LEP CALLER: Yes, please.
CRUISE LINE: OK, we'll be sending an information packet, along with your tickets and vouchers to your address in Springfield within the next seven to ten business days. Would there be anything else I could do for you?
LEP CALLER: No, that's all I needed. Thank you!
CRUISE LINE: Thank you, and have a great day!

Chapter 18
Practice Scenarios: Telecommunications

Telecommunications Scenario 1: Cellular Phone Plan

PROVIDER: Thank you for calling Global Cellular Sales. How may I help you?

LEP CALLER: Yes, I'm calling about the commercial on TV that says I can get two free camera phones if I sign up for new service with you.

PROVIDER: That's right. If you enroll in the new family plan and purchase one of our new camera phones at the price of $99.99, you'll receive two more for free.

LEP CALLER: OK, I will actually need four phones, one for my mother, one for myself, and one for each of my two children.

PROVIDER: That's no problem, but you'll still only get the two phones for free. The fourth phone will be an additional cost of $99.99.

LEP CALLER: OK, and what does it cost per month?

PROVIDER: That depends on the plan you choose. The monthly cost for the most affordable plan is $39.99, plus $9.99 for each additional line.

LEP CALLER: How many minutes does it include?

PROVIDER: It includes 400 minutes of peak minutes per month, plus unlimited off-peak minutes.

LEP CALLER: Is off-peak evenings and weekends?

PROVIDER: Yes, off-peak hours start at 8:00pm each evening, and from 8:00pm on Friday until 6:00am on Monday.

LEP CALLER: How much does it cost per minute if I go over?

PROVIDER: 33 cents per minute.

LEP CALLER: I think I might want a plan with more minutes, because my daughters like to talk on the phone a lot.

PROVIDER: OK, the next plan we have includes 700 minutes of peak minutes per month, unlimited off-peak minutes, and costs $49.99 per month, plus $9.99 for each additional line.

LEP CALLER: Is there any way to avoid paying the fees for the extra lines?

PROVIDER: No, there's not. However, the standard contract is for 24 months. If you'd like to extend yours to 36 months, we can credit the price of the fourth phone to you on your monthly bill after you've had your account open for 90 days.

LEP CALLER: OK, that sounds good.

PROVIDER: Great, to set this up today over the phone, I'll just need your name, address, social security number and a major credit card.

LEP CALLER: I don't have credit cards. I pay cash for everything.

PROVIDER: OK, well we can also accept a check by phone.

LEP CALLER: I don't have a checking account. I only deal with cash.

PROVIDER: Well, you can still open an account with us, but you'll need to go into one of our stores.

LEP CALLER: OK, there is one here in my local mall. Will they be able to give me the credit you mentioned for the fourth phone?

PROVIDER: Yes, they should be able to do that. Just let them know you'd like to extend the contract to 36 months instead of 24, and that you were offered a credit for the fourth phone when you called into the telesales department.

LEP CALLER: OK, and can I get your name?

PROVIDER: Yes, my name is Jason Jones, and my agent ID number is 4215.

LEP CALLER: Thank you!

PROVIDER: Have a great day, and thank you for using Global Cellular.

Telecommunications Scenario 2: International Long Distance Plan

PROVIDER: Hello, thank you for calling Global Long Distance. How may I help you?

LEP CALLER: Hello, I'm calling to find out what your rates are for international calls.

PROVIDER: OK, we'll be happy to help you with that. Just one moment while I transfer you to the appropriate office.

LEP CALLER: OK.

PROVIDER: Please hold one moment, and a representative from the international plan office will be with you shortly.

LEP CALLER: Fine.

PROVIDER: Thank you for holding. I understand that you'd like information on our rates for international calls. Is that correct?

LEP CALLER: Yes. I received a bill, and the rates were sky-high, so I called my local company, and they told me that I didn't have a long distance carrier on my line, and that I'd need to add one. They offered to add one for me, but I wanted to call first and compare rates.

PROVIDER: That's a very wise choice, Sir/Ma'am. Well, let me ask you this: do you dial several regions throughout the world, or are your calls primarily being placed to one region of the world?

LEP CALLER: Why do you need to know?

PROVIDER: Well, we have two types of plans. One plan includes discounted flat rates for all countries, and the other type of plan focuses on a single region. If you call one region primarily, the second type of plan would give you the greatest savings.

LEP CALLER: I see. Well, the region I'd be calling most often is Europe.

PROVIDER: Excellent, and what countries in Europe would you be calling?

LEP CALLER: Russia and Germany.

PROVIDER: OK, if I enroll you in our regional plan for Europe, you'll receive a rate of 0.33 cents per minute for calls to Russia and 0.18 cents per minute for calls to Germany. That rate is valid no matter what time of day you call, and no matter what day of the week.

LEP CALLER: Isn't there a single flat rate for both countries?

PROVIDER: No, unfortunately those are the flat rates, but they vary depending on the country. Also, it is important for you to know that if you place an international call to a wireless phone, there may be additional charges. Also, per-call surcharges may apply.

LEP CALLER: OK, that's all right. I don't plan to call cellular phones that often.

PROVIDER: In addition, if Global Long Distance deems it necessary to protect your account from fraudulent activity, calling to certain destinations may be temporarily blocked without prior notice.

LEP CALLER: Fine, and what is the fee for this plan?

PROVIDER: In addition to the per-minute rate, you'd pay an extra three-dollar monthly service charge. This monthly fee will allow you to enjoy substantially lower rates than our basic international rates.

LEP CALLER: OK, and I can sign up for this over the phone?

PROVIDER: Yes, but you'd have to be a current Global Long Distance customer.

LEP CALLER: I don't understand. If I am calling to enroll, it means I want to be a customer. If I were already a customer, I wouldn't be calling you.

PROVIDER: No, actually, you would have to be a current subscriber to Global Long Distance's domestic long distance. In other words, we would need to be your provider for your regular long distance services, which you use to place domestic long distance calls.

LEP CALLER: But I don't place any long distance calls in the country. I only need to call overseas.

PROVIDER: I understand, Sir/Ma'am, but in order for you to sign up for one of our international calling plans, you would need to be a current Global Long Distance customer, and to do that, you would need to be enrolled in one of our domestic calling plans.

LEP CALLER: And how much will that cost me?

PROVIDER: There are a variety of plans available for you to choose from, but unfortunately, I am in the international plan office, so I would need to transfer you to the domestic plan office.

LEP CALLER: You're kidding! I've already been transferred once. If you really want my business, you should make this process simpler. I am not so sure I want to do this.

PROVIDER: My apologies, Sir/Ma'am, but we are a large organization with many different departments. I'll be happy to transfer you to the domestic plan office, so that we can get this process started.

LEP CALLER: And then, after I do that, how will I get my international plan?

PROVIDER: They will have to transfer you back to us so that we can enroll you.

LEP CALLER: This is all too complicated. Look, I can't spend all afternoon on the phone. I'm going to see if I can go into one of your local offices and get all of this done at the same time.

PROVIDER: As you wish, Sir/Ma'am. We'll be happy to help you, either in one of our local offices, or by phone. If you change your mind, feel free to call back to the same number you dialed, and we'll be happy to take care of everything so that you can start enjoying low rates on your calls to Russia and Germany.

LEP CALLER: OK, thank you for your time.

PROVIDER: Thank you for calling Global Long Distance, and have a great afternoon.

LEP CALLER: Thank you, goodbye.

PROVIDER: Goodbye.

Telecommunications Scenario 3: Calling Card

PROVIDER: Thank you for calling National Calling Cards. Are you calling to purchase a new pre-paid card today, or are you calling to recharge an existing card?

LEP CALLER: I'm calling to purchase a new pre-paid card, but it depends on the rates. A friend of mine gave me your number and said you had the best rates.

PROVIDER: We do strive to give our customers the best rates, Sir/Ma'am, and we'll definitely give you several options to make sure that we are meeting your needs.

LEP CALLER: OK. My friend said you have a card with a rate of 1.4 cents per minute. Is that right?

PROVIDER: Yes, we do, that's correct. That would be for the card we offer that has a surcharge of $1.95 for each call placed. When you call, do you tend to talk for more than 15 minutes each time, or less than 15 minutes?

LEP CALLER: More than 15 minutes.

PROVIDER: OK, well this card might work for you then. We normally don't advise people to buy this card if they will be making multiple calls of short duration, due to the surcharges, but if you are speaking for longer than 15 minutes, it does not make such a big impact on the amount you are spending.

LEP CALLER: What other cards do you offer?

PROVIDER: Well, we have a surcharge-free card, but the rate for that card is 2.6 cents per minute.

LEP CALLER: That is a much higher rate. I don't think I am interested.

PROVIDER: Now, we also have a card that gives you a rate of 1.5 cents per minute, which is a slightly higher rate, but that card enables you to have PIN-less dialing.

LEP CALLER: I don't understand what you mean.

PROVIDER: The PIN-less dialing feature enables you to place each call without the need to enter a separate PIN number. All you would enter is the card number itself.

LEP CALLER: OK, I think I would like that feature. That would save me a lot of hassle.

PROVIDER: OK, and the final card we have available gives you a rate of 2 cents per minute, also comes with PIN-less dialing, and has no connection fee.

LEP CALLER: How much is the connection fee with the other cards, such as the one you just told me about that costs 1.5 cents per minute?

PROVIDER: The connection fee for all of the cards, except for the one with the 2-cent rate, would be 0.99 cents per connection.

LEP CALLER: So that means that I could talk for nearly 50 minutes longer with the 2-cent card?

PROVIDER: Pretty much. The 2-cent card has a higher per-minute rate, but you have no surcharges, no connection fees, and PIN-less dialing.

LEP CALLER: OK, I think I'd like to order that card.

PROVIDER: You can purchase the card in the amounts of 10, 25, 50 or 75 dollars.

LEP CALLER: Did you say 10 dollars?

PROVIDER: Yes, we have them available in 10-dollar amounts.

LEP CALLER: In that case, I think I might like to get some for my wife/husband and children too. I'll need to talk to them and then call you back.

PROVIDER: That's fine. We are open at this number 24/7, so feel free to call us anytime to place your order.

LEP CALLER: OK, I will probably call back in the next few hours.

PROVIDER: Excellent, we are looking forward to hearing from you.

LEP CALLER: Very well, thank you for your help!

PROVIDER: Have a great day. Goodbye!

LEP CALLER: Goodbye.

Telecommunications Scenario 4: Repair Request

PROVIDER: Thank you for calling Local Phone Repair. How may we help you today?

LEP CALLER: Yes, I'm calling to report some trouble on my line. I keep hearing voices on the line, and I am really getting tired of it. I will be in the middle of a conversation, and all of a sudden, these other voices come onto the line. I'm not sure what's going on, but I think my lines are crossed with someone else's.

PROVIDER: OK, Sir/Ma'am. How long has this been happening?

LEP CALLER: Ever since I moved in to this house. We've only been here two months, but it's been getting worse, especially in the past few weeks.

PROVIDER: OK, and do you have any cordless phones attached to the line?

LEP CALLER: Yes, we have one in the kitchen.

PROVIDER: OK, Sir/Ma'am. The cordless phone may be causing the interference. Many times, the cordless phone is the root of this problem.

LEP CALLER: No, it isn't this phone. We've had this phone in two other houses, and it never caused a problem before. I'm sure it's the line.

PROVIDER: Each location is different, but it could still be the phone that's causing the problem.

LEP CALLER: No, you don't understand. This problem occurs no matter what phone I'm using. Even if I use one of the other phones in the house that aren't cordless, this problem keeps happening no matter what.

PROVIDER: To find out if it's the phone or not, I suggest that you do a test. Unplug the cordless phone and leave it unplugged. Then, try using one of the other phones in the house to make a call. If the problem clears up, then we know the cordless phone was the cause.

LEP CALLER: OK, I'll try it. But if the problem continues? What do I do?

PROVIDER: If the problem continues, call us back and we'll schedule a technician to come out and investigate the line, but first let's try this and see if it solves the problem.

LEP CALLER: Have you ever had calls like this before?

PROVIDER: Yes, we receive them all the time, and 9 times out of 10, it is the customer's phone equipment that is causing the interference, but please do call us back if you continue to have this trouble.

LEP CALLER: OK, thank you for letting me know. I've never had a problem like this before.

PROVIDER: OK, best of luck!

LEP CALLER: Thank you, goodbye!

PROVIDER: Goodbye.

Chapter 19
Practice Scenarios: Finance

Like other practice scenarios in this book, the scenarios that follow include terminology that is representative of calls and situations that are common in the United States. For example, the term 'IRA' is a commonly used acronym in the USA that stands for 'individual retirement account', but this type of terminology may be unfamiliar in other countries where government pensions or other funds are the main sources of retirement income. Terms such as 'ARM' (adjustable rate mortgage) and 'W-2 form' (a form required by the US government for tax purposes) are also part of everyday speech for most individuals in the US, but reflect cultural and societal practices that may not be typical in other locations.

As an exercise to make the scenarios more relevant for practice, it is recommended that readers scan the scenarios before translating them and replace these terms, phrases or utterances with ones that are more reflective of everyday language in the country where interpreting will be provided. This will ensure that the practice scenarios are more useful and helpful to the interpreter.

Finance Scenario 1: 401K Rollover

INSTITUTION: Thank you for calling Global Finance. You've reached the Retirement Services Division. How may I assist you today?

LEP CALLER: Yes, I've just switched jobs and wanted to know how to transfer my retirement investments over to you.

INSTITUTION: Did you already set up a Rollover IRA?

LEP CALLER: Yes, my son helped me set that up last week. I thought my employer would transfer everything automatically after that, but they told me I needed to call you.

INSTITUTION: So, now you need to consolidate your assets into your existing IRA. OK, so you did already notify your plan administrator that you are rolling over your assets into the Rollover IRA with Global Finance?

LEP CALLER: Yes, I did that already.

INSTITUTION: Did you already complete the distribution forms required by your former employer?

LEP CALLER: Yes, I did that too.

INSTITUTION: And did they provide you with the benefits contact name and phone number?

LEP CALLER: Yes, I have it here. Do you need it from me?

INSTITUTION: No, I don't need it, but you'll need to hang onto that. Do you know when your plan administrator will distribute the funds?

LEP CALLER: They said they can distribute the funds on the 15th of next month.

INSTITUTION: OK, then what you need to do is contact your plan administrator and ask them to write the Global Finance IRA account number on your distribution check and make it payable to us. They also need to mark it with the letters 'FBO' and put your name after those letters.

LEP CALLER: Yes, now that you mention it, I'm looking at the information you sent me in the mail, and I think it has these instructions here as well, only I couldn't really understand them because they were sent to me in English.

INSTITUTION: OK, Sir/Ma'am. Once you contact your plan administrator and take care of the rollover, you can call us back after the 15th to check on the status. Once the distribution has taken place and you've rolled over your assets to Global Finance, I would recommend that you call us back so that a Retirement Analyst can help you create an investment plan that will meet your needs.

LEP CALLER: OK, I'll do that.

INSTITUTION: Also, you may want to consider professional money management services from Global Finance. We can offer a carefully selected model portfolio of mutual funds based on your goals, risk tolerance and time frame.

LEP CALLER: Yes, I went through that with my previous account, so I would like to match it somewhat to the way I had it allocated before.

INSTITUTION: We'll be happy to assist you with that when the time comes.

LEP CALLER: Great, thank you so much. I appreciate your help.

INSTITUTION: No problem at all, and thank you for your time.

LEP CALLER: Thank you, goodbye.

INSTITUTION: Thanks again, and goodbye.

Finance Scenario 2: Mortgage Loan Rate Request

INSTITUTION: Thank you for calling National Mortgage Bank. How can I help you this afternoon?

LEP CALLER: Yes, I'd like to apply for a home loan, and I'm calling to find out what today's current rates are.

INSTITUTION: Do you know what type of loan you're applying for?

LEP CALLER: Yes, a mortgage loan.

INSTITUTION: OK, but do you know what term you're interested in? A 30-Year Fixed, for example?

LEP CALLER: I'd like the rates for all of your loans, if possible.

INSTITUTION: OK, please hold one moment.

LEP CALLER: Fine.

INSTITUTION: The rates I am about to quote are for your information only, and are only valid during the duration of this call. For actual rates, you would be subject to full credit approval and would need to complete the full loan application.

LEP CALLER: I understand. What are the rates?

INSTITUTION: Our current APR for a 15 Year Fixed ranges from 6.0 to 6.34%. For a 30-Year Fixed, it ranges from 6.2 to 6.5%. For a 5 year ARM, the rate ranges from 6.0 to 7.2%, and for a Home Equity Loan, the rate ranges from 6.7 to 7.1%.

LEP CALLER: OK. That's all I needed to know. Thank you very much.

INSTITUTION: Thank you for calling, and have a good afternoon.

LEP CALLER: Goodbye.

INSTITUTION: Goodbye.

Finance Scenario 3: Home Equity Loan Inquiry

INSTITUTION: Thank you for calling National Mortgage Bank's Home Equity Hotline. How may I help you today?

LEP CALLER: Yes, I'm calling to find out how to apply for a home equity loan.

INSTITUTION: OK, well I can give you a basic list of things you'll need to have ready prior to doing an application. How does that sound?

LEP CALLER: Perfect.

INSTITUTION: OK, first of all, we'll need some personal information about yourself and any co-applicants that are applying with you. We'll need you to have the social security number and date of birth for each applicant.

LEP CALLER: OK.

INSTITUTION: We'll also need you to have the current and previous addresses for the last 24 months for each applicant.
LEP CALLER: OK, got it.
INSTITUTION: And we'll need you to provide the current and previous employment information for the last 24 months for each applicant.
LEP CALLER: What kind of employment information?
INSTITUTION: For past employers, we'll need job titles, start date and end date of employment, and names and addresses of those employers. For current employers, we'll need the gross salaries of all applicants.
LEP CALLER: Where do I find that information?
INSTITUTION: You can get this from a W-2 form of a pay stub. If you or a co-applicant are self-employed, then you'll need to determine your monthly gross income from an average of the most recent 2 years of personal tax returns.
LEP CALLER: OK.
INSTITUTION: We'll also need to know the monthly amount of any other income that you or a co-applicant may receive and that you wish to include in your application.
LEP CALLER: What do you mean by 'other income'?
INSTITUTION: Well, that refers to any child support, alimony, retirement, trust income, rental income or any other income that you receive in addition to your main source of income.
LEP CALLER: Oh, OK. We do have a rental property.
INSTITUTION: OK, then we'll need the property address, the lien holder and the value of the property.
LEP CALLER: What else do I need to have ready?
INSTITUTION: We'll need the information about your collateral property, including the address, estimated value, and the original purchase price and date purchased.
LEP CALLER: OK, anything else?
INSTITUTION: No, once you have that information ready, we can begin your application.
LEP CALLER: How do I start the application process?
INSTITUTION: You can start the process by calling the same number you dialed today, or you can go onto our website and begin the process online. Or, if you'd prefer, we can send you hard copies of an application form via regular mail.
LEP CALLER: OK, I think I'll call back once I have all of the information ready. Thank you very much for your help!
INSTITUTION: It's our pleasure, Sir/Ma'am. Have a great day, and thank you for calling!

LEP CALLER: Thank you, goodbye.
INSTITUTION: Goodbye.

Finance Scenario 4: On Line Banking

INSTITUTION: Thank you for calling Global Finance's On Line Banking Help Line. How may I help you today?

LEP CALLER: Yes, I'm trying to make a payment on line, and the system won't allow me to go in and change it.

INSTITUTION: OK, I have your account information in front of me. Would you please verify your pass code?

LEP CALLER: Yes, it's X74J23P9C.

INSTITUTION: OK, Sir/Ma'am. I see the amount of your last payment was $32.81 to National Credit Processing, and that the payment was made successfully at 3:24 pm today. Is this the payment you had a question about?

LEP CALLER: Yes, that's the one. I meant to make the payment in the amount of $328.81, but I must have entered it in wrong.

INSTITUTION: OK, I'll be happy to walk you through this. Are you logged into your account at this time?

LEP CALLER: Yes, I am. I'm on the home page for my accounts.

INSTITUTION: OK, go ahead and click on the account ending in 7152, which is the checking account. You wanted to make this payment from the checking account, is that correct?

LEP CALLER: Yes, that's correct.

INSTITUTION: OK, after you click on that, it should bring you to a page that gives you the current account balance.

LEP CALLER: Yes, that's what I see.

INSTITUTION: Do you see some tabs on the side of the page with blue lettering?

LEP CALLER: Yes, I do.

INSTITUTION: OK, right below where it says, 'Make a Payment', do you see the tab that says 'Payment History'? It's the fourth button from the top.

LEP CALLER: Yes.

INSTITUTION: OK, click on that. Now, when it loads the new window, you should see a list of all of your most recent payments.

LEP CALLER: Yes, I can see the amounts of the payments I made.

INSTITUTION: OK, do you see that some of the payments have a little red star next to them? Those are the payments that are still being processed.

LEP CALLER: Yes, I see three payments with stars by them.

INSTITUTION: OK, now look for the amount that you gave me before of $32.81.
LEP CALLER: OK, I see it, it's at the top of the list.
INSTITUTION: That's right. Now click on that payment amount.
LEP CALLER: I am trying, but nothing is happening.
INSTITUTION: Make sure you are clicking on the actual amount, not on the red star. Click directly on the amount, right on the $32.81.
LEP CALLER: OK, now it's opening.
INSTITUTION: Great! OK, now, you will see that you have four choices at the top of the screen in red buttons. If you count over from the left, the third button says 'Edit Payment'. Do you see that button?
LEP CALLER: Yes, I think this is the right one.
INSTITUTION: OK, click on that button, and it should open up a new window.
LEP CALLER: Yes, now I see the information about the payment, and the amount appears in a little box with the cursor flashing.
INSTITUTION: OK, go ahead and enter the correct amount of the payment in that box.
LEP CALLER: OK, just one second, I'm typing it in. I'm going to make sure this time that I type it correctly.
INSTITUTION: No problem, Sir/Ma'am. I'm standing by. Take your time.
LEP CALLER: OK, I'm ready.
INSTITUTION: Fine, now what you need to do, once you've verified that you've entered the correct amount, is to click on the big blue button below that box that says 'Change Payment Amount'.
LEP CALLER: OK, I'm clicking it now.
INSTITUTION: Great. Now, you should be at a confirmation page that shows you that the correct amount has been entered into the system. Also, from this page, you can navigate back to the main page and make more payments if you'd like.
LEP CALLER: Actually, I just want to log off now.
INSTITUTION: OK, do you know how to do that?
LEP CALLER: Yes, I just click the button in the upper right hand corner.
INSTITUTION: That's correct.
LEP CALLER: OK, great.
INSTITUTION: Now, don't hesitate to call us if you have questions in the future about using the on line banking tools. We're happy to assist you.
LEP CALLER: Excellent. It's hard for me because I am not used to it yet, so I appreciate your help.
INSTITUTION: Anytime. Have a great day!

LEP CALLER: Thank you, same to you. Goodbye!
INSTITUTION: You're welcome anytime, goodbye.

Chapter 20
Practice Scenarios: Insurance

Prior to using the scenarios in this section, it may be helpful to make some adaptations. The term 'deductible' is a commonly used term in the United States that describes the payment required by the insured driver prior to the point at which the insurance will begin to cover damages and expenses.

In order to make the scenarios more relevant for practice, scan the scenarios prior to translating them and replace these terms, phrases or utterances with items that are more reflective of everyday language in the country where interpreting will be provided. This will ensure that the practice scenarios are more useful and helpful to the interpreter.

Insurance Scenario 1: Auto Insurance Quote

AGENCY: Thank you for calling National Auto Insurance. How may I help you?

LEP CALLER: I'd like to get a quote for automobile insurance.

AGENCY: OK, certainly. I'd like to start by asking a few basic questions about the drivers in your household.

LEP CALLER: OK.

AGENCY: During the past 7 years, has any driver or household member had a major traffic violation?

LEP CALLER: No.

AGENCY: Has anyone had auto insurance refused, canceled, or received notice of intent to refuse or cancel insurance in the past 7 years?

LEP CALLER: No. We all have good driving records.

AGENCY: In the last 7 years, has anyone had a driver's license suspended, revoked or refused?

LEP CALLER: No.

AGENCY: Does any driver have a physical or mental condition that could

affect or impede the safe operation of a motor vehicle?
LEP CALLER: No.
AGENCY: What about any at fault accidents or violations within the last 3 years?
LEP CALLER: No, none.
AGENCY: Do you have at least one driver in the household with 3 or more years of experience driving in the US or Canada?
LEP CALLER: Yes, both of us have had our licenses for at least 5 years.
AGENCY: And does each driver have at least 1 year of continuous automobile insurance coverage?
LEP CALLER: Yes, we've been insured ever since getting our licenses.
AGENCY: And what date would you like the insurance to take effect?
LEP CALLER: Immediately.
AGENCY: Today, then. And how many drivers in the household would we be quoting today?
LEP CALLER: Two.
AGENCY: And how many vehicles?
LEP CALLER: One.
AGENCY: Is there any vehicle in the household that has been driven without insurance in the last 3 years?
LEP CALLER: No.
AGENCY: Are any of the vehicles in the household currently insured with us?
LEP CALLER: No.
AGENCY: Does any household member being quoted currently have any other policies with us?
LEP CALLER: No.
AGENCY: What is the address where the vehicle is principally garaged?
LEP CALLER: We park it in a few different places. Which one should I give you?
AGENCY: The location where it is garaged at least six months out of the year.
LEP CALLER: OK, that would be 101 North Main St.
AGENCY: Fine, thank you. And how many vehicles will we be quoting today?
LEP CALLER: Just one.
AGENCY: OK, may I have the year, make and model please?
LEP CALLER: It's a 1994 Nissan Sentra.
AGENCY: Is that a 4-door, and if so, is it Limited or Custom?
LEP CALLER: 4-door, Limited.

AGENCY: And what is the primary use of the vehicle?
LEP CALLER: To drive to work and back.
AGENCY: And how many miles do you drive it per year?
LEP CALLER: About 10,000.
AGENCY: How many miles each way to work?
LEP CALLER: 45 miles each way.
AGENCY: And how many days per week do you drive it?
LEP CALLER: 5 days.
AGENCY: OK, and what percentage of the time does each person drive the car?
LEP CALLER: Each of us drives it 50% of the time.
AGENCY: We have to list one driver as the primary driver. Who would you say would be the primary driver?
LEP CALLER: You can put me down as the primary driver.
AGENCY: OK. And who is the registered owner for the vehicle?
LEP CALLER: I am.
AGENCY: Now, for your coverage limits, what would you like for your bodily injury? Bodily injury pays for bodily injuries to others if you are responsible. If you are sued, it pays for your court costs as well. Some examples of this are lost wages, medical expenses, and pain and suffering.
LEP CALLER: What we have on the current policy is $50,000 per person, $100,000 per accident.
AGENCY: OK, I'll put you down for the same. And what about property damage?
LEP CALLER: We have a $100,000 limit on our current policy.
AGENCY: Fine, I'll keep that at $100,000 then. Now, what would you like your deductible to be for your comprehensive coverage?
LEP CALLER: I believe my current deductible is $250.
AGENCY: OK, and what about for collision coverage? Would that be $250 as well?
LEP CALLER: Yes.
AGENCY: And how about your limit for medical payments?
LEP CALLER: We have a limit of $5,000.
AGENCY: OK, and did you want emergency roadside service on this policy?
LEP CALLER: No, no thank you. I don't have the coverage currently.
AGENCY: Fine, and did you want car rental and travel expense coverage?
LEP CALLER: No, I don't believe it's necessary.
AGENCY: OK, just one second while I generate that quote for you,

Sir/Ma'am.

LEP CALLER: Thank you.

AGENCY: Before I give you the quote, I need to read a legal disclaimer to you.

LEP CALLER: OK.

AGENCY: The rate quote generated in our over-the-phone quote request process today is based on the information you provided and does not constitute a contract, binder or an agreement to extend insurance coverage to you or to any other party.

LEP CALLER: OK.

AGENCY: A final quote would require obtaining additional underwriting information from other reporting sources, including state motor vehicle records, prior insurance claims and credit history, if necessary. Do you wish to proceed?

LEP CALLER: Yes.

AGENCY: The total premium for the 1994 Nissan Sentra would be $507.81, to be paid semi-annually.

LEP CALLER: Wow, that is a lot more expensive than my current rate. I think I will stay with my current company.

AGENCY: You may qualify for additional discounts upon application that would make that rate go down a bit.

LEP CALLER: That's OK. This is already quite a bit higher than my current premium, so I think I will stick with my current provider. Thank you anyway.

AGENCY: It's our pleasure, and thank you for calling.

LEP CALLER: Goodbye.

Insurance Scenario 2: Homeowner's Insurance Quote

AGENCY: Thank you for calling National Home Insurance. How may I help you?

LEP CALLER: I'd like to get a quote for homeowner's insurance.

AGENCY: Very well, Sir/Ma'am. I'd like to start by asking a few basic questions. What is the address of the residence?

LEP CALLER: 101 North Main.

AGENCY: OK, thank you. How many applicants will be on the application?

LEP CALLER: 2.

AGENCY: In the last 3 years, has any insurance agency canceled or refused to issue or renew insurance to any household member?

LEP CALLER: No.

AGENCY: In the last 5 years, has any applicant had any insured or uninsured losses?

LEP CALLER: What do you mean by losses?

AGENCY: Have there been any occurrences that caused direct physical damage to property?

LEP CALLER: No.

AGENCY: And has any applicant been convicted of fraud, arson or other offenses related to insurance?

LEP CALLER: No, of course not.

AGENCY: And is any applicant insured by us on an automobile policy?

LEP CALLER: No.

AGENCY: And has any applicant had any other kind of insurance with us in the past 3 years?

LEP CALLER: No.

AGENCY: OK, Sir/Ma'am. The quote we will provide assumes that the amount of coverage you select for your dwelling is at least equal to 100% of the replacement cost estimate of your home. The replacement cost estimate and the actual coverage amount you select could affect the coverages available to you and your annual premium.

LEP CALLER: OK.

AGENCY: What is the current value of your home?

LEP CALLER: $150,000.

AGENCY: OK, I have the dwelling amount as $150,000. What percentages would you like for your property coverages?

LEP CALLER: Whatever is considered mandatory or customary.

AGENCY: For increased dwelling, we can use 20% of the dwelling amount, which would be 30,000. For dwelling extension, we can use 10%, which is 15,000. Are those amounts OK with you?

LEP CALLER: Yes.

AGENCY: For contents amount, we can use 75% of the dwelling amount, which is 112,500. Would that be acceptable?

LEP CALLER: Yes.

AGENCY: What percentage would you like for your deductible?

LEP CALLER: I currently have 1%.

AGENCY: OK, and how about personal liability and medical payments to others?

LEP CALLER: 100,000 and 2,000 are what I currently have.

AGENCY: OK, thank you. Now I'd like to ask a series of questions about protective devices.

LEP CALLER: Fine.

AGENCY: Do you have deadbolt locks on the doors?

LEP CALLER: Yes, on both the front and back doors.

AGENCY: Do you have a fire extinguisher?
LEP CALLER: Yes.
AGENCY: Sprinkler system?
LEP CALLER: No.
AGENCY: Fire or smoke alarm?
LEP CALLER: Smoke alarm.
AGENCY: Central or local?
LEP CALLER: Local.
AGENCY: And do you have a burglar alarm?
LEP CALLER: No.
AGENCY: OK, and in what year was the home built?
LEP CALLER: 1987.
AGENCY: And what construction type? Is it fire-resistant, frame, log, masonry or masonry veneer?
LEP CALLER: Masonry.
AGENCY: How many units are in the building?
LEP CALLER: Two.
AGENCY: Does the dwelling have any unrepaired damage?
LEP CALLER: No.
AGENCY: Is the dwelling located within 15 miles of a responding fire department?
LEP CALLER: Yes. That's actually just down the street.
AGENCY: Does the dwelling have water available for fire protection all year long?
LEP CALLER: Yes.
AGENCY: Is it accessible for fire department protection all year long?
LEP CALLER: Yes. We live here all year long.
AGENCY: Are there any detached structures?
LEP CALLER: No.
AGENCY: Is there a wood or coal stove, fireplace insert or freestanding fireplace on the residence premises?
LEP CALLER: No.
AGENCY: Is there any business conducted on the premises of the residence?
LEP CALLER: No.
AGENCY: Do you have any boarders or renters on the premises?
LEP CALLER: No.
AGENCY: Are any of the doors or windows fitted with burglar bars?
LEP CALLER: No.
AGENCY: Are there any dogs in the household?
LEP CALLER: No.

AGENCY: Are there any wild animals retained as pets in the household?

LEP CALLER: No.

AGENCY: Would you like to add any special options to your policy for jewelry and furs, business property, home computers, firearms or silverware and goldware?

LEP CALLER: No thank you.

AGENCY: Earthquake coverage is not included in this policy. Would you like to add earthquake coverage to your policy?

LEP CALLER: No.

AGENCY: OK, Sir/Ma'am, just one moment, while I wait for the computer to generate the quote for you.

LEP CALLER: OK.

AGENCY: The total premium would be $737.00 annually, or $61.42 with the monthly payment plan.

LEP CALLER: That sounds like a very reasonable rate. Is there any way you could send me a copy of the quote?

AGENCY: Yes, I'd be happy to do so. Shall I use the address of the residence?

LEP CALLER: That would be perfect, yes.

AGENCY: OK, this quote is valid for 30 days, and if you'd like to accept it, we'd just need a few additional details when you call in to do a final application.

LEP CALLER: OK, I appreciate your time. Thank you very much!

AGENCY: Thank you. Was there anything else I could help you with?

LEP CALLER: No, that's all. Goodbye!

AGENCY: Goodbye, and thank you again for calling.

Chapter 21
Practice Scenarios: Government (Social Services & Education)

Government Scenario 1: Child Support

AGENCY: Thank you for calling the Child Support hotline. How may I help you?

LEP CALLER: Yes, I need some information about getting Child Support.

AGENCY: OK, what questions do you have?

LEP CALLER: Well, how can you help me get child support for my two children? Their father left us six years ago, and he has not given me a penny.

AGENCY: Well, in this department, there are a few main areas that we help people with. We monitor child support awards to ensure compliance with financial, insurance and child care orders.

LEP CALLER: OK.

AGENCY: We also initiate enforcement actions, such as withholding income and contempt applications.

LEP CALLER: Well, I don't even know where he is. I don't have any idea where to begin. Can you still help me?

AGENCY: We might be able to. We help locate non-custodial parents. We can also help establish paternity, establish orders for financial and medical support, and we can help enforce those orders.

LEP CALLER: But I don't even know where to start. I'm really not even sure it is worth my time. It sounds like a lot of trouble.

AGENCY: Well, in order to receive child support, you need to have a court order. This will help establish the monetary support order, and make sure that there is support for health insurance and child care.

LEP CALLER: Can't I just ask their father to put something in writing? I don't want to go to court.

AGENCY: Actually, even if he is willing to sign a voluntary agreement, it needs to be approved by a court.
LEP CALLER: How do I get a court order then?
AGENCY: Well, you can do it one of three ways. You can hire an attorney to pursue the case for you, you can represent yourself, or you can apply for child support services free of charge through social services.
LEP CALLER: There is no way I can represent myself, and I cannot afford an attorney. How do I contact social services?
AGENCY: If you'd like to come into the office, I can give you the address of the location nearest you.
LEP CALLER: OK, that sounds like a good idea.
AGENCY: The location nearest you is at 101 North Main Street.
LEP CALLER: Oh, is that across from the pharmacy?
AGENCY: Yes, it is.
LEP CALLER: I know where it is then. Can you tell me how much money I will be getting for my two children? It is almost time to enroll them in school, and they want to play soccer this year, but I am not sure if we'll have the extra money.
AGENCY: Well, I can't really tell you what the amount would be until we do some more paperwork. There are state regulations to determine the amount owed in arrears, as well as the monthly payment, and for that we would need to know the father's income. It is a process that might take some time.
LEP CALLER: What if he doesn't want to pay?
AGENCY: We can help enforce an order by withholding income. We could also find the father in contempt of court if he willfully failed to obey a court order. Also, the court could suspend his driver's license and other professional licenses if he does not obey the order.
LEP CALLER: I am not even sure if he still lives in this state anymore. He has moved a few times. I think he was here last year, but I haven't spoken with him since.
AGENCY: Well, we do have processes for interstate enforcement. We can register the order in another state. That will give the new state authority to enforce the order, withhold income, seize financial assets and take other measures.
LEP CALLER: If he doesn't pay, what will happen?
AGENCY: We will continue to use all tools possible to enforce any outstanding orders. Also, the Attorney General's office periodically publishes names and photos of parents who owe child support and have a civil warrant for their arrest.
LEP CALLER: OK, I think it is time for me to do something about this.

I've been waiting for years now and I want to make sure I provide for my children.

AGENCY: We look forward to helping you.

LEP CALLER: Thank you.

AGENCY: You're welcome. Goodbye.

Government Scenario 2: Education

SCHOOL: Hello, is this Mario's [mother/father]?

LEP CALLER: Yes, speaking.

SCHOOL: Good afternoon. I'm calling regarding your son Mario, from Public Elementary School.

LEP CALLER: OK. Is there any trouble?

SCHOOL: Well, I'm calling to speak to you about a problem we've noticed with Mario.

LEP CALLER: What kind of problem? Is it because he's missed a lot of school lately?

SCHOOL: No, but we think that might be a related issue. Apparently, some of the other children are bullying him.

LEP CALLER: What do you mean, bullying him? He hasn't been in any fights at school, has he?

SCHOOL: No, he hasn't been in any physical fights that we are aware of. However, bullying can take on several different forms.

LEP CALLER: I don't understand.

SCHOOL: Well, some of the children are using their mobile phones to send text messages to him. Even though they are supposed to turn off the phones during class, we've noticed on more than one occasion that he's stormed out of the classroom after checking his phone.

LEP CALLER: How do you know that means he's being bullied?

SCHOOL: Well, some of the other students have reported to us that other children are sending messages to his phone, to make fun of him.

LEP CALLER: Why would they do that?

SCHOOL: It's really a new form of bullying, but the truth is, when children want to bully another child, they will often find many ways of doing it.

LEP CALLER: Is anything else going on?

SCHOOL: Well, yes. We think your son is showing some signs that are worrisome.

LEP CALLER: Like what?

SCHOOL: For example, he's been going into the boys' rest room at lunchtime instead of going into the cafeteria. We sent one of the male teachers in to see him, and he was sitting on the floor, listening to his MP3 player.

LEP CALLER: I knew he'd lost weight! He hasn't been eating lunch, has he? I knew that was why he is feeling so sick all the time!

SCHOOL: Actually, that was one of the things I wanted to discuss with you. We've noticed that Mario has been out of school more than 10 days already since the start of the semester.

LEP CALLER: Yes, he's been telling me he feels sick, and he stays in bed all day while I am at work, and doesn't even get out of bed when I come home. I think he is becoming weak because he is not eating right, and now I know why! He is skipping lunches.

SCHOOL: That might be part of it, but he also might be fibbing about his symptoms in order to stay home from school. That is a sign that we see often from children who are being bullied at school. It is a way of escaping it.

LEP CALLER: Really? I guess I never doubted him, because he never lied about being sick before. I would not have guessed he was making it up.

SCHOOL: It is hard sometimes to tell, but we do have a lot of experience with regard to bullied students. Would you like me to share some suggestions with you, so that you can do your best as a parent to help your son?

LEP CALLER: Yes, I would really like that.

SCHOOL: OK, well one of the first things you can do to help him is try to talk with him. If you can ask him about how he is feeling, he may share his problems with you, and this will help him to feel better.

LEP CALLER: Yes, but I already do ask him how things go at school, and he just says everything is fine.

SCHOOL: Yes, that is a typical response, but you might try phrasing the question differently and more directly. For example, after he says things are fine, you might ask him if he's made any friends at school. Then, you can ask if he's having trouble getting along with anyone in particular.

LEP CALLER: Hmmm. I guess I should have been asking him those things all along.

SCHOOL: Also, something very important. Here at the school, we are going to talk with Mario and try to give him some important techniques that he can use when he is being bullied. If you agree, we'd like to see if you can reinforce these with him at home when and if you speak with him about the bullying.

LEP CALLER: I guess so. What techniques?

SCHOOL: First of all, we need to make sure that Mario does not react with anger or physical violence. That can only make things worse.
LEP CALLER: Has he done that in the past?
SCHOOL: We heard from another student that he threw his books at another child in the hallway between classes.
LEP CALLER: Oh, I see.
SCHOOL: Aside from teaching Mario not to react with violence or anger, another thing you can help us reinforce with him is to act brave and walk away. The sooner he leaves the scene, the less likely something physical is to happen.
LEP CALLER: OK, I'll remember to tell him that.
SCHOOL: Finally, is there something that Mario is very good at? Something that might make him feel good about himself and help build his self-esteem?
LEP CALLER: Well, he's not very good at sports, because of his weight, but he used to be very good at drawing. He used to sit and draw for hours, and he was very good, but in the last few years, he's stopped doing it.
SCHOOL: That's great! I believe he's always received high grades in his art classes, too. Well, perhaps that is something that you can encourage him to do.
LEP CALLER: Yes, actually, there is an art club for kids here in our community. I always thought that might be fun for him, but I never mentioned it to him because he stopped drawing.
SCHOOL: That sounds like a good idea! If Mario can start building a social network for himself and develop some friendships, that might help him with his self-esteem and confidence. This could prevent some of the bullying, too.
LEP CALLER: OK, well I am going to try these things. I am really grateful that you called. I had no idea my son was going through this.
SCHOOL: Many parents don't, so please don't feel bad about yourself as a parent. I want you to feel free to get in touch with me if you have any questions. Do you have my number?
LEP CALLER: Yes, it's here on the caller ID.
SCHOOL: OK, well in addition to you calling me if you have any questions, I'm going to check back with you next week to see how things are going, and to let you know the results of our discussions with him as well. Is this a good time of day to reach you?
LEP CALLER: Yes, but only on weekdays. I have a different job that I work on the weekends, and then I work a different shift.
SCHOOL: That's fine. I will only call during the week then. Thank you so

much for speaking with me about Mario, and best of luck in helping him.

LEP CALLER: Thank you for taking the time. I really appreciate your help.

SCHOOL: Any time. Have a nice afternoon.

LEP CALLER: Goodbye!

Chapter 22
Practice Scenarios: Health Care

As in other chapters, the scenarios in this chapter represent calls and situations that are common in the United States. To make them most useful, readers from other countries may wish to replace some of the terminology with words and phrases that are more commonly used in the reader's own country of origin or are more reflective of everyday language in the country where interpreting will be provided.

Health Care Scenario 1: Children's Health Plan

HEALTH PLAN: Thank you for calling the Children's Health Plan information line. How may I help you?

LEP CALLER: Good afternoon. I have some questions about eligibility and enrollment.

HEALTH PLAN: OK, what questions do you have?

LEP CALLER: Well, first of all, I want to know if my children are eligible for the plan.

HEALTH PLAN: OK, first let me ask how many people are in your household?

LEP CALLER: Six people. Two adults and four kids.

HEALTH PLAN: And what is your annual income?

LEP CALLER: We made 33,000 dollars last year.

HEALTH PLAN: Well, that definitely puts you within the eligible range. You have four children?

LEP CALLER: That's right.

HEALTH PLAN: OK, the plan would cost 8 dollars per child for the first three children, so that means a monthly premium of 24 dollars for your family. You won't have to pay an additional premium for the fourth child.

LEP CALLER: OK. That is a lot of money. I don't know if we will be able to afford it.

HEALTH PLAN: Well, that is true. But it could save you a lot of money if your children get sick.

LEP CALLER: Can you tell me more about the plan?

HEALTH PLAN: Yes, would you like to hear about the benefits?

LEP CALLER: Yes, please.

HEALTH PLAN: Well, for doctor office visits, you would pay 5 dollars. For urgent care, you would pay 5 dollars. For emergency visits, you would pay 35 dollars.

LEP CALLER: Wow, that is great! I still have a huge bill from the last time my baby had to go to the emergency room. I've been making payments on that for two years.

HEALTH PLAN: For prescriptions, you pay 5 dollars for generic medications and 20 dollars for brand-name.

LEP CALLER: Is that for a one-month supply?

HEALTH PLAN: No, that is for a three-month supply.

LEP CALLER: Oh, that is really good then.

HEALTH PLAN: Also, there is no charge for laboratory and X-ray services.

LEP CALLER: Really? OK, and what about vision and hearing tests? They have to have those every few years for school.

HEALTH PLAN: Those are 5 dollars each.

LEP CALLER: OK, let me ask you this. My oldest daughter has some problems with depression. I have wanted to take her to a psychologist but we don't have the money.

HEALTH PLAN: Is your daughter one of the four children you mentioned?

LEP CALLER: Yes.

HEALTH PLAN: Is she under 18?

LEP CALLER: Yes, she is 15.

HEALTH PLAN: OK, well through the plan, for outpatient visits, there is a co-payment of 5 dollars for each individual therapy visit. There is a limit of 20 visits per calendar year. For inpatient care, there is no charge, up to 30 days per calendar year.

LEP CALLER: What about my son's glasses? Will the plan help me pay for them? He needs some new ones, but I have been putting it off because they are so expensive.

HEALTH PLAN: Yes, the plan gives you an allowance of 125 dollars for eyeglasses for each child every 24 months.

LEP CALLER: This sounds like it would save us a lot of money.

HEALTH PLAN: Not only that, but you have a co-payment maximum of

250 dollars per child or 500 per family per calendar year.
LEP CALLER: That is great. By the way, will this plan cover the dentist?
HEALTH PLAN: Yes, there is also a dental plan included at no additional premium.
LEP CALLER: How can I enroll?
HEALTH PLAN: You can enroll over the phone with me now if you like.
LEP CALLER: Well, I want to talk to my husband first. We have to look at our budget, because it will still be a lot of money. I'm also going to look at our medical bills and see if this plan will save us money in the long run.
HEALTH PLAN: OK, well once you have looked it over, if you would like to enroll, please just dial the same number you called.
LEP CALLER: Thank you!
HEALTH PLAN: Thank you for calling, goodbye!

Health Care Scenario 2: Prescription Information Line

PHARMACY: Thank you for calling the prescription information line. How may I help you?
LEP CALLER: Yes, my doctor gave me two prescriptions for my daughter, and he gave us some information on the side effects, but it's in English and I can't read it, so I wanted to call and see if I could get information over the phone.
PHARMACY: Did your doctor call the prescriptions into our pharmacy?
LEP CALLER: Yes, he did.
PHARMACY: OK, how many prescriptions did you have?
LEP CALLER: Two.
PHARMACY: OK, can you give me the prescription numbers please?
LEP CALLER: Yes. The first one is ... let me see ... it's R-X-4-9-8-M-U-3-4-1-5.
PHARMACY: That's R-X-4-9-8, M as in Mary, U as in Unicorn, 3-4-1-5?
LEP CALLER: That's right. And the second one, just let me find the number.
PHARMACY: OK, and you don't need to read the R-X. That's actually not part of the number.
LEP CALLER: OK, it's 3-7-3-T-Y-3-8-9-7.
PHARMACY: 3-7-3, T as in Tom, Y as in Yellow, 3-8-9-7?
LEP CALLER: Yes, that's correct.
PHARMACY: OK, can you confirm the medications for me?
LEP CALLER: Yes, one is an acne medication, and the other is a birth control pill. The doctor said that this medicine would require that she take a birth control pill. I was really against it, but he's saying she has

to because of the side effects.

PHARMACY: OK, I will be happy to read the interaction information to you. However, first I need to read you a disclaimer.

LEP CALLER: OK, go ahead.

PHARMACY: The information I am about to read may not cover all possible drug interactions or side effects that may occur. Individuals respond to medications in different ways. You should consult with your health care professional if you have questions about the medication you are taking.

LEP CALLER: OK. I'm ready to hear about the interactions.

PHARMACY: Would you like me to read all of the interactions, or just the ones with a severity ranking of 'high'?

LEP CALLER: Just the high ones for now please.

PHARMACY: Well, first, what your doctor told you is right. The medication for acne does have some side effects and the severity ranking is 'high'. Would you like me to read you a description of the side effects?

LEP CALLER: Yes, please.

PHARMACY: Interpreter, I will stop after every sentence or two to give you a chance to interpret. I'll begin now. This medication can cause serious birth defects. If you are of childbearing age, you should use two forms of reliable birth control while taking this drug. You must avoid getting pregnant while on this drug.

PHARMACY: Progestin-only products may not be sufficient to prevent pregnancy while you are on this drug. You should consider using more effective birth control.

PHARMACY: Pregnancy is also possible for women using injectable/implantable progestin-only birth control or combination birth control pills. If you are sexually active, it is recommended that you use two reliable kinds of birth control at the same time.

PHARMACY: While taking this medication, you should use an additional method of birth control to prevent unwanted pregnancy. Please discuss your needs and options with your health care provider in order to find a birth control combination that is right for you.

LEP CALLER: OK. That is pretty much what I remember the doctor telling me. Is that all? Or are there any other side effects?

PHARMACY: Those are the side effects listed here as high severity for the acne medication. Would you like to hear about the side effects for the birth control pill?

LEP CALLER: Yes, please.

PHARMACY: Now, here is another high-severity interaction that I can read to you for the birth control pill. You should not smoke while taking this medication. Smoking tobacco can increase your risk of a heart attack, stroke or blood clot while taking this medication, especially if you are 35 years old or older.

PHARMACY: Also, if you smoke more than fifteen cigarettes per day, you are at an increased risk. If you experience abdominal pain, chest pain, frequent headaches or migraines, eye pain or severe leg pain, you should report these to your prescriber.

LEP CALLER: OK, I didn't know about that.

PHARMACY: Would you like me to read the others? All of them are low severity.

LEP CALLER: OK, thank you.

PHARMACY: If you take the birth control pill, you may experience increased side effects from caffeine. Consuming too much caffeine can cause nervousness, sleeplessness or nausea. An interaction may occur, but these drugs are often used together without significant problems.

PHARMACY: In some females, foods containing grapefruit and grapefruit juice may increase the side effects of the birth control pill. These side effects may include nausea, headache, breast tenderness or fluid retention. There may be no interaction.

PHARMACY: And here is one more about the acne drug. If you drink alcoholic beverages while taking this drug, the side effects may get worse. You should avoid alcoholic drinks for at least thirty-six hours before any drug tests, because alcohol may alter the results of the blood tests performed to monitor treatment.

LEP CALLER: OK, thank you.

PHARMACY: Was there anything else I could help you with?

LEP CALLER: No, that's all I needed. Oh, once I fill the prescription, will I be able to refill them automatically?

PHARMACY: Yes, you can call the Refill Line after you've filled it for the first time. The number will be on the sticker on your medication packaging.

LEP CALLER: OK, thank you for your help.

PHARMACY: Have a great day, and thank you for calling the Prescription Information Line.

Health Care Scenario 3: Medical Equipment Catalog

CATALOG: Hello, how may I help you today?

LEP CALLER: I received your catalog in the mail, and it has a coupon for 50 dollars off any blood glucose monitor.

CATALOG: Yes, that is a very popular offer. Actually, at the bottom of the coupon, it specifies that the coupon may be used for one of three specific models.

LEP CALLER: OK, which models are those? Can you tell me what page they're on?

CATALOG: Yes, of course. The first one is our compact model. It's on page 11.

LEP CALLER: OK, I'm turning to that page now.

CATALOG: Can you read the features of that model? They are listed in the column on the right side of the page.

LEP CALLER: Well, the catalog is in English, so I really don't understand it very well. Also, my eyesight is not so great. If you can just tell me what the main features are, that will be fine.

CATALOG: Oh, of course, I'll be happy to do that for you.

LEP CALLER: Thank you.

CATALOG: Well, this is our smallest model, and it is very convenient. Also, you won't have to handle any strips with this, because it comes with a preloaded drum of 20 strips.

LEP CALLER: Oh, that would be so nice. The arthritis in my fingers makes it hard to grasp the individual strips.

CATALOG: There is also a detachable lancet device. The device can be detached from the meter.

LEP CALLER: That's a good idea. I wish my current meter had that feature.

CATALOG: This meter also has very fast results. Test results show up on the screen in only seven seconds.

LEP CALLER: Can I test from any site?

CATALOG: You can test from your fingertip, palm, forearm, upper arm, thigh or calf.

LEP CALLER: Will it give me the average? My nurse likes me to call with my averages each month.

CATALOG: Yes, it will keep your 7-, 14- and 30-day averages. It also shows your high and low test results over the same periods.

LEP CALLER: OK, that sounds like a nice meter. Can you tell me about the other two that I could purchase with the coupon?

CATALOG: Sure, if you turn to page 15, I will tell you about our special contoured model.

LEP CALLER: OK, I see the photo. This one looks bigger than the last one.

CATALOG: This meter uses a wide strip that absorbs a very tiny drop of blood. This helps to avoid re-testing, which can be painful.

LEP CALLER: Yes, it can. I have to retest a lot with my current meter.

CATALOG: Well, this model has more than 200 automatic checks to help identify and prevent problems that cause unreliable results. That can help prevent re-testing too.
LEP CALLER: What about the lancets? Does it take one at a time?
CATALOG: This model actually has a pre-loaded eight-lancet drum, so it saves you from handling individual lancets.
LEP CALLER: Oh, that's nice. Can I test from various sites?
CATALOG: Yes, you can test on any of the sites that I mentioned for the first one: fingertip, palm, forearm, upper arm, calf or thigh.
LEP CALLER: And how fast do the results appear?
CATALOG: It is a bit faster than the other one. The results appear in 5 seconds.
LEP CALLER: I like that it looks bigger than the other one. I have a hard time holding the smaller ones because of my arthritis.
CATALOG: Yes, and this has rubber grips that make it easy to hold.
LEP CALLER: That would be so nice. I really like the look of this one.
CATALOG: Well, this is bigger than both of the other two models that you can purchase with the coupon.
LEP CALLER: In that case, I don't need to hear about the third model. I think I like this one the best. The reason I have to buy a new one is because I've dropped my meter because it is too small. I'd like the bigger one.
CATALOG: OK, would you like to place an order now?
LEP CALLER: No, I'd rather wait until my daughter comes home, because she is the one who can read my credit card number to you. How late are you open today?
CATALOG: Our order line is open 24 hours.
LEP CALLER: OK, then I'll have her call after dinner to order this one for me.
CATALOG: Very well, then. Thank you very much for calling!
LEP CALLER: Thank you for your help!
CATALOG: Have a nice day, and goodbye!
LEP CALLER: Goodbye!

Chapter 23
Practice Scenarios: Legal

The scenarios in this chapter represent calls and situations that are common in the United States. To make them most useful, readers from other countries may wish to replace some of the terminology with words and phrases that are more commonly used in the reader's own country of origin or are more reflective of everyday language in the country where interpreting will be provided.

Legal Scenario 1: Jury Duty Information

COURT: Thank you for calling the Superior Court. How may I help you?

LEP CALLER: Hello, I am calling because I received a Jury Summons and have a few questions.

COURT: OK, how may I help you?

LEP CALLER: Well, my friend told me that I would be paid for jury duty. Can you tell me what I get paid?

COURT: Yes, you will be paid 15 dollars per day starting on the second day of service. You will also be paid 34 cents per mile for mileage.

LEP CALLER: Where do I pick up my payment?

COURT: Your check will be computed at the completion of service. You won't need to pick it up. We'll mail it to you at your home address. You will receive it within two weeks after you complete service.

LEP CALLER: I may need proof of my jury duty for my boss. Can you provide me with some type of letter or certificate?

COURT: Yes, we will provide you a form certifying the number of days you performed jury service. If you require a weekly certification for your employer, you can request it from our staff.

LEP CALLER: One of my friends went for jury duty and they made her go home because her skirt was too short. Can you tell me about any other things I should avoid wearing in court?

COURT: Yes, dress code should be casual, but still respectful. You should not wear shorts, beach attire, halter or tank tops, sandals or t-shirts with inappropriate pictures or sayings.

LEP CALLER: OK, is there anything I should avoid bringing with me to court?

COURT: When you come to the courthouse, you will need to go through the metal detector. Your purse, briefcase or backpack will be checked or X-rayed. If you have any metal objects, such as scissors, pocket knives, weapons or nail clippers, they will be removed by the security officers.

LEP CALLER: OK.

COURT: Also, you cannot bring any electronic recording devices, cameras or camera phones inside the courthouse. Alcoholic beverages are also not allowed.

LEP CALLER: Thank you. I have another question for you. I know you have interpreters at the court, but do I need to do anything special to request one?

COURT: Yes, you will need to call the Jury Coordinator and request an interpreter.

LEP CALLER: OK, well those are all the questions I have for now. Thank you very much.

COURT: Thank you for calling. Goodbye.

Legal Scenario 2: Traffic Court

COURT: Thank you for calling the Traffic Court. How may I help you?

LEP CALLER: Yes, I received a citation here and I want to make sure I understand what to do with it. It's only in English and I don't understand everything it says.

COURT: OK, do you see the citation number in the top left corner?

LEP CALLER: Ummm, let me see ... I'm looking.

COURT: It should start with the letter J or the letter T.

LEP CALLER: Here it is. T-5-3-6-2-3-2-2-9-0-5.

COURT: OK, your initials are M.S.?

LEP CALLER: Yes, that's right.

COURT: OK, on the right side, you'll see the date and the time of the citation.

LEP CALLER: Yes.

COURT: And below that, you'll see a list of the violations for which you were cited, along with the location of the violation.

LEP CALLER: Well, what I was cited for is debatable, but that's why I'm

coming to court. And what is the other information here?
COURT: You'll also see the issuing officer, and at the bottom in the grey box, you'll see the place and time at which you promised to appear.
LEP CALLER: OK, and can you tell me about the actual violations?
COURT: Yes, all the violations on this citation are infraction violations.
LEP CALLER: What does that mean?
COURT: An infraction is a failure to comply with or a violation of the Vehicle Code, local ordinance or other law or statute. The maximum sentence on most infractions is a fine of two hundred fifty dollars, plus fees.
LEP CALLER: Could I go to jail?
COURT: You may not be sentenced to jail time on an infraction unless it is combined with a misdemeanor charge.
LEP CALLER: A misdemeanor? I see that my appearance date is next Wednesday, but I don't think I will be able to pay my fees. What happens if I don't resolve this by that date?
COURT: Failure to appear on or before your due date could result in the Department of Motor Vehicles placing a hold on your driver's license, or a warrant could be issued for your arrest.
LEP CALLER: Wow. But I may not have enough money to pay. I don't earn very much.
COURT: You may be eligible for a Waiver of Court Fees and Costs. You'll need to look at the information form that describes eligibility requirements. I would be glad to send you one.
LEP CALLER: OK, thank you. Please do send me one. Those are all the questions I have.
COURT: OK, thank you for calling. Goodbye.
LEP CALLER: Thank you. Goodbye.

Legal Scenario 3: Small Claims Court

COURT: Small Claims. How may I help you?
LEP CALLER: I am thinking of taking my landlord to small claims court, but I have a few questions.
COURT: OK, what questions do you have?
LEP CALLER: Well, do I need to hire a lawyer?
COURT: No, in small claims court, you cannot have a lawyer. However, you may ask a lawyer for advice.
LEP CALLER: Is there any maximum amount that I can sue for?
COURT: Since you are an individual, you cannot ask for more than 7500 dollars in a claim.
LEP CALLER: What court will I need to go to?

COURT: You must sue in the right court and district, according to the rule of venue. If you file in the wrong court, the court will dismiss the claim unless all defendants personally appear at the hearing and agree that the claim may be heard. In your case, this will probably be where the defendant lives or where the contract was signed

LEP CALLER: Where can I find out the different court locations?

COURT: I can send you a list of court locations so that you can determine the correct court in which to file.

LEP CALLER: I don't get it. Am I the defendant?

COURT: No, you would be the person filing the lawsuit, so you are the plaintiff. The defendant would be your landlord.

LEP CALLER: OK. So my landlord is the defendant.

COURT: Yes, and you must sue using the defendant's exact legal name.

LEP CALLER: How will my landlord find out about the claim?

COURT: You are responsible for the defendant being informed about your lawsuit. The correct way of telling the defendant about the lawsuit is called having him served through a service of process. This means giving the defendant a copy of the claim.

LEP CALLER: OK, I can give him a copy.

COURT: You cannot do this yourself. There are three ways to serve the defendant. The first is having a law officer, a marshal or sheriff serve your landlord, and a fee will be charged.

LEP CALLER: OK.

COURT: You can also go through a process server. This person must personally give a copy of your claim to the defendant, and has to sign a proof of service form showing when the defendant was served.

LEP CALLER: OK.

COURT: You can also notify the defendant through certified mail. You can ask the clerk to do this for you. You can check back to find out when the defendant was served.

LEP CALLER: OK, I guess I understand.

COURT: You have to make sure that the defendant is served by a certain date or the trial will be postponed. If the defendant lives in the county, service must be completed at least 15 days before the trial date. This period is 20 days if the defendant lives outside the county.

LEP CALLER: OK, thank you. I think I know what I need to do. If I have any more questions, can I call you back?

COURT: Yes, we are here to answer calls in Small Claims from 8:30 to 4:30, Monday through Friday.

LEP CALLER: OK, thank you!

COURT: Thank you for calling.
LEP CALLER: Goodbye.

Part 5
Client Considerations

Chapter 24
Selecting a Telephone Interpreting Provider

As is the case when shopping for any service or product, it is important to become an informed consumer. Therefore, a good first step when comparing telephone interpreting providers is to understand as much as possible about the industry. Reading this book is an important first step. Another beneficial strategy is to visit a call center where telephone interpreting is taking place, in order to see the company in action, or to request the opportunity to listen to sample calls, or better yet, to try out the service.

It is always advisable to develop a good relationship with any vendor, in order to stay updated on industry trends, new technologies, company developments and general advice. In general, a telephone interpreting company that places an importance on building a strong relationship with its customers and having frequent and open communication with its clients is often best suited to providing high-quality service that is tailored to its client's needs.

Although reading this book will provide an insight into how some telephone interpreting providers operate, it is important that consumers of telephone interpreting services ask the right questions. The sections that follow provide questions that consumers may wish to ask their providers in order to gain a better understanding of the company and its services prior to making a purchasing decision.

Company Background

It is always a good idea to conduct research and find out more about the company itself. There are many telephone interpreting vendors to choose from and it is important to know if the one you choose is a high-quality company. The following section will help you gauge the quality and of the telephone interpreting provider and its ability to meet your needs.

- *Review the company website.* It is beneficial to go onto the company's website to learn more about the company and the services it provides. If the website is well organized, and if the company is transparent with its customers and the public, many of the questions outlined in this section will be answered on its pages. In fact, you may be able to download brochures, white papers and press releases to learn more. In addition, a true sign of a multilingual telephone interpreting company is a multilingual website. If the company's website is available in multiple languages, that is a sign that the company cares about projecting a multilingual image, and reaching audiences in other languages.
- *Where is the company headquarters located?* If the company headquarters is located near you, you may be able to arrange for a visit. Visiting the main office building can give you insight into how the company is organized. Many telephone interpreting companies house a call center in their main office. If this is the case for your provider, you may be able to see telephone interpreters in action.
- *What other branch locations does the company have?* Perhaps the company headquarters is not located near you, but there may be other locations or call centers nearby. If so, you may be able to set up a tour of one of them in order to become more familiar with the operations of a telephone interpreting company.
- *In what countries does the company currently do business?* If your own organization has branches or business dealings in other countries, it may be help to be aware that your telephone interpreting provider can provide services in those countries as well.
- *Does the company have call centers for its interpreters?* If the company is one of the large-scale providers, it will probably have several call centers. Having multiple call centers is important for redundancy purposes; in other words, if one call center loses its ability to provide services (because of a power failure or natural disaster, for example) all calls can be distributed to other call centers. As technology changes and telecommunications continue to take advantage of Internet telephony, this model may evolve. For example, as technology allows interpreters to work more effectively from home offices, call centers may not be as important, so long as other arrangements are made to ensure that calls can be routed to other interpreter resources, should a particular geographic area be affected by a natural disaster or other emergency.
- *How many other call centers does it have, and where are they located?* The number of call centers may help to give you an idea of the company's redundancy.
- *How many years has the company been in business?* If the company

is a start-up company, this may indicate a lack of experience. If it is a relatively new company, find out how the company's leaders obtained experience in the field of telephone interpreting.

- *How many years has the company provided language services?* Perhaps the company has been around for many years, but has only recently begun providing language services. Even if the company has been in business for 20 years, this does not necessarily mean that it has a background in the language services industry.
- *How many years has the company been providing telephone interpreting services?* Perhaps the company has been providing localization, translation or interpreting services for the past five years, but has only recently begun to provide telephone interpreting. As with any novice to the field, be prepared to ask how the company gained experience in telephone interpreting, and how long it has been providing this specific service.
- *Is it a public or private company?* It may be helpful to know if the company is privately held or publicly traded. In the latter case, consumers of interpreting services should be able to access financial statements, investor calls and other publicly-available information.
- *Does the company employ interpreters directly?* If not, it may be helpful to ask the company what percentage of their calls are handled by contractors.
- *What is the company's financial situation?* It is often useful to get at least a basic understanding of the company's financial picture. Has the company been profitable quarter after quarter, and year after year? If not, why is this? What is its average rate of growth? Is the company burdened by debt, or is it debt-free?
- *Has the company been involved in any lawsuits?* It may also help to see if the company has been involved in any litigation. Depending on the nature of the litigation, this may influence a consumer's desire to work with that company.
- *Who are the leaders of the company (CEO, President)?* It is also helpful to have a good understanding of the company's leadership. Who is the CEO and/or President and what is their business background?
- *Do the company's leaders speak other languages?* Much as the executives of a leading technology company are likely to include technology buffs, the executive management team of a language services company is likely to speak other languages. This is often an indication that the leaders have a good understanding of their business.
- *Does the company have an advisory board?* If a telephone interpreting company has a panel of advisors or consultants who represent a

cross-section of academic and industry experts, this is a sign that the company has a strong commitment to quality.

- *Does the company have the ability to handle volume surges in the event of natural disasters or national emergencies?* Often the true test of a telephone interpretation firm is their ability to handle sudden emergencies. For example, if a client closes a Spanish-language call center, the interpreting firm should be able to quickly and easily handle the volume surge.

Insurance

- *What kind of insurance does the company carry?* The company should have an insurance policy that provides complete coverage to protect its customers, including Errors and Omissions (E&O) coverage, Crime Insurance and Professional Liability.
- *Does the company's insurance apply to all employees?* The policy should cover all employees (financial services staff, management, customer service staff, etc.), not just the individuals who interpret.
- *Does the company's insurance apply to independent contractors?* The insurance should cover all individuals who work for the company, even independent contractors. In addition, the company may require that independent contractors have additional coverage, above and beyond what is offered by the company confidentiality.

Confidentiality

- *Has a claim ever been made against the company for a breach of third-party confidentiality or a theft of third-party information?* If such a claim has been made, the company should disclose this and inform you of what steps were taken to prohibit a further occurrence of such a breach of confidentiality.
- *Is confidentiality covered in the company's interpreter code of ethics?* Confidentiality should be a core component of the interpreter code of ethics. If possible, request a copy of the code of ethics.
- *Is confidentiality addressed in the company's standards of practice for interpreters?* In addition to confidentiality being part of the code of ethics, the standards of practice should provide explicit guidance for interpreters on issues of confidentiality.
- *What kind of training do interpreters receive in confidentiality and nondisclosure?* Interpreters must be trained in confidentiality and nondisclosure. It is important that these are actual training topics, and not just words on a piece of paper sent to the interpreters.
- *Do interpreters sign a confidentiality agreement? If so, how often?*

As an additional protection for their customers, some telephone interpreting providers take the step of ensuring that each interpreter has signed a confidentiality agreement.

- *Are back ground checks and fingerprints obtained for interpreters?* Many government agencies now require background checks and fingerprint processing for security clearance.
- *What kind of screenings take place for interpreters?* Some telephone interpreting companies conduct criminal background checks, financial/credit history checks and drug/alcohol screening.
- *What are the procedures for handling confidential information?* Providers should be able to show you copies of security procedures for their call center workers as well as for the individuals who may work from home. Most large interpretation firms will have strict procedures in place for confidentiality.

Interpreter Recruiting

- *What kind of recruitment process is in place for interpreters?* The process the company outlines should indicate the type of recruiting staff that works for the company, along with the process used for recruiting.
- *From what sources does the company recruit interpreters?* Telephone interpreting companies cannot recruit from 'telephone interpreter schools', since very few universities and colleges offer courses in the subject. High-quality providers also recruit from professional interpreting and translation associations. However, providers often have relationships with academic institutions, to provide scholarships, internships and workshops.
- *Does the company require a minimum level of experience?* Beware of companies that place recruiting advertisements that state, 'no experience necessary'. Very few interpreters have experience in the specifics of telephone interpreting prior to working with a company. However, companies should recruit individuals with prior experience of working as interpreters and/or in bilingual environments. While interpreting experience is always desired, for some rare languages this may not always be possible. When the interpreter has no prior experience as an interpreter, recruiters should look for other very strong qualifications, such as working as a translator and professional experience using both languages.
- *Does the company require a minimum level of education?* Again, this may vary according to language. For certain language groups, it may be easy to find college-educated interpreters, but for others, this may not be as common. However, providers should require at least a

high school diploma and, when possible, the highest standards for education should be sought.

- *Does the company require past immersion in both languages?* It is extremely important that interpreters are familiar with more than one culture. If the interpreter learned a language through study alone, he or she may speak the 'textbook' version of the language, but this is not sufficient for interpreting. In the course of his or her work, the interpreter will encounter many references to popular culture from both languages, and therefore must have experience living in more than one language setting.
- *Does the company have any requirements for language proficiency?* Interpreters should have native or near-native proficiency in both languages.

Interpreter Testing

- *What types of tests does the company use for interpreters?* Interpreters should be tested for interpreting skills, as well as language proficiency.
- *What do the tests cover?* The telephone interpreting company should be able to provide you with an outline of the major areas covered in its tests. Many tests are proprietary, but you can ask your provider to share a copy of a sample test or a sample outline with you.
- *Who developed the company's tests?* If the company developed the tests on its own, it may not have subjected them to the academic rigor that is required by the testing community. When reviewing the test developers' qualifications, you should be able to identify one or more individuals whose specialty is language test design.
- *Who administers and rates the tests?* Are the tests administered and rated by staff that works remotely or in-house? How were they trained? Do they receive follow-up training?
- *Does the company work with the test designers on an ongoing basis?* To reflect the ever-changing needs of the company's business and the types of calls that interpreters receive, it is important for individuals involved in test design to continue to help inform the decisions that the company makes about the future revisions of the test.
- *What are the scoring criteria?* It is important to see how the interpreter's performance is scored. Is numerical scoring available? On what categories is the interpreter's performance rated? Are there various levels of scoring?
- *What is the minimum passing score?* The passing score for many interpreting tests is in the 70–75% range. However, remember that

the scoring criteria will define what that percentage actually means. In other words, tests could be 'weighted' in terms of difficulty. The minimum passing score alone is not necessarily a valid indicator of the quality of the interpreting service.

Interpreter Training

- *What kind of training programs does the company have in place?* Ask for a description of the training-program syllabus for any course that the provider delivers to its interpreters. Providers should offer a range of programs, from new interpreter orientation to more advanced and/or specialized programs.
- *How many hours of training are required?* The number of hours of training for telephone interpreters can vary widely. Some providers offer only a basic orientation that lasts for a few hours. This would not be a good guarantee of quality. Others offer more in-depth and complex programs that intersperse training with practice, monitoring, feedback and mentoring. The number of hours of training is often not as important as the quality of the training program itself and the variety of its components.
- *How often is training required?* Frequency of training is important. Interpreters should have access to quality assurance staff, to answer their questions and address their ongoing needs. Training should be a constant part of the provider's workforce development efforts. On-the-job training for telephone interpreters never ends.
- *Do interpreters receive one-on-one training?* Interpreters can benefit tremendously from one-on-one training, which often includes role-play scenarios and practice situations. In this setting, the trainer can gain a better understanding of the interpreter's unique areas of development, and tailor a plan to the interpreter's needs.
- *Do interpreters receive group training?* Interpreters may also participate in group training. When providing training on subjects (such as code of ethics and standards) that apply to all interpreters within the company, this type of training is often carried out in a group setting. If the company has call centers, this training may be delivered in person by a lead trainer. For remote workers, training may be conducted via telephone or via web-based training.
- *Does the training cover specific industries?* Telephone interpreters should be trained to interpret for all the settings in which they will receive calls. In addition, some providers offer client-specific training to interpreters each time a new client is added. This can be extremely helpful since, even within the same industry, one client may use

terminology that is completely different from others.

- *What are the credentials of the trainers?* Some companies have full-time training staff in their offices. You should be able to request copies of resumes for these individuals. They should have college degrees and/or certificates in interpreting, and should have extensive experience in the field of telephone interpreting.

Interpreter Monitoring

- *How often are interpreters monitored?* Interpreters should be monitored frequently. However, the definition of 'frequently' may vary from one company to another. It is difficult to assign a number of calls as a minimum standard, because if an interpreter receives three calls, but each one is only a few minutes long, this does not provide enough data from which to evaluate the interpreter's performance. Therefore, it may be helpful to ask for the average number of monitoring sessions per year per interpreter. Within that number, it may be useful to find out the number of average minutes per call. This will provide a better sense of the length of the monitoring period.
- *What standards are in place for monitoring?* In other words, how is the interpreter's performance measured? You may wish to ask for copy of the telephone interpreting provider's monitoring scoring grid in order to gain a better understanding of how scores are calculated.
- *Does the company record calls for monitoring purposes?* Telephone interpreting calls are ideally recorded for monitoring purposes. When calls are recorded, the monitoring specialist can rewind portions of the call to verify the interpreter's rendition. The monitor may also be able to play back the session for the interpreter to point out areas of improvement. This is a very powerful tool for training interpreters and improving quality.
- *Can I elect for my calls to not be recorded?* If the company does record calls, you should be able to request that they configure their monitoring software to prevent your calls from being recorded. However, unless there are concerns about confidentiality that are not addressed to your satisfaction through the provider's insurance coverage, it is advisable to let the company record your calls, so that you can be sure that they will be used for quality assurance and monitoring.
- *Can I listen to or play back my recorded calls?* Some telephone interpreting companies will allow you to play back calls that have been recorded and monitored through an external web client, so that you can listen to the interpreted session first-hand.
- *Does the company also do live monitoring?* If the provider does record

calls, they should also have live monitoring available for customers who do not wish to have their calls recorded, and as a back-up in case there are problems with the monitoring software.

Interpreter Certification

- *What are the requirements of the company's certification program?* Look for a diverse array of requirements from your provider. Certification should not just be based on passing a test. The program should include training, testing and monitoring components.
- *What is the certification procedure?* Request a copy of the company's brochures and materials that describe the certification process, including a diagram of the process.
- *What languages are offered for certification?* The company should offer certification in at least the ten most commonly requested languages. Often, the top ten languages will make up more than 90% of the call volume. If the company offers certification in a minimum of these languages, this guarantees that the overwhelming majority of your calls will be handled by interpreters who have obtained certification.

Other Quality Issues

- *What is the procedure when an interpreter does not meet standards for quality?* Your provider should be able to share the process that indicates how low-performing interpreters are handled. For example, what happens when you register a complaint about an interpreter? At what point is the interpreter dismissed?
- *Are all calls interpreted using first-person interpretation?* One of the most important indicators of a high-quality service is the exclusive use of first-person interpretation. This means that the interpreter says exactly what was stated in the other language, using the pronouns 'I' or 'me'. When the interpreter starts the sentence with 'he says ...' or 'she's saying ...', this is an indication of a poor-quality service. 'Reported speech' or 'indirect speech' is strictly prohibited by many interpreting associations, so if your telephone interpreting provider does not use first person exclusively, this is a sign that the provider that does not place an emphasis on quality.
- *Can the provider share sample interpreter resumes?* Your provider should be able to provide resumes of interpreting staff, to enable you to see the qualifications and experience of the individuals who will be taking calls for your company on an ongoing basis.
- *Does the firm allow interpreters to take calls on a cell phone?* Professional providers do not allow this practice due to the background

noises and interference this can cause. Some firms in the industry use their telecommunications technology to ensure that this never happens and have strict procedures in place to control and monitor this issue.

Interpreters and Languages

- *How many languages does the company support?* In the United States, all major providers support at least 150 languages.
- *Can the company provide a list of the languages it supports?* It is also important to ask for a list of languages, since each provider may refer to languages differently. In fact, some providers might list regional varieties of a language as completely separate languages. It is important to be aware of this so that you can compare providers directly and make sure your language needs are met.
- *How many interpreters are available?* Your provider should be able to give you at least an estimate of the total number of interpreters that work with the company. A company with a very large number of interpreters might not be able to give you an exact figure because hiring and recruiting is a constant process and the number of interpreters will change all the time.
- *How many interpreters are available for the top ten languages that my company requires?* Most of these interpreters will probably be full-time interpreters, and this number may actually be more important to you than the total number of interpreters, if you are trying to ascertain a company's ability to support your needs. However, many companies recruit from the same pool of interpreters, and a company's historical ability to 'scale up' and add interpreters may be more important than the total number of interpreters currently working for the company.
- *Where are the interpreters located (in what cities, regions and countries)?* If the company primarily uses call centers, the interpreters will be concentrated in those regions. However, some interpreters are remote workers, who are located elsewhere. If you need the interpreters to be located within the country where your services are being provided, you may wish to check with the telephone interpreting company to see if this is possible.

Performance and Technology

The following questions are self-explanatory, and may provide additional insight into technology and performance factors, and their importance when selecting a provider:

- What kind of technology does the company have in place?

- What are the advantages of this type of technology over other types?
- What is the average connection time?
- Does it vary by language?
- If so, how?
- How is the average speed of answer computed?
- What percentage of calls is successfully routed to an interpreter?
- Are there any financial penalties if performance standards are not met?
- If so, how are these computed?
- What are the hours of operation?
- What kind of call center redundancy plan is in place?
- Is there an emergency contingency plan or standby escalation plan in place?
- How does the company accommodate volume surges?
- What is the company's maximum capacity?
- What is the capacity for increasing call activity?
- How are calls routed to interpreters?
- How does the company prevent power outages?
- What kind of technical support does the company offer?
- When is technical support available?
- How many engineers are on the company staff?
- What kinds of performance checks are carried out?
- How often are performance checks carried out?
- Has the company's ability to provide services ever been affected by natural disasters?
- What percentage of calls is answered successfully via live agents?
- What percentage of calls is answered successfully through an interactive voice response system?
- What percentage of calls is successfully transferred to an interpreter?

Customer Service

- *How are customer service issues handled?* Ideally, you should have a designated individual, or a team of individuals, assigned to your account. The account management team should provide you with training, not just on how to use the service, but on the process that will ensue once you begin service, so that you understand how your needs will be met.
- *How are customer service complaints handled?* The company should have a concrete process in place for customer service issues. For all issues, you should receive a guaranteed response time, along with a

guaranteed resolution time frame.

- *How are billing disputes handled?* You will need to know where to direct billing inquiries. Do you call a separate department, or is this handled through your account management team? What is the typical process?
- *How often will the provider communicate with my company regarding performance?* Your provider should offer flexibility here, but the communication should be consistent and frequent. If you are a large-scale user, you may wish to have a monthly performance review. If your needs are smaller, you may only want to meet quarterly to discuss performance.
- *What kind of training is available for training staff how to use interpretation services?* Again, your provider should offer flexibility. Training is most often provided via telephone, but training should be accessible in many formats: hard copies of materials, electronic materials, web-based training, and in-person training.
- *Is the provider willing to provide references?* Your provider should be able to provide you with references. If you are a large-scale user, you may want to speak with one of the company's large-scale customers, to learn more about that customer's experience. If you are a small-scale user, you may want to speak with other users whose needs are similar to yours.
- *What is your annual customer retention rate?* The rate of customer retention can provide a strong indication of customer satisfaction.

Account Set-Up

- *How are client identification codes issued?* Does the provider assign numbers, or can you choose your own identification number? Will the code be alpha-numeric, or only numeric?
- *Are user identification codes issued as well?* If you require unique user identification codes to track the different individuals who are accessing the service, your provider should be able to facilitate this for you.
- *Is there dedicated toll-free access for each customer account?* To protect your account, you should have your own dedicated toll-free number.
- *What does the account set-up process entail?* You will need to find out what the process is for establishing the account. Do individual branch locations need to follow the process separately? Do you simply configure your auto-dialed to dial the number of the new provider? The process may vary depending on your company's current method for accessing the service.

- *How do I test the system to verify that the service is working?* Your provider should walk you through the various steps that will take place in order for you to verify that your service is working properly.
- *How long does the service implementation process take?* This depends greatly on your organization, and varies from one organization to the next. If you have 50 call centers that will each require unique identification codes and user codes, it may be a more time-consuming set-up process than for a company that requires only one access code.
- *How does the company minimize risk during the transition phase?* Your provider should work with you to create a plan for transition. This might involve converting several locations at a time, to minimize risk.

Reporting

- *What kinds of reports are provided?* Your provider should be able to show you a sample report, so that you can determine if the information presented will meet your needs. If you require hard copies of your reports, your provider should grant that request.
- *Do reports include volume trend analysis?* Your provider should include an analysis of volume trends. This will enable you to identify patterns that could affect your own business needs.
- *Do reports include answer-time analysis?* The reports you receive should include answer-time analysis, especially if this is included in your service agreement, so that you can ensure that your provider is upholding its commitment.
- *Do reports include customer complaint and dispute analysis?* If any disputes or complaints were presented, this should be listed on your reports.
- *Do reports include a breakdown of language usage?* Your provider should include language usage information on the reports.
- *Is billing information available electronically?* All customer billing information should be available to you in electronic format.
- *Does the company have a web-based customer extranet tool?* Some providers allow access to all billing data through a secure customer extranet. This allows the customer to do more in-depth analysis of trends in usage at the click of a mouse.
- *What categories of usage are listed?* Reports should indicate usage according to a minimum of the following categories: date, interpreter ID, customer ID, user ID, language, start time and end time.

Pricing

- *Is there an account set-up fee?* Some providers charge a nominal account set-up fee. For large customers, this amount can be waived.
- *Is there a recurring monthly fee?* Some providers charge a monthly 'subscription' fee that includes a certain number of minutes per month. If the customer goes over this amount, the customer pays a per-minute rate. This type of price structure is more common for small-volume users (100 minutes or less per month).
- *What is the per-minute rate?* Within the United States, prices vary widely. The cost of providing services has decreased over the past two decades, but some organizations still pay premium prices in excess of $5.00 per minute, while others (often large-scale users) pay rates that hover around $1.00 per minute.
- *Does the price-per-minute vary by language?* Sometimes, providers may offer different rates for different languages. This is largely because the cost of providing the service may vary somewhat across languages. Because providers guarantee customers the ability to conference in an interpreter for one of 150 languages within seconds, this means that interpreters are often paid a 'retainer' or a per-hour rate, even though they may be rarely called upon to interpret.
- *Does the price-per-minute rate vary according to volume?* Some large providers may offer discounted rates for larger volumes.

Industry-Specific Expertise

- *How long has the company provided services for companies such as yours?* It may be helpful to gain a better understanding of the experience the company has with your specific industry. You may want to ask to speak with the provider's current customers from within your own industry in order to get their perspective.
- *Are there any special service packages available for customers from your industry?* If the vendor offers multiple types of language services, such as document translation and on-site (in-person) interpreting, it may be able to offer you all of these services in a bundled package. Sometimes, this may result in discounted rates and free trials of other services that your organization may require.
- *Does the provider endorse codes of ethics and standards that are published for your industry?* If there are codes of ethics and standards published for your industry, check to see if your provider has endorsed them. If this is the case, the provider will most likely state this in its marketing materials.
- *Does the company provide interpreters with copies of codes of ethics*

and standards that are published for your industry? The provider should provide interpreters with copies of codes of ethics and standards for the industry in question.

- *Is the company a member of associations that support interpreting for your industry?* The telephone interpreting company should be a member of the major interpreting associations for the industry in question. This demonstrates familiarity with industry best practices for interpreting.

Language Services Support

- *Does the company provide on-site interpreters?* If you have a need for telephone interpreting services, it is likely that you may also require in-person interpreters from time to time. If this is the case, check with your providing company to see if it offers this service and also check on the interpreters' qualifications. Also, check to find out what the qualifications are of the interpreters. The interpreters should be qualified for the setting in which they are working (e.g. if interpreters are working in a court setting, they should hold a court certification).
- *Does your company offer translation services?* If you are providing services via telephone to customers in other languages, you will require assistance with written documents as well. If the company offers this service, find out about the qualifications of their staff. Find out whether or not the company provides this service directly or out sources it to another company. If the company out sources the work to a separate agency, you will most likely pay more for it. Also, make sure that the company is using qualified, professional translators – not interpreters – to do the translation work.
- *Does the company offer localization services?* If your own company has a website, you may wish to learn more about localizing the site into other languages. Again, if the telephone interpreting provider offers this service, find out more about the qualifications of its staff. Localization is a field that requires expertise, and should be performed only by experts.
- *Does the company offer terminology management services?* If the company is a high-quality provider of translation services, it is likely that it will offer terminology management services as well. Terminology management allows you to take advantage of the terminology from written documents and ensure that the same terminology is used consistently throughout your organization. This terminology can be shared with the telephone interpreters, to ensure utmost consistency when dealing with speakers of other languages.

- *Does the company offer cultural competence training services?* With legislation that mandates cultural competence training for certain professions in some states, you may wish to ask your provider if it offers cultural competence training. Some cultural competence training programs include modules on language access, which cover how to work with an interpreter, as well as information on key legislation with regard to providing culturally and linguistically appropriate services.
- *Does the company offer video remote interpreting (VRI) services?* For sign language, video remote interpreting is another service that is commonly requested of telephone interpreting providers. If you deal with deaf customers, you may wish to learn more about this service.
- *Does the company offer any other services that will help you serve your customers in other languages?* telephone interpreting providers sometimes offer other important language services, such as multilingual transcription, multilingual monitoring or language proficiency testing. It may be wise to research companies in advance in order to determine what services you require and to determine what benefits (both in terms of cost savings and quality improvement) might be obtained by working with a full-service provider, compared with the option of working with multiple vendors.
- *Does the company provide 24/7 or 24/5 customer service?* Some companies log all customer service calls and provide clients with a status report on open items.
- *What are the standards for getting back to you with any issues?* Providers should give you a clear idea of when to expect a response – whether that is within one hour, one day or one week.

Chapter 25
Working Effectively with Telephone Interpreters

A unique combination of knowledge, skills and experience is required to work as a telephone interpreter. Likewise, to work with a telephone interpreter in an effective manner, the client can benefit from gaining additional information, practicing specific skills, and gaining experience. In this chapter, you can gain knowledge and learn about the skills that are necessary to have the most productive and efficient sessions possible when working with a telephone interpreter. Much of the information in this chapter can also be useful when working with in-person interpreters.

Organizational Preparation

An important, yet often overlooked, part of preparation for working with telephone interpreters occurs at an organizational level, long before an interpreted phone call ever takes place. When an organization is at the initial stages of a new relationship with a telephone interpreting company, this is the ideal time to take steps to ensure the best possible efficiency and eventual outcomes for all of the interpreted sessions that will be taking place over the phone throughout the course of the relationship. The following guidelines will help the client to reduce the need for clarification on calls, thereby potentially saving hundreds, if not thousands, of billed minutes over time.

Find a telephone-interpreting company with a partnership approach

Your telephone-interpreting provider should have a dedicated account management team that works with you to understand not only the nature of your business, but also the details and unique facets of your company. As a true extension of the service you provide to your customers, the telephone interpreting provider should be constantly informed of any changes that occur in your business that could affect the service provided.

For example, a hospital has recently decided to launch a new public awareness campaign regarding childhood obesity. When the marketing department makes the various departments aware of this campaign, the department in charge of interpreting services should communicate this to the telephone-interpreting provider and send a copy of any relevant materials to the provider.

On the hospital's part, this will take only a matter of seconds to do. However, once the telephone-interpreting provider receives this information, here is what happens. The account management team will notify the quality assurance department. The quality assurance department will disseminate this information to the interpreter trainers and/or monitoring specialists, who will in turn, share this information with the interpreters. Interpreters may then begin discussing the best ways of interpreting the key terminology from the materials into the various languages. When the campaign is launched and calls begin coming in, the interpreters are already familiar with the terminology and will be less likely to request clarification, resulting in a more effective and efficient communication experience for all involved.

Not all telephone-interpreting providers take a partnership approach to working with their customers, so it is important to ask the company representative if this is possible. When providers do offer this service, however, it results in a higher quality of interpretation and a more expedient session for all involved.

Give the telephone-interpreting company a profile of your organization

It will be extremely helpful for the telephone interpreting provider to have as much information as possible about your organization. If available, a percentage breakdown of the languages requested and the anticipated volume of calls can help the telephone-interpreting provider ensure adequate staffing and forecasting.

It is especially helpful for the client organization to provide information that is relevant to the types of calls that will be interpreted. For example, an emergency (911/999) call center may want to give the telephone-interpreting provider a list of major streets and landmarks in the area it services.

The LEP caller will often find it difficult to pronounce street names, and if the interpreter is unfamiliar with the area, the LEP caller's rendition of the street name or other proper noun may seem unintelligible. However, if the interpreter has previously studied a list of street names that, this will help facilitate the communication process.

In addition to the concern for the LEP caller's pronunciation, keep in mind that regional accents in English could also be confusing for the interpreter.

For example, if a dispatcher pronounces a proper noun such as 'Clark Street' in the way that is common in certain parts of the east coast of the USA, the interpreter may incorrectly assume that the dispatcher said, 'Clock Street', and could render it as such phonetically into the other language, which could cause additional confusion for all parties. Having a list of common street names on hand may help to prevent this type of confusion.

Some clients, especially those with call centers, use scripts for many of their calls. It is often helpful to provide copies of such scripts to the telephone interpreting provider. This way, the provider's training and quality assurance staff members can provide these materials to the interpreters. In some cases, when customers provide extensive materials, the quality assurance team may simply provide the interpreters with recommended translations or in-language glossaries for the customer in question. This way, interpreters can study these materials in advance, and when calls come in, interpreters can refer to some of these materials as needed.

Create a list or glossary of jargon

If your organization uses proper names or terms that are unique or uncommon, it is helpful to give these to your telephone interpreting partner, so that they can be shared with the interpreters, who will then be prepared to interpret them when they come up during calls. In addition, while telephone interpreters are accustomed to taking calls from a variety of industries, some telephone interpreting clients have niche terminology and may require services only occasionally.

For example, an auto parts catalog may receive an occasional call from someone in another country who wishes to place an order. The interpreter may not come across terms such as 'vertically driven diamond plate tonneau cover', 'stick-on hatch weatherstripping', and 'big-bore cylinder replacement ring' on a daily basis. These terms would not be understood by a layperson and can be difficult to interpret, especially since relatively little context is given. To render them in another language would require some research and thoughtful consideration even by certified technical translators. If the company provides a catalog to the telephone-interpreting provider in advance, the quality assurance department will be able to generate a glossary and/or list of terms that may come up during a call.

Become more familiar with the profession

For any organization interested in working with a telephone interpreting provider, it is imperative to become an informed consumer. When the choice of telephone-interpreting provider is being made by a team of individuals, it may be helpful for each team member to read a copy of this book, in order to become more familiar with the subject matter. When reading the book, special attention should be focused on the chapters directed at the client, as well as the chapters that provide model codes of ethics and standards. These chapters should serve to provide good insight into the world of telephone interpreting, thereby allowing the client to make an informed decision.

20 Tips for Working Effectively With Telephone Interpreters

The suggestions that follow are most useful for individuals who work with telephone interpreters. Following these tips and distributing them widely to end users of telephone-interpreting services will help to improve quality and maximize efficiency, resulting in decreased call lengths and more effective communication.

1. *Tell the interpreter the context.* It is extremely important to provide the interpreter with a context, so that he or she will know what to expect and be better prepared to interpret the information. If the organizational preparation described above has taken place, this will be of tremendous help. However, it is also helpful to give a brief description of the call to the interpreter. For example, you might say, 'I am taking a loan application with Mr. Yamashita, who is here with me in the bank branch today', or 'Miss Lourenco is calling regarding her son's prescription'.

2. *Explain the interpreter's role.* The beginning of the call is a perfect time to introduce the interpreter to the LEP speaker and provide an explanation of the interpreter's role. You may also clarify both the purpose of the session and the expected outcome. For example, after you conference both parties together, you may say to the LEP speaker, 'Mr. Perez, I have your interpreter, Maria, on the line. Maria will be interpreting everything we say to each other, so please address all your comments directly to me, and Maria will interpret them.'

3. *Limit the use of gestures and facial expressions.* You may be accustomed to using expressions and gestures along with your words to help convey meaning. Because the meaning of gestures varies drastically

from one culture to another, it is normally best to avoid using them when speaking with an LEP party. The LEP person could become confused by your gestures, find them offensive or misinterpret them, especially because he or she will not hear the interpretation of your statement until after the gestures have already been used, so they will not be immediately associated with the words you originally intended to emphasize or convey. Instead, focus on choosing your words carefully to convey meaning so that the interpreter will be able to render the entire meaning accurately. Likewise, if you are with the LEP speaker and he or she makes gestures or expressions, do not make assumptions, as you might be misinterpreting them as well. Listen carefully to the interpreter's rendition of the meaning, and focus on that instead.

4. *Ensure that the LEP speaker understands.* When you are working through an interpreter, you are less likely to be able to pick up on non-verbal cues such as hesitations, pauses and intonation that might indicate a lack of understanding. It is helpful, therefore, for you to verify understanding, especially regarding the most important pieces of information. Rather than just say, 'Do you understand?' (which may not help you obtain the most accurate picture of the party's level of understanding), it is helpful to get the LEP speaker to rephrase or repeat key information back to you. For example, you might say, 'Mrs. Chen, I want to make sure you understand. How often will you be giving your daughter the medication?'

5. *Pace your speech appropriately.* You should speak at a natural pace. However, try to avoid speaking too quickly, as it may be harder for the interpreter to understand you. At the opposite end of the spectrum, avoid speaking too slowly. Sometimes, clients speak very slowly, as if they are speaking to children, and this artificial rhythm can actually detract from the meaning and make the interpreter's job more difficult. It is best to speak at the same pace that you would normally speak to an adult. Also, be aware that, if you are reading scripted text or reciting information that you commonly use, you are likely to speak at a faster pace than normal. When you are reading or reciting prewritten material, make a conscious effort to slow down your rate of speech. You may also want to advise the LEP speaker in advance by saying, for example, 'I am about to read a legal disclosure. I will read you one or two sentences at a time, so that the interpreter can interpret the information accurately.'

6. *Have sufficient time available.* When you are working with an interpreter, every part of the conversation will be stated twice (once in each language). Also, what may take only a few words in one language may require paraphrasing in another. If you are placing an outbound call to the LEP speaker, be sure to allow sufficient time – at least twice the normal amount that you would allow. Obviously, for inbound calls, such as emergency calls placed by LEP speakers, you cannot plan for each call in advance. However, by using the usage information provided by your telephone-interpreting partner, you can more accurately forecast the numbers of calls that come in from LEP callers, and this will hopefully allow you to adjust your staffing as needed.

7. *Ask only one question at a time.* It is best not to ask more than one question at once. If you do ask multiple questions at once, you may not be able to match up the answers with the original questions. If you give the interpreter a list of questions to ask, the interpreter will most likely be interrupted by the LEP speaker, who will want to provide an answer to the questions immediately after each question is asked. This increases the amount of information that the interpreter will have to relay back to you, and therefore increases the chance of information being omitted. Also, if you ask the interpreter multiple questions, the interpreter will have to add additional words when rendering the answers back to you to clarify. For example, suppose you want to ask, 'What day did you mail your last payment?' and 'What was the amount?' The LEP speaker might answer, 'the 23rd' and '$23.00'. If the interpreter renders these back as, 'the 23rd, $23.00', this could lead to confusion and require additional clarification. So the interpreter would most likely say instead, 'the payment was sent on the 23rd, in the amount of $23.00'. This requires the interpreter to use additional words to clarify. If the client had asked, 'What day did you mail your last payment?', the response would have been 'the 23rd', and to the question 'What was the amount?', the interpreter can render the exact response immediately, '$23.00'. Obviously, the greater the number of questions asked at one time, the less efficient the communication process becomes, and the greater the likelihood of errors, omissions and the need for clarification. In addition, a 'pile-up' of questions for the interpreter to render will require additional phrases of clarification, which lengthens the conversation and means a higher cost to the customer.

8. *Note the interpreter's name and ID number.* There are many benefits to documenting the interpreter's identifying information. For example, if your customer calls back immediately to ask an additional question, you will need to contact the interpreter again, and you may be able to provide the interpreter ID number to be connected to the same interpreter. This will require less explanation to the interpreter at the beginning of the call, since the interpreter will already be familiar with the scenario. In addition, you may be able to request the same interpreter for a future call or encounter with the same LEP speaker. Also, if you have any feedback (either positive or negative) to share regarding the interpreter's performance, your telephone-interpreting provider will be able to follow up on your comments more easily if it knows exactly which interpreter your feedback refers to.

9. *Enunciate words and speak audibly.* Try your best to pronounce your words clearly and in audibly. You may also want to check that interpreter can hear you clearly. Avoid yelling into the phone or speaking too loudly, as this can also be problematic for the interpreter. Checking on audibility at the beginning of a call can help prevent requests for repetition or clarification later on in the call, thereby saving you time.

10. *Incorporate first person or direct speech.* Address your statements directly to the LEP speaker. Remember that the interpreter is simply rendering what you say, so when you want to say something to the LEP party, there is no need to address the interpreter. For example, instead of saying, 'Interpreter, ask Mr. Lopez for his address,' say, 'Mr. Lopez, what is your address?'

11. *Notice and work through additional communication problems.* Do not automatically assume that a communication barrier or lack of understanding is related to the interpreter's performance. Just as misunderstandings often take place between two people who speak the same language, they will also sometimes happen when working with an interpreter. If you notice that a response does not seem to relate to what you originally stated, you may want to repeat your original statement in a different way, to make sure that your point is understood. Also, double-check to make sure that you have also understood what the LEP party is trying to convey. Some communication problems go beyond language barriers, and are due to personality issues or differences in communication styles. It may be easy to point the finger at the interpreter when communication

goes awry, but sometimes the communication barriers have nothing whatsoever to do with the interpreter.

12. *Take turns speaking.* It is important that only one party speaks at a time. When multiple parties speak simultaneously, the interpreter will not be able to hear everyone clearly and may lose parts of the meaning. It is important that you avoid interrupting either speaker, but if you notice the LEP speaker interrupting the interpreter, you should direct him or her to wait until the interpreter finishes before interrupting. When all parties take turns speaking in this way, it will allow for the best possible communication, especially if there is more than one LEP speaker in the room or on the line. However, in your goal to make sure the communication flows in an organized fashion, be sure not to become overzealous or 'coach' the interpreter. If you constantly say things like, 'Go ahead interpreter', or 'You can interpret now', this may interrupt the flow of the conversation.

13. *Encourage requests for clarification.* If an interpreter stops you to clarify something you have said, or to verify accuracy, this is, in most cases, a sign of a professional interpreter who is committed to providing an accurate and complete interpretation. If you know that you will be covering highly technical information, you may want to encourage the interpreter to clarify with you if he or she has any questions or needs you to provide an explanation or definition. Also, you may proactively offer clarification. In many languages, exact linguistic equivalents may not exist for certain terms. If you provide a definition or explanation of the term when you use it, this will serve to help the LEP speaker and the interpreter gain a clearer understanding of the message.

14. *Refrain from using figures of speech and cultural references.* Some phrases might be extremely difficult to render, even if they are easy for the interpreter to understand. For example, if you say, 'She isn't the sharpest knife in the drawer,' or 'He went postal', it is unlikely that even a very experienced interpreter would be able to spontaneously find a perfect equivalent for that phrase. More likely, the interpreter would have to paraphrase in order to convey the same meaning in the other language. You can decrease the difficulty of the interpretation task by simply avoiding such references.

15. *Protect and respect the role of the interpreter.* The interpreter's primary role is to render the communication from one language into another.

It is never appropriate to ask the interpreter to take on part of your job. For example, if the LEP speaker says, 'I don't understand what you mean by liability insurance', it is not appropriate to say, 'Interpreter, go ahead and explain liability insurance to him.' That would fall outside the interpreter's role. Likewise, if the LEP speaker asks the interpreter a question and the interpreter alerts you to this, support the interpreter by asking the LEP speaker to refrain from making such requests of the interpreter.

16. *Remain present for all communication.* Do your best not to leave the LEP speaker 'alone' with the telephone interpreter. If you need to place both parties on hold or leave the LEP speaker in a room while the telephone interpreter is still on the line, you should advise the LEP speaker not to have a conversation with the interpreter without your presence. For example, you may say, 'I need to go grab a brochure for you, I'll be right back. Please wait until I am back to continue with the conversation', or 'I need to put you on hold for a moment. We will continue speaking when I return to the line.' If you do not do this, the LEP speaker may be tempted to initiate a private conversation with the interpreter. Often when this happens, the LEP speaker will feel that he or she may safely confide in the interpreter. For example, he or she may say, 'Do you think I am really getting the best rate, or should I switch to another company?', or 'I'm not going to take the medicine my doctor is prescribing. I don't trust him.' This puts the interpreter in an awkward position. You can prevent this by forewarning both parties that no conversation should take place when you are not present.

17. *Exercise awareness of the words you say aloud.* Because you know that the LEP speaker is not able to understand you, it may sometimes be tempting to 'think out loud' in front of the interpreter, or say things that you might not really want to have interpreted. Remember that everything you say will be interpreted. For example, instead of saying, 'It's so frustrating that this guy is not understanding me; I guess I'll just have to come up with another way of explaining the process', say, 'It seems you are still not understanding me. Please give me a moment while I think of another way to explain the process to you.'

18. *Talk in short utterances.* By pausing frequently to allow the interpreter to render what you have stated, you will help to reduce the risk of errors and omissions. A general rule of thumb is to provide one long sentence or three to four shorter ones. Then, you should pause to let the interpreter render the information. Make sure that you stop in a

natural place, such as the end of a sentence. If you stop in the middle of a sentence, the interpreter will often not be able to render it until he or she hears the rest of the sentence, because of differences in grammar and syntax in the other language. In addition, the complexity of your speech will affect the ideal length of an utterance. If you have even a short sentence that includes highly technical vocabulary, you may want to stop after that sentence, so that the interpreter can render it immediately.

19. *Eliminate vague expressions and words that have double meanings.* In lieu of terms that are vague or easily confused, use descriptive language whenever possible. If you use words such as 'this' and 'that' or 'here' and 'there', the meaning may not be clear enough. Instead, identify objects and places by name, and be more descriptive when using the telephone interpreter. This is especially important if you are demonstrating something with an LEP speaker that is present with you. For example, instead of saying, 'Please sign here', say, 'Please sign the line on the bottom right corner of the page'. Instead of saying, 'Take these to the pharmacy', say, 'Take a copy of these two prescriptions to the pharmacy'. Remember that the interpreter is not present in the room with you and cannot see the same things that you are seeing. By being more descriptive, you are providing clearer communication and allowing the interpreter to do a better job.

20. *Relieve or replace your interpreter as needed.* Interpreting is a very demanding activity that is both mentally and physically draining. If a call goes beyond 30 minutes, you may wish to check with the interpreter to see if he or she needs to rest for a minute or two, or if you should call back and request a fresh interpreter. Keep in mind also that the interpreter may have been taking call after call in the hours leading up to your call, and perhaps he or she was due for a break right before your call came in. While that cannot be avoided, and the interpreter will get a break after the call ends, you may wish to check in with him or her. A short rest will also allow the interpreter to achieve a greater performance.

The table below can be used as an at-a-glance reminder of these 20 tips for working effectively with telephone interpreters.

Twenty tips for working with telephone interpreters

Tell the interpreter the context.
Explain the interpreter's role.
Limit the use of gestures and facial expressions.
Ensure the LEP speaker's understanding.
Pace your speech appropriately.
Have sufficient time available.
Offer only one question at a time.
Note the interpreter's name and ID number.
Enunciate words and speak audibly.
Incorporate first person or direct speech.
Notice and work through additional communication problems.
Take turns speaking.
Encourage requests for clarification
Refrain from using figures of speech and cultural references.
Protect and respect the role of the interpreter.
Remain present for all communication.
Exercise awareness of the words you say aloud.
Talk in short utterances.
Eliminate vague expressions and words that have double meanings.
Relieve or refresh your interpreter as needed.

Additional Suggestions

In addition to the top 20 tips that can be used during an interpreted session with a telephone interpreter, here are some other considerations to take into account.

- *Reinforce verbal information with written materials.* Often, people will call back to request the same information that was already provided, or they may forget information or need additional clarification. To prevent this, it is a good idea to provide written materials in the LEP party's native language. This may help to reduce the number of calls that come in requesting the same type of information. If you partner a telephone interpreting company, ask it to support you in producing commonly requested information in other languages. It is important to take into account the literacy levels of the target audience when providing materials. In some cases, you may need to rewrite the materials at a lower reading level, or you may need to request support for this from your language services provider.
- *Avoid competing with the interpreter.* If you have some experience

with the language in question, be careful not to interject or interrupt the interpreter. Allow the interpreter to finish the rendition. Likewise, if the LEP caller knows some English and tries to answer before listening to the entire interpretation, instruct him or her to wait until the interpreter finishes. You may also recommend to the LEP individual, 'I appreciate your attempt to speak English. However, while the interpreter is with us, let's communicate through a professional.'

- *Make sure the setting is quiet.* Try to eliminate any background noise, and avoid using speaker-phones whenever possible. If background noise persists, you may have to pick up the receiver and pass it back and forth. Ideally, you should work with a provider that offers dual handset phones.
- *Think twice before 'replacing' the telephone interpreter.* If a bilingual colleague arrives on the scene while you are working with a telephone interpreter, this is not necessarily a valid reason to end the call with the interpreter. Unless the bilingual employee is a trained interpreter, it is better to keep using the telephone interpreter. Your telephone interpreting provider is accountable for providing you with a qualified interpreter. If you use a colleague whose interpreting skills have not been verified, this could result in errors and omissions. No matter what, never use children or family members to interpret for the LEP individual. A telephone interpreter is always a preferable option.

Bibliography

The following works were consulted in the preparation of this book.

ASTM (2001) ASTM F2089-01 Standard Guide for Language Interpretation Services.

American Society of Testing and Materials (website at www.astm.org).

Angelelli, C. (2000) Interpretation as a communicative event: A look through Hymes' lenses. META XLV (4), 580–592.

Angelelli, C. (2000) Interpretation pedagogy: A bridge long over due. ATA Chronicle,

November/December.

Angelelli, C. (2004) Medical Interpreting and Cross-cultural Communication. Cambridge: Cambridge University Press.

Angelelli, C. (2004) Revisiting the Interpreter's Role: A Study of Conference, Court, and Medical Interpreters in Canada, Mexico, and the United States. Benjamins Translation Library. Amsterdam: John Benjamins.

Anderson, C.C. and Anderson, M.P.A. (2002) Linguistically Appropriate Access and Services: An Evaluation and Review for Healthcare Organizations. The National Council on Interpreting in Health Care Working Paper (Vol. 6).

Avery, M-P.B., Chun, A., Downing, B., Maynard, M. and Ruschke, K. (2001) Guide to Initial Assessment of Interpreter Qualifications. The National Council on Interpreting in Health Care Working Paper..

Avery, M-P.B. (2001) The Role of the Health Care Interpreter: An Evolving Dialogue. The National Council on Interpreting in Health Care Working Paper.

Baker, D. and Puebla Fortier, J. (1998) Interpreter use and satisfaction with interpersonal aspects of care for Spanish-speaking patients. Medical Care 36 (10), 1461–1470

Bancroft, MA. (2005) The Interpreter's World Tour: An Environmental Scan of Standards of Practice for Interpreters. Woodland Hills, CA:

The California Endowment.

Barsky, R. (1996) The interpreter as intercultural agent in Convention Refugee Hearings. The Translator 2 (1), 45–63.

Butler, F., Sawyer, D., Turner, J. and Stone, I. (2001) Quality assessment of telephone interpreters: Preview to the process of identifying, training and certifying telephone interpreters. ATA Annual Conference, October 31–November 3.

Butler, F., Sawyer, D., Turner, J. and Stone, I. (2002) A quality assurance model for remote language mediation. ATA Chronicle XXI (8), 31–36.

Cambridge, J. (1999) Information loss in bilingual medical interviews through an untrained interpreter. The Translator 5 (2), 201–219.

Canadian Centre for Occupational Health Safety (2003) Lighting ergonomics: Survey and solutions. Ergonomics, November 7.

Chang, P.H. and Fortier J.P. (1995) Language barriers to health care: An overview. Journal of Health Care for the Poor and Underserved 1998 (9: Supplement), S5–S20.

Comstock, J. (1999) Telephonic interpreting access: Grant application report. A report submitted to the Idaho Supreme Court. Rauch Companies website. Available online at http://www.rauchcom.com/idgrantreport.html. Accessed 02.02.07.

Davidson, B. (2000) The interpreter as institutional gatekeeper: The social-linguistic role of interpreters in Spanish-English medical discourse. Journal of Sociolinguistics 4 (3), 379–405.

Davidson, B. (2001) Questions in cross-linguistic medical encounters: The role of the hospital interpreter. Anthropological Quarterly 74 (4) 170–178.

Davidson, B. (2002) A model for the construction of conversational common ground in interpreted discourse. Journal of Pragmatics 34, 1273–1300.

Department of Health and Human Services Office of Minority Health and the National Council on Interpreting in Health Care (NCIHC) (2002) The Terminology of Health Care Interpreting, A Glossary of Terms. Working Paper Series (Vol. 6).

Department of Immigration and Multicultural and Indigenous Affairs (DIMIA) (2003) Report of the Review of Settlement Services for Migrants and Humanitarian Entrants (p. 278). Available online at: http://www.immi.gov.au/living-in-Australia/delivering-assistance/government-programs/settlement-policy/reviewsettlement-services.htm. Accessed 02.02.07.

Dispatch Monthly (1995) History of 911. Available online at: http://

www.911dispatch.com/911/history. Accessed 19.01.06

Duncan, L. (2001) Remote court interpreting: Development of a pilot project in California. National Center for State Courts. Available online at: http://www.ncsconline.org/D_ICM/Abstracts_2001/Remote_Court_Interpreting.pdf. Accessed 02.02.07.

El Boghdady, D. (2005) Healing touch by telephone: Medicare program uses call centres. Washington Post, 2 August, p. D04.

Englund Dimitrova, B. (1997) Degree of interpreter responsibility in the interaction process in community interpreting. In S.E. Carr, R. Roberts, A. Dufour and D. Steyn. The Critical Link: Interpreters in the Community (pp. 147–164). Philadelphia: John Benjamins

Gambier, Y., Gile, D. and Taylor, C. (1997) Conference Interpreting: Current Trends in Research. Philadelphia: John Benjamins.

Geertsen, D., Romero, N. and Mikkelson, H. (2000) Testing for certification: A holistic approach to an interpreter certification program at language line services. Proceedings of the 41st Annual Conference of the American Translators Association (pp. 113–134). Orlando, September 20–23.

Gentile, A., Ozolins, U. and Vasilakakos, M. (1996) Liaison Interpreting: A Handbook. Victoria: Melbourne University Press.

Gile, D. (1995) Basic Concepts and Models for Interpreter and Translator Training. Philadelphia: John Benjamins.

Gillies, A. (2005) Note-taking for consecutive interpreting: A short course. Manchester: St Jerome Publishing.

González, R., Vásquez, V. and Mikkelson, H. (1991) Fundamentals of Court Interpretation: Theory, Policy and Practice. Durham, NC: Carolina Academic Press.

Gracia-García, R.A. (2002) Telephone interpreting: A review of pros and cons. Proceedings of the 43rd Annual Conference of the American Translators Association (pp. 195–218). Atlanta, November 2002.

Gracia-García, R.A. (2003) The new industry of telephone interpreting: A comprehensive study. Master's thesis.

Hardt E.J. (1995) The bilingual interview and medical interpretation. In M. Lipkin Jr, S.M. Putnam and A. Lazare (eds) The Medical Interview: Clinical Care, Education, and Research. Ann Arbor: Braum-Brumfield.

Heh, Y-C. and Hu Qian (1997) Over-the-phone interpretation: A new way of communication between speech communities. Proceedings of the 38th Annual Conference of the American Translators Association (pp. 51–62). San Francisco, November.

Herman,Mand Bryant, D. (2000) Language Interpreting in the Courts: Telephonic Interpreting: Report on Trends in the State Courts (1999–

2000 edition). National Center for State Courts. Available online at http://www.ncsconline.org/WC/Publications/KIS_CtInte_Trends99-00_Pub.pdf. Accessed 02.02.07.

Hertog, E. (ed.) (2003) Aequalitas: Equal Access to Justice across Language & Culture in the EU. Grothis Project 2001/GRP/015. Antwerpen: Lessins Hogenschool.

Hewitt, W.E. (1995) Court Interpretation: Model Guides for Policy and Practice in the State Court., Williamsburg, VA: National Center for State Courts.

Heynold, C. (1995) La Videoconférence multilingue: Premières expérience à la Commission Europeéenne. Nouvelle de la FIT- FIT Newsletter N.s.14 (3/4), 337–42.

Jacob, J.A. (2001) Better interpretation is just a phone call away.AMNews. June 11.

Karpf, A. (2006) The Human Voice. New York: Bloomsbury Publishing.

Kelly, N. (2007) Interpreter certification programs in the United States: Where are we headed? ATA Chronicle, January.

Kelly, N., Bancroft, M.A. and Willet, K. (2006) Bridging the cultural divide: Cultural competence in public safety. Emergency Number Professional Magazine, May.

Language Line Services (2008) History. Available online at http://www.languageline.com/page/history/. Accessed 02.14.08.

Leman, P. (1998) NHS Direct should provide a national telephone interpreter service. British Medical Journal. E-letters. October 23. Available online at http://www.bmj.com/cgi/eletters/317/7165/1026. Accessed 02.02.07.

Killian, W.C. (1998) Interpreting by phone.OACReports 1–3, July 6. Olympia, WA: Office of the Administrator of the Courts.

Mason, I. (ed.) (2001) Triadic Exchanges: Studies in Dialogue Interpreting. Manchester: St Jerome Publishing.

Mikkelson, H. (1998) Towards a redefinition of the role of the court interpreter. Interpreting: International Journal of Research and Practice in Interpreting 3(1), 21–46.

Mikkelson, H. (2000) Introduction to Court Interpreting. Manchester: St Jerome Publishing.

Mintz, D. (1998) Hold the phone: Telephone interpreting scrutinized. NAJIT. PROTEUS VII (1) Winter 1998.

Moser-Mercer, B. (2003) Remote Interpreting: Assessment of Human Factors and Performance Parameters. Geneva: International Telecommunication Union-Ecole de Traduction et d'Interpretation, Université de Genève.

Mousourakis, P. (1996) Videoconferencing: Techniques and challenges. Interpreting: International Journal of Research and Practice in Interpreting 1 (1), 21–38.

NAJIT (2004) NAJIT Position Paper on Direct Speech in Legal Settings. National Association of Judiciary Interpreters and Translators, July 10.

NAJIT (undated) Code of Ethics and Professional Responsibilities. National Association of Judiciary Interpreters and Translators. Available online at http://najit.org/ethics.html. Accessed 25.01.07.

National Council on Interpreting in Health Care (2004) A National Code of Ethics for Interpreters in Health Care. July, 2004.

National Council on Interpreting in Health Care (2005) National Standards of Practice for Interpreters in Health Care. October, 2005.

Oviatt, S.L. and Cohen, P.R. (1992) Spoken language in interpreted telephone dialogues. Computer Speech and Language 6, 277–302.

Phelan, M. (2001) The Interpreter's Resource. Clevedon: Multilingual Matters Ltd.

Pointon, T. (1996) Telephone interpreting service is available. British Medical Journal 312, 53.

Pointon, T., Ozolins, U. and Doucouliagos, C. (1998) TIS in Europe 1976–2001. Victoria: Deakin University.

Pressman, S.D., Cohen, S., Miller, G.E., Rabin, B., Barkin, A. and Traynor, J. (2005) Loneliness, social isolation and antibody response to the influenza immunization. Health Psychology 24 (3), 297–306.

Putsch, R.W.I. (1985) Cross-cultural communication: The special case of interpreters in health care. JAMA 254 (23), 3344–3348.

Roat, C.E. (2003) Health Care Interpreter Training in the State of California Including an Analysis of Trends and a Compendium of Training Programs. Woodland Hills, CA: The California Endowment.

Rozan, J-F. (1956) La prise de notes en interprétation consécutive. Genève: Georg. RSI (1998) Remote Simultaneous Interpretation Project at Santa Clara Valley Medical Center. Summary administrative report. Stanford University School of Medicine, Department of Health Research and Policy. January 15.

Saint-Louis, L., Friedman, E., Chiasson, E., Quessa, A. and Novaes, F. (2003) Testing New Technologies in Medical Interpreting. Cambridge, MA: Cambridge Health Alliance.

Stejskal, J. (2003) International Certification Study. Alexandria, VA: American Translators Association.

Stone, I. (2001) New concepts for telephone interpreting. ATA Chronicle XXX (1), January 2001.

Stone, I. (2001) If you cannot see it, how can you tell? The meaning and significance of voice in telephone interpreting. ATA Chronicle. October 2001.

Swaney, I. (1997) Thoughts on live vs. telephone and video interpretation. NAJIT. PROTEUS VI (2), Spring.

Wadensjö, C. (1999) Telephone interpreting and the synchronisation of talk in social interaction. The Translator: Studies in Intercultural Communication 5 (2), 247–264.

Coming Soon!

From Our Lips to Your Ears: How Interpreters are Changing the World

Communication. Not much in this world can happen without it. Yet day after day, millions of people around the world communicate in spite of the fact that they do not share a common language.

And it's largely thanks to interpreters.

Whether it's rendering the nurse's encouraging words as a woman delivers a baby in the local hospital, carefully conveying the messages of foreign diplomats, converting the judge's decision accurately into another language in the courtroom, or interpreting a phone call as an international tourist faces a life-threatening emergency, interpreters are helping our world go 'round.

The *From Our Lips to Your Ears* project is a testament to the important work that interpreters do each and every day.

This compendium of real-life interpreter anecdotes is a first-of-its-kind project that aims to memorialize the experiences of interpreters in order to enable readers to gain a greater appreciation of this incredibly complex and fascinating profession.

Interpreters are helping our world go 'round. Isn't it time the world knew about it?

View the call for submissions and learn how to participate:

www.fromourlips.com

Future Editions

Have a question about telephone interpreting that you didn't find an answer to in this book?

Submit it for potential inclusion in a future edition.

Visit
www.telephoneinterpreting.net
to learn more.

Lightning Source UK Ltd.
Milton Keynes UK
UKOW030144230313

208075UK00007B/139/P